THE AUTOBIOGRAPHY OF BERTRAND RUSSELL
VOLUME III

ι

THE
AUTOBIOGRAPHY
OF
BERTRAND
RUSSELL

1944–1967

(VOLUME III)

LONDON

GEORGE ALLEN AND UNWIN LTD

RUSKIN HOUSE   MUSEUM STREET

PRINTED IN GREAT BRITAIN
in 11 *point Bell type*
BY UNWIN BROTHERS LTD
WOKING AND LONDON

ACKNOWLEDGEMENTS

ACKNOWLEDGEMENTS are due to the following for permission to include certain letters, articles, and illustrations in this volume: Baron Cecil Anrep, for the letters of Bernard Berenson; the Estate of Albert Einstein; Valerie Eliot, for the letters of T. S. Eliot; the *Evening Standard*, for the cartoon by Jak; Dorelia John, for the letter of Augustus John; *The New York Times* Company, for 'The Best Answer to Fanaticism-Liberalism' (© 1951); *The Observer*, for 'Pros and Cons of Reaching Ninety'; *Punch* magazine, for the cartoon by Ronald Searle. The above list includes only those who requested formal acknowledgement; many others have kindly granted permission to publish letters.

PREFACE TO VOLUME III

THIS BOOK is to be published while the great issues that now divide the world remain undecided. As yet, and for some time to come, the world must be one of doubt. It must as yet be suspended equally between hope and fear.

It is likely that I shall die before the issue is decided—I do not know whether my last words should be:

> The bright day is done
> And we are for the dark,

or, as I sometimes allow myself to hope,

> The world's great age begins anew,
> The golden years return. . . .
> Heaven smiles, and faiths and empires gleam,
> Like wrecks of a dissolving dream.

I have done what I could to add my small weight in an attempt to tip the balance on the side of hope, but it has been a puny effort against vast forces.

May others succeed where my generation failed.

*   *   *

During the year 1944, it became gradually clear that the war was ending, and was ending in German defeat. This made it possible for us to return to England and to bring our children with us without serious risk except for John, who was liable for conscription whether he went home or stayed in America. Fortunately, the end of the war came soon enough to spare him the awkward choice which this would have entailed.

My life in England, as before, was a mixture of public and private events, but the private part became increasingly important. I have found that it is not possible to relate in the same manner private and public events or happenings long since finished and those that are still continuing and in the midst of which I live. Some readers may be surprised by the changes of manner which this entails. I can only hope that the reader will realize the inevitability of diversification and appreciate the unavoidable reticences necessitated by the law of libel.

CONTENTS

ILLUSTRATIONS

CHAPTER I

RETURN TO ENGLAND

CROSSING THE ATLANTIC in the first half of 1944 was a complicated business. Peter and Conrad travelled on the *Queen Mary* at great speed but with extreme discomfort, in a ship completely crowded with young children and their mothers, all the mothers complaining of all the other children, and all the children causing the maximum trouble by conduct exposing them to the danger of falling into the sea. But of all this I knew nothing until I myself arrived in England. As for me, I was sent in a huge convoy which proceeded majestically at the speed of a bicycle, escorted by corvettes and aeroplanes. I was taking with me the manuscript of my *History of Western Philosophy*, and the unfortunate censors had to read every word of it lest it should contain information useful to the enemy. They were, however, at last satisfied that a knowledge of philosophy could be of no use to the Germans, and very politely assured me that they had enjoyed reading my book, which I confess I found hard to believe. Everything was surrounded with secrecy. I was not allowed to tell my friends when I was sailing or from what port. I found myself at last on a Liberty ship, making its maiden voyage. The Captain, who was a jolly fellow, used to cheer me up by saying that not more than one in four of the Liberty ships broke in two on its maiden voyage. Needless to say, the ship was American and the Captain, British. There was one officer who whole-heartedly approved of me. He was the Chief Engineer, and he had read *The ABC of Relativity* without knowing anything about its author. One day, as I was walking the deck with him, he began on the merits of this little book and, when I said that I was the author, his joy knew no limits. There was one other passenger, a business man, whom the ship's officers did not altogether like because they felt that he was young enough to fight. However, I found him pleasant and I quite enjoyed the three weeks of inactivity. There was considered to be no risk of submarines until we were approaching the coast of Ireland, but after that we were ordered to sleep in trousers. However, there was no incident of any kind. We were a few days from the end of our journey on D-day, which we learned about from

15

the wireless. Almost the whole ship's crew was allowed to come and listen. I learned from the wireless the English for 'Allons, enfants de la patrie, le jour de gloire est arrive'. The English for it is: 'Well, friends, this is it.'

They decanted us at a small port on the northern shore of the Firth of Forth on a Sunday. We made our way with some difficulty to the nearest town, where I had my first glimpse of Britain in that war-time. It consisted, so far as I could see at that moment, entirely of Polish soldiers and Scotch girls, the Polish soldiers very gallant, and the Scotch girls very fascinated. I got a night train to London, arrived very early in the morning, and for some time could not discover what had become of Peter and Conrad. At last, after much frantic telephoning and telegraphing, I discovered that they were staying with her mother at Sidmouth, and that Conrad had pneumonia. I went there at once, and found to my relief, that he was rapidly recovering. We sat on the beach, listening to the sound of naval guns off Cherbourg.

Trinity College had invited me to a five-year lectureship and I had accepted the invitation. It carried with it a fellowship and a right to rooms in College. I went to Cambridge and found that the rooms were altogether delightful; they looked out on the bowling green, which was a mass of flowers. It was a relief to find that the beauty of Cambridge was undimmed, and I found the peacefulness of the Great Court almost unbelievably soothing. But the problem of housing Peter and Conrad remained. Cambridge was incredibly full, and at first the best that I could achieve was squalid rooms in a lodging house. There they were underfed and miserable, while I was living luxuriously in College. As soon as it became clear that I was going to get money out of my law-suit against Barnes,[1] I bought a house at Cambridge, where we lived for some time.

VJ-day and the General Election which immediately followed it occurred while we were living in this house. It was also there that I wrote most of my book on *Human Knowledge, its Scope and Limits.* I could have been happy in Cambridge, but the Cambridge ladies did not consider us respectable. I bought a small house at Ffestiniog in North Wales with a most lovely view. Then we took a flat in London. Though I spent much time in visits to the Continent for purposes of lecturing, I did no work of importance during these years. When, in 1949, my wife decided that she wanted no more of me, our marriage came to an end.

Throughout the 'forties and the early 'fifties, my mind was in a state of confused agitation on the nuclear question. It was obvious to me that a nuclear war would put an end to civilization. It was also

[1] Cf. Vol. II.

obvious that unless there were a change of policies in both East and West a nuclear war was sure to occur sooner or later. The dangers were in the back of my mind from the early 'twenties. But in those days, although a few learned physicists were appreciative of the coming danger, the majority, not only of men in the streets, but even of scientists, turned aside from the prospect of atomic war with a kind of easy remark that 'Oh, men will never be so foolish as that'. The bombing of Hiroshima and Nagasaki in 1945 first brought the possibility of nuclear war to the attention of men of science and even of some few politicians. A few months after the bombing of the two Japanese cities, I made a speech in the House of Lords pointing out the likelihood of a general nuclear war and the certainty of its causing universal disaster if it occurred. I forecast and explained the making of nuclear bombs of far greater power than those used upon Hiroshima and Nagasaki, fusion as against the old fission bombs, the present hydrogen bombs in fact. It was possible at that time to enforce some form of control of these monsters to provide for their use for peaceful, not war-like, ends, since the arms race which I dreaded had not yet begun. If no controls were thought out, the situation would be almost out of hand. It took no great imagination to foresee this. Everybody applauded my speech; not a single Peer suggested that my fears were excessive. But all my hearers agreed that this was a question for their grandchildren. In spite of hundreds of thousands of Japanese deaths, nobody grasped that Britain had escaped only by luck and that in the next war she might be less fortunate. Nobody viewed it as an international danger which could only be warded off by agreement among the Great Powers. There was a certain amount of talk, but no action was taken. This easy-going attitude survives among the laity even down to the present day. Those who try to make you uneasy by talk about atom bombs are regarded as trouble-makers, as people to be avoided, as people who spoil the pleasure of a fine day by foolish prospects of improbable rain.

Against this careless attitude I, like a few others, used every opportunity that presented itself to point out the dangers. It seemed to me then, as it still seems to me, that the time to plan and to act in order to stave off approaching dangers is when they are first seen to be approaching. Once their progress is established, it is very much more difficult to halt it. I felt hopeful, therefore, when the Baruch Proposal was made by the United States to Russia. I thought better of it then, and of the American motives in making it, than I have since learned to think, but I still wish that the Russians had accepted it. However, the Russians did not. They exploded their first bomb in August, 1949, and it was evident that they would do all in their power to make themselves the equals of the United States in destructive—or, politely, defensive—power. The arms race became inevitable unless drastic measures were taken to avoid it. That is why, in late 1948, I suggested that the remedy might be the threat of immediate war by the United States on Russia for the purpose of forcing nuclear disarmament upon her. I have given my reasons for doing this in an Appendix to my *Common Sense and Nuclear Warfare*. My chief defence of the view I held in 1948 was that I thought Russia very likely to yield to the demands of the West. This ceased to be probable after Russia had a considerable fleet of nuclear planes.

This advice of mine is still brought up against me. It is easy to understand why Communists might object to it. But the usual criticism is that I, a pacifist, once advocated the threat of war. It seems to cut no ice that I have reiterated *ad nauseam* that I am not a pacifist, that I believe that some wars, a very few, are justified, even necessary. They are usually necessary because matters have been permitted to drag on their obviously evil way till no peaceful means can stop them. Nor do my critics appear to consider the evils that have developed as a result of the continued Cold War and that might have been avoided, along with the Cold War itself, had my advice to threaten war been taken in 1948. Had it been taken, the results remain hypothetical, but so far as I can see it is no disgrace, and shows no 'inconsistency' in my thought, to have given it.

None the less, at the time I gave this advice, I gave it so casually without any real hope that it would be followed, that I soon forgot I had given it. I had mentioned it in a private letter and again in a speech that I did not know was to be the subject of dissection by the press. When, later, the recipient of the letter asked me for permission to publish it, I said, as I usually do, without consideration of the contents, that if he wished he might publish it. He did so. And to my surprise I learned of my earlier suggestion. I had, also, entirely forgotten that it occurred in the above-mentioned speech. Unfortunately, in the meantime, before this incontrovertible evidence was set before me, I had hotly denied that I had ever made such a suggestion. It was a pity. It is shameful to deny one's own words. One can only defend or retract them. In this case I could, and did, defend them, and should have done so earlier but from a fault of my memory upon which from many years' experience I had come to rely too unquestioningly.

My private thoughts meanwhile were more and more disturbed. I became increasingly pessimistic and ready to try any suggested escape from the danger. My state of mind was like a very much exaggerated nervous fear such as people are apt to feel while a thunder-storm gathers on the horizon and has not yet blotted out the sun. I found it very difficult to remain sane or to reject any suggested measures. I do not think I could have succeeded in this except for the happiness of my private life.

For a few years I was asked yearly to give a lecture at the Imperial Defence College in Belgrave Square. But the invitations stopped coming after the lecture in which I remarked that, knowing that they believed you could not be victorious in war without the help of religion, I had read the Sermon on the Mount, but, to my surprise, could find no mention of H-bombs in it. My audience appeared to be embarrassed, as they were good Christians as well as, of course, warriors. But, for myself, I find the combination of Christianity with war and weapons of mass extinction hard to justify.

In 1948, the Western Powers endeavoured to create a union which should be the germ of a World Government. The Conservative Party approved and wished Britain to become a member. The Labour Party, after some hestitation, opposed the scheme, but left individual members free to support it or not, as they thought fit. I joined and made a possibly somewhat excessive attack upon one of the few Communists present at the international Congress assembled at The Hague to consider the scheme. In his speech he had maintained that Communists have a higher ethic than other men. This was just after the fall of the Democratic Government of Czechoslovakia and my remarks had the complete agreement of the bulk of the people present. The younger Masaryk's suicide as a result of his rough handling by the Communists had shocked us all, and almost all of us had the conviction that co-operation with the East was for the present impossible. I said: 'If you can persuade me that hounding your most eminent citizen to his death shows a higher ethical outlook than that of the West, I shall be prepared to support you, but, till that time comes, I shall do no such thing.'

Towards the end of the war, after my return to England, and for sometime thereafter, the Government used me to lecture to the Forces. The Forces had become more pacific than I expected as the war neared its end, and I remember that Laski and I were sent together on one occasion to speak to some of the air men. Laski was more radical than I was, and they all agreed with him. In the middle of my lecture I suddenly realized that half of my audience was creeping out of the hall and I wondered if I had offended them in some way more drastic than merely failing to be sufficiently radical. Afterwards, I was told that the men had been called away to combat the last of the German air raids against England.

At the time of the Berlin air lift, I was sent by the Government to

Berlin to help to persuade the people of Berlin that it was worth while to resist Russian attempts to get the Allies out of Berlin. It was the first and only time that I have been able to parade as a military man. I was made a member of the armed forces for the occasion and given a military passport, which amused me considerably.

I had known Berlin well in the old days, and the hideous destruction that I saw at this time shocked me. From my window I could barely see one house standing. I could not discover where the Germans were living. This complete destruction was due partly to the English and partly to the Russians, and it seemed to me monstrous. Contemplation of the less accountable razing of Dresden by my own countrymen sickened me. I felt that when the Germans were obviously about to surrender that was enough, and that to destroy not only 135,000 Germans but also all their houses and countless treasures was barbarous.

I felt the treatment of Germany by the Allies to be almost incredibly foolish. By giving part of Germany to Russia and part to the West, the victorious Governments ensured the continuation of strife between East and West, particularly as Berlin was partitioned and there was no guarantee of access by the West to its part of Berlin except by air. They had imagined a peaceful co-operation between Russia and her Western allies, but they ought to have foreseen that this was not a likely outcome. As far as sentiment was concerned, what happened was a continuation of the war with Russia as the common enemy of the West. The stage was set for the Third World War, and this was done deliberately by the utter folly of Governments.

I thought the Russian blockade was foolish and was glad that it was unsuccessful owing to the skill of the British. At this time I was *persona grata* with the British Government because, though I was against nuclear war, I was also anti-Communist. Later I was brought around to being more favourable to Communism by the death of Stalin in 1953 and by the Bikini test in 1954; and I came gradually to attribute, more and more, the danger of nuclear war to the West, to the United States of America, and less to Russia. This change was supported by developments inside the United States, such as McCarthyism and the restriction of civil liberties.

I was doing a great deal of broadcasting for the various services of the BBC and they asked me to do one at the time of Stalin's death. As I rejoiced mightily in that event, since I felt Stalin to be as wicked as one man could be and to be the root evil of most of the misery and terror in, and threatened by, Russia, I condemned him in my broadcast and rejoiced for the world in his departure from the scene. I forgot the BBC susceptibilities and respectabilities. My broadcast never went on the air.

In the same year that I went to Germany, the Government sent me to Norway in the hope of inducing Norwegians to join an alliance against Russia. The place they sent me to was Trondheim. The weather was stormy and cold. We had to go by sea-plane from Oslo to Trondheim. When our plane touched down on the water it became obvious that something was amiss, but none of us in the plane knew what it was. We sat in the plane while it slowly sank. Small boats assembled round it and presently we were told to jump into the sea and swim to a boat—which all the people in my part of the plane did. We later learned that all the nineteen passengers in the non-smoking compartment had been killed. When the plane had hit the water a hole had been made in the plane and the water had rushed in. I had told a friend at Oslo who was finding me a place that he must find me a place where I could smoke, remarking jocularly, 'If I cannot smoke, I shall die'. Unexpectedly, this turned out to be true. All those in the smoking compartment got out by the emergency exit window beside which I was sitting. We all swam to the boats which dared not approach too near for fear of being sucked under as the plane sank. We were rowed to shore to a place some miles from Trondheim and thence I was taken in a car to my hotel.

Everybody showed me the utmost kindness and put me to bed while my clothes dried. A group of students even dried my matches one by one. They asked if I wanted anything and I replied, 'Yes, a strong dose of brandy and a large cup of coffee'. The doctor, who arrived soon after, said that this was quite the right reply. The day was Sunday, on which day hotels in Norway were not allowed to supply liquor—a fact of which I was at the time unaware—but, as the need was medical, no objection was raised. Some amusement was caused when a clergyman supplied me with clerical clothing to wear till my clothes had dried. Everybody plied me with questions. A question even came by telephone from Copenhagen: a voice said, 'When you were in the water, did you not think of mysticism and logic?' 'No', I said. 'What did you think of?' the voice persisted. 'I thought the water was cold', I said and put down the receiver.

My lecture was cancelled as the man who had been intended to be the Chairman had been drowned. Students took me to a place in the nearby mountains where they had an establishment. In going and coming, they walked me about in the rain and I remarked that Trondheim was as wet out of the water as in it, a remark which seemed to please them. Apart from the rain, which turned to snow in the region of the mountains, I found Trondheim a pleasant place, but I was a little puzzled when I learnt that the Bishop pronounced the place one way and the Mayor another. I adopted the Bishop's pronunciation.

I was astonished by the commotion caused by my part in this adventure. Every phase of it was exaggerated. I had swum about one hundred yards, but I could not persuade people that I had not swum miles. True, I had swum in my great-coat and lost my hat and thrown my attaché case into the sea. The latter was restored to me in the course of the afternoon—and is still in use—and the contents were dried out. When I returned to London the officials all smiled when they saw the marks of sea water on my passport. It had been in my attaché case, and I was glad to recover it.

When I had returned to England in 1944, I found that in certain ways my outlook had changed. I enjoyed once more the freedom of discussion that prevailed in England, but not in America. In America, if a policeman addressed us, my young son burst into tears; and the same was true (*mutatis mutandis*) of university professors accused of speeding. The less fanatical attitude of English people diminished my own fanaticism, and I rejoiced in the feeling of home. This feeling was enhanced at the end of the 'forties when I was invited by the BBC to give the first course of Reith lectures, instead of being treated as a malefactor and allowed only limited access to the young. I admired more than ever the atmosphere of free discussion, and this influenced my choice of subject for the lectures, which was 'Authority and the Individual'. They were published in 1949 under that title and were concerned very largely with the lessening of individual freedom which tends to accompany increase of industrialism. But, although this danger was acknowledged, very little was done either then or since to diminish the evils that it was bringing.

I proposed in these lectures to consider how we could combine that degree of individual initiative which is necessary for progress with the degree of social cohesion that is necessary for survival. This is a large subject, and the remarks that I shall make upon it here are no more than annotations on the lectures and sometimes expansions of subjects that have interested me since writing the book.

The problem comes down, in my view, to the fact that society should strive to obtain security and justice for human beings and, also, progress. To obtain these it is necessary to have an established framework, the State, but, also, individual freedom. And in order to obtain the latter, it is necessary to separate cultural matters from the Establishment. The chief matter in which security is desirable now is security of nations against hostile enemies, and to achieve this a world government must be established that is strong enough to hold sway over national governments in international matters.

Since no defence is possible for a single nation against a more powerful nation or a group of such nations, a nation's safety in international matters must depend upon outside protection. Aggression against a single nation by another nation or group of nations must be opposed by international law and not left to the wilful initiative of some warlike State. If this is not done, any State may at any moment be totally destroyed. Changes in weapons may frequently alter the balance of power. It happened, for example, between France and England in the fifteenth century when the Powers ceased to defend castles and came to depend upon moving armies with artillery. This put an end to the feudal anarchy which had until then been common. In like manner, nuclear weapons must, if peace is to exist, put an end to war between nations and introduce the practical certainty of victory for an international force in any possible contest. The introduction of such a reform is difficult since it requires that the international Power should be so armed as to be fairly certain of victory in warfare with any single State.

Apart from this connection with the dangers of war now that weapons of mass destruction were being developed, these lectures were important in my own life because they give the background of a subject which has absorbed me in one way and another, especially since 1914: the relation of an individual to the State, conscientious objection, civil disobedience.

The prevention of war is essential to individual liberty. When war is imminent or actually in progress various important liberties are curtailed and it is only in a peaceful atmosphere that they can be expected to revive. As a rule, the interference with liberty goes much further than is necessary, but this is an inevitable result of panic fear. When Louis XVI's head was cut off other monarchs felt their heads insecure. They rushed to war and punished all sympathy with the French Revolution. The same sort of thing, sometimes in a less violent form, happened when Governments were terrified by the Russian Revolution. If the individual is to have all the liberty that is his due, he must be free to advocate whatever form of government he considers best, and this may require the protection of an international authority, especially since nuclear weapons have increased the power of nations to interfere with each other's internal affairs. Individual liberty in war-time should extend to personal participation in war.

In the course of these lectures, I gave a brief résumé of the growth and decay of governmental power. In the great days of Greece there was not too much of it: great men were free to develop their capacities while they lived, but wars and assassinations often cut short their labours. Rome brought order, but at the same time brought a considerable degree of eclipse to the achievement of individuals. Under the Empire, individual initiative was so curtailed as to be incapable of resisting new attacks from without. For a thousand years after the fall of Rome, there was too little authority and also too little individual initiative. Gradually, new weapons, especially gunpowder, gave strength to governments and developed the modern State. But with this came excessive authority. The problem of preserving liberty in a world of nuclear weapons is a new one and one for which men's minds are not prepared. Unless we can adapt ourselves to a greater search for liberty than has been necessary during the last few centuries, we shall sink into private lethargy and fall a prey to public energy.

It is especially as regards science that difficult problems arise. The modern civilized State depends upon science in a multitude of ways. Generally, there is old science, which is official, and new science, which elderly men look upon with horror. This results in a continual battle between old men, who admire the science of their fathers, and the young men who realize the value of their contemporaries' work. Up to a point this struggle is useful, but beyond that point it is disastrous. In the present day, the most important example of it is the population explosion, which can only be combated by methods which to the old seem impious.

Some ideals are subversive and cannot well be realized except by war or revolution. The most important of these is at present economic justice. Political justice had its day in industrialized parts of the world and is still to be sought in the unindustrialized parts, but economic justice is still a painfully sought goal. It requires a world-wide economic revolution if it is to be brought about. I do not see how it is to be achieved without bloodshed or how the world can continue patiently without it. It is true that steps are being taken in some countries, particularly by limiting the power of inheritance, but these are as yet very partial and very limited. Consider the vast areas of the world where the young have little or no education and where adults have not the capacity to realize elementary conditions of comfort. These inequalities rouse envy and are potential causes of great disorder. Whether the world will be able by peaceful means to raise the conditions of the poorer nations is, to my mind, very doubtful, and is likely to prove the most difficult governmental problem of coming centuries.

Very difficult problems are concerned with the inroads of war against liberty. The most obvious of these is conscription. Military men, when there is war, argue that it cannot be won unless all men on our side are compelled to fight. Some men will object, perhaps on religious grounds or, possibly, on the ground that the work they are doing is more useful than fighting. On such a matter there is liable to be, or at any rate there ought to be, a division between the old and the young. The old will say they are too aged to fight, and many of the young ought to say that their work is more useful towards victory than fighting.

The religious objection to taking part in warfare is more widespread. Civilized people are brought up to think it is wicked to kill other people, and some do not admit that a state of war puts an end to this ethical command. The number who hold this view is not very large, and I doubt whether any war has ever been determined by their action. It is good for a community to contain some people who feel the dictates of humanity so strongly that even in war-time they still obey them. And, apart from this argument, it is barbarous to compel a man to do acts which he considers wicked. We should all admit this if a law were proposed to punish a man for being a vegetarian, but when it is a human being whose life is at stake, we begin to wonder whether he is a friend or an enemy and, if the latter, we think we are justified in compelling the law to punish him.

In addition to those who consider all war wrong, there are those who object to the particular war that they are asked to fight. This happened with many people at the time of the Korean War and later in regard to the Vietnam War. Such people are punished if they refuse to fight. The law not only punishes those who condemn all war, but also those who condemn any particular war although it must be obvious that in any war one side, at least, is encouraging evil. Those who take this position of objecting to a certain war or a certain law or to certain actions of governments may be held justified because it is so doubtful that they are not justified. Such considerations, it will be said, since they condemn the punishment of supposed malefactors, throw doubt upon the whole criminal law. I believe this is true and I hold that every condemned criminal incurs a certain measure of doubt, sometimes great and sometimes small. This is admitted when it is an enemy who is tried, as in the Nuremberg Trials. It was widely admitted that the Nuremberg prisoners would not have been condemned if they had been tried by Germans. The enemies of the German Government would have punished with death any soldier among themselves who had practised the sort of civil disobedience the lack of which among Germans they pleaded as an excuse for condemning Germans. They refused to accept the plea made by many of those whom they condemned that they had committed criminal acts only under command of those in superior authority. The judges of Nuremberg believed that the Germans should have committed civil disobedience in the name of decency and humanity. This is little likely to have been their view if they had been judging their own countrymen and not their enemies. But I believe it is true of friend as well as foe. The line between proper acceptable civil disobedience and inacceptable civil disobedience comes,

I believe, with the reason for it being committed—the seriousness of the object for which it is committed and the profundity of the belief in its necessity.

Some years before I gave the Reith Lectures, my old professor and friend and collaborator in *Principia Mathematica*, A. N. Whitehead, had been given the OM. Now, by the early part of 1950, I had become so respectable in the eyes of the Establishment that it was felt that I, too, should be given the OM. This made me very happy for, though I daresay it would surprise many Englishmen and most of the English Establishment to hear it, I am passionately English, and I treasure an honour bestowed on my by the Head of my country. I had to go to Buckingham Palace for the official bestowal of it. The King was affable, but somewhat embarrassed at having to behave graciously to so queer a fellow, a convict to boot. He remarked, 'You have sometimes behaved in a way which would not do if generally adopted'. I have been glad ever since that I did not make the reply that sprang to my mind: 'Like your brother.' But he was thinking of things like my having been a conscientious objector, and I did not feel that I could let this remark pass in silence, so I said: 'How a man should behave depends upon his profession. A postman, for instance, should knock at all the doors in a street at which he has letters to deliver, but if anybody else knocked on all the doors, he would be considered a public nuisance.' The King, to avoid answering, abruptly changed the subject by asking me whether I knew who was the only man who had both the KG and the OM. I did not know, and he graciously informed me that it was Lord Portal. I did not mention that he was my cousin.

In the February of that year I had been asked to give an address, which I called 'L'Individu et l'Etat Moderne', at the Sorbonne. In the course of it I spoke warmly and in most laudatory terms of Jean Nicod, the brilliant and delightful young mathematician who died in 1924.[1] I was very glad after the lecture that I had done so, for I learnt that, unknown to me, his widow had been in the audience.

At the end of June, 1950, I went to Australia in response to an invitation by the Australian Institute of International Affairs to give lectures at various universities on subjects connected with the Cold War. I interpreted this subject liberally and my lectures dealt with speculation about the future of industrialism. There was a Labour Government there and, in spite of the fact that the hatred and fear of China and, especially, Japan, was understandably fierce, things seemed better and more hopeful than they appeared to become in the following sixteen years. I liked the people and I was greatly impressed by the size of the country and the fact that ordinary private conversations, gossips,

[1] Cf. Vol. II.

were conducted by radio. Because of the size, too, and people's relative isolation, the libraries and bookshops were impressively numerous and good, and people read more than elsewhere. I was taken to the capitals, and to Alice Springs which I wanted to see because it was so isolated. It was a centre for agriculture and inhabited chiefly by sheep owners. I was shown a fine gaol where I was assured that the cells were comfortable. In reply to my query as to why, I was told: 'Oh, because all the leading citizens at one time or another are in gaol.' I was told that, expectedly and regularly, whenever possible, they stole each other's sheep.

I visited all parts of Australia except Tasmania. The Korean War was in full swing, and I learnt to my surprise that the northern parts of Queensland had, when war broke out, been evacuated, but were again inhabited when I was there.

The Government, I found, treated the Aborigines fairly well, but the police and the public treated them abominably. I was taken by a public official whose duty it was to look after Aborigines to see a village in which all the inhabitants were native Australians. One complained to us that he had had a bicycle which had been stolen, and he displayed marked unwillingness to complain to the police about it. I asked my conductor why, and he explained that any native who appealed to the police would be grossly ill-treated by them. I observed, myself, that white men generally spoke abusively to the Aborigines.

My other contact with the Government concerned irrigation. There is a chain of hills called 'Snowy Mountains' and there was a Federal scheme to utilize these mountains for purposes of irrigation. When I was there the scheme was bogged down by the operation of States which would not benefit by it. A scheme was being pushed to advocate the proposed irrigation on the grounds of defence rather than of irrigation, thus avoiding conflicts of States which are a standard problem in Australian politics. I spoke in favour of this scheme.

I was kept very busy making speeches and being interviewed by journalists and, at the end of my stay, I was presented with a beautifully bound book of press cuttings which I cherish, though I do not like much of what the journalists report me as saying of myself. I had advocated birth control on some occasion and naturally the Roman Catholics did not approve of me, and the Archbishop of Melbourne said publicly that I had been at one time excluded from the United States by the United States Government. This was not true; and I spoke of suing him, but a group of journalists questioned him on the point and he admitted his error publicly, which was a disappointment, since it meant that I had to relinquish the hope of receiving damages from an Archbishop.

On my way home to England my plane stopped at Singapore and

Karachi and Bombay and other places. Though I was not permitted to visit any of these places, beyond their airports, as the plane did not stop long enough, I was called upon to make radio speeches. Later, I saw from a cutting from *The Sydney Morning Herald* for August 26th, an account of my speech at Singapore. It reported my saying: 'I think that Britain should withdraw gracefully from Asia, as she did in India, and not wait to be driven out in the event of a war. . . . In this way good-will will be won and a neutral Asian bloc could be formed under the leadership of Pandit Nehru. This is the best thing that can happen now, and the strongest argument in its favour is that it would be a strategic move.' This, though unheeded, seems to me to have been good advice.

Soon after my return from Australia, I went again to the United States. I had been asked to 'give a short course' in philosophy for a month at Mt Holyoak College, a well-known college for women in New England. From there I went to Princeton where I, as usual, delivered a lecture and again met various old friends, among them Einstein. There I received the news that I was to be given a Nobel Prize. But the chief memory of this visit to America is of the series of three lectures that I gave on the Matchette Foundation at Columbia University. I was put up in luxury at the Plaza Hotel and shepherded about by Miss Julie Medlock, who had been appointed by Columbia to bear-lead me. Her views on international affairs were liberal and sympathetic and we have continued to discuss them, both by letter and when she visits us as she sometimes does.

My lectures, a few months later, appeared with other lectures that I had given originally at Ruskin College, Oxford, and the Lloyd Roberts Lecture that I had given in 1949 at the Royal Society of Medicine, London, as the basis of my book called *The Impact of Science on Society*. The title is the same as that of the three lectures that Columbia University published separately, which is unfortunate as it causes bewilderment for bibliographers and is sometimes a disappointment to those who come upon only the Columbia publication.

I was astonished that, in New York, where I had been, so short a time before, spoken of with vicious obloquy, my lectures seemed to be popular and to draw crowds. This was not surprising, perhaps, at the first lecture, where the audience might have gathered to have a glimpse of so horrid a character, hoping for shocks and scandal and general rebelliousness. But what amazed me was that the hall should have been packed with enthusiastic students in increasing numbers as the lectures proceeded. There were so many that crowds of those who came had to be turned away for lack of even standing room. I think it also surprised my hosts.

The chief matter with which I was concerned was the increase of human power owing to scientific knowledge. The gist of my first lecture was contained in the following sentence: 'It is not by prayer and humility that you cause things to go as you wish, but by acquiring a knowledge of natural laws.' I pointed out that the power to be acquired in this way is very much greater than the power that men formerly sought to achieve by theological means. The second lecture was concerned with the increase of power men achieve by the application of scientific technique. It begins with gunpowder and the mariners' compass. Gunpowder destroyed the power of castles and the mariners' compass created the power of Europe over other parts of the world. These increases of governmental power were important, but the new power brought by the Industrial Revolution was more so. I was largely concerned in this lecture with the bad effect of early industrial power and with the dangers that will result if any powerful State adopts scientific breeding. From this I went on to the increase of the harmfulness of war when scientific methods are employed. This is, at present, the most important form of the application of science in our day. It threatens the destruction of the human race and, indeed, of all living beings of larger than microscopic size. If mankind is to survive, the power of making scientific war will have to be concentrated in a supreme State. But this is so contrary to men's mental habits that, as yet, the great majority would prefer to run the risk of extermination. This is the supreme danger of our age. Whether a World Government will be established in time or not is the supreme question. In my third lecture I am concerned chiefly with certain views as to good and evil from which I dissent although many men consider that they alone are scientific. The views in question are that the good is identical with the useful. I ended these lectures with an investigation of the kind of temperament which must be dominant if a happy world is to be possible. The first requisite, I should say, is absence of dogmatism, since dogmatism almost inevitably leads to war. I will quote the paragraph summing up what I thought necessary if the world is to be saved: 'There are certain things that our age needs, and certain things that it should avoid. It needs compassion and a wish that mankind should be happy; it needs the desire for knowledge and the determination to eschew pleasant myths; it needs, above all, courageous hope and the impulse to creativeness. The things that it must avoid and that have brought it to the brink of catastrophe are cruelty, envy, greed, competitiveness, search for irrational subjective certainty, and what Freudians call the death wish.'

I think I was mistaken in being surprised that my lectures were liked by the audience. Almost any young academic audience is liberal and likes to hear liberal and even quasi-revolutionary opinions expressed by someone in authority. They like, also any jibe at any received opinion, whether orthodox or not: for instance, I spent some time making fun of Aristotle for saying that the bite of the shrewmouse is dangerous to a horse, especially if the shrewmouse is pregnant. My audience was irreverent and so was I. I think this was the main basis of their liking of my lectures. My inorthodoxy was not confined to politics. My trouble in New York in 1940 on sexual morals had blown over but had left in any audience of mine an expectation that they would hear something that the old and orthodox would consider shocking. There were plenty of such items in my discussion of scientific breeding. Generally, I had the pleasant experience of being applauded on the very same remarks which had caused me to be ostracized on the earlier occasion.

I got into trouble with a passage at the tail end of my last Columbia lecture. In this passage, I said that what the world needs is 'love, Christian love, or compassion'. The result of my use of the word 'Christian' was a deluge of letters from Free-thinkers deploring my adoption of orthodoxy, and from Christians welcoming me to the fold. When, ten years later, I was welcomed by the Chaplain to Brixton Prison with the words, 'I am glad that you have seen the light', I had to explain to him that this was an entire misconception, that my views were completely unchanged and that what he called seeing the light I should call groping in darkness. I had thought it obvious that, when I spoke of *Christian* love, I put in the adjective 'Christian' to distinguish it from sexual love, and I should certainly have supposed that the context made this completely clear. I go on to say that, 'If you feel this you have a motive for existence, a guide in action, a reason for courage, and an imperative necessity for intellectual honesty. If you feel this, you have all that anybody should need in the way of religion.' It seems to me totally inexplicable that anybody should think the above words a description of Christianity, especially in view, as some Christians will remember, of how very rarely Christians have shown Christian love. I have done my best to console those who are not Christians for the pain that I unwittingly caused them by a lax use of the suspect adjective. My essays and lectures on the subject have been edited and published in 1957 by Professor Paul Edwards along with an essay by him on my New York difficulties of 1940, under the title *Why I am not a Christian*.

When I was called to Stockholm, at the end of 1950, to receive the Nobel Prize—somewhat to my surprise, for literature, for my book *Marriage and Morals*—I was apprehensive, since I remembered that, exactly three hundred years earlier, Descartes had been called to Scandinavia by Queen Christina in the winter time and had died of the cold. However, we were kept warm and comfortable and, instead of snow, we had rain, which was a slight disappointment. The occasion, though very grand, was pleasant and I enjoyed it. I was sorry for another prize winner who looked utterly miserable and was so shy that he refused to speak to anyone and could not make himself heard when he had to make his formal speech as we all had to do. My dinner companion was Madame Joliot-Curie and I found her talk interesting. At the evening party given by the King, an Aide-de-Camp came to say that the King wished to talk with me. He wanted Sweden to join with Norway and Denmark against the Russians. I said that it was obvious, if there were a war between the West and the Russians, the Russians could only get to Norwegian ports through and over Swedish territory. The King approved of this observation. I was rather pleased, too, by my speech, especially by the mechanical sharks, concerning whom I said: 'I think every big town should contain artificial waterfalls that people could descend in very fragile canoes, and they should contain bathing pools full of mechanical sharks. Any person found advocating a preventive war should be condemned to two hours a day with these ingenious monsters.' I found that two or three fellow Nobel prize-winners listened to what I had to say and considered it not without importance. Since then I have published it in Part II of my book *Human Society in Ethics and Politics* and a gramophone record has been made of it in America. I have heard that it has affected many people more than I had thought which is gratifying.

1950, beginning with the OM and ending with the Nobel Prize, seems to have marked the apogee of my respectability. It is true that I began to feel slightly uneasy, fearing that this might mean the onset of blind orthodoxy. I have always held that no one can be respectable without being wicked, but so blunted was my moral sense that I could not see in what way I had sinned. Honours and increased income which began with the sales of my *History of Western Philosophy* gave me a feeling of freedom and assurance that let me expend all my energies upon what I wanted to do. I got through an immense amount of work and felt, in consequence, optimistic and full of zest. I suspected that I had too much emphasized, hitherto, the darker possibilities threatening mankind and that it was time to write a book in which the happier issues of current disputes were brought into relief. I called this book *New Hopes for a Changing World* and deliberately, wherever there were two possibilities, I emphasized that it *might* be the happier one which would be realized. I did not suggest that either the cheerful or the painful alternative was the more probable, but merely that it is impossible to know which would be victorious. The book ends with a picture of what the world may become if we so choose. I say:

'Man, in the long ages since he descended from the trees, has passed arduously and perilously through a vast dusty desert, surrounded by the whitening bones of those who have perished by the way, maddened by hunger and thirst, by fear of wild beasts, by dread of enemies, not only living enemies, but spectres of dead rivals projected on to the dangerous world by the intensity of his own fears. At last he has emerged from the desert into a smiling land, but in the long night he has forgotten how to smile. We cannot believe in the brightness of the morning. We think it trivial and deceptive; we cling to old myths that allow us to go on living with fear and hate—above all, hate of ourselves, miserable sinners. This is folly. Man now needs for his salvation only one thing: to open his heart to joy, and leave fear to gibber through the glimmering darkness of a forgotten past. He must lift up his eyes and say: "No, I am not a miserable sinner; I am a being who, by a long and arduous road, have discovered how to make intelligence master natural obstacles, how to live in freedom and joy, at peace with myself and therefore with all mankind." This will happen if men choose joy rather than sorrow. If not, eternal death will bury man in deserved oblivion.'

But my disquietude grew. My inability to make my fellow men see the dangers ahead for them and all mankind weighed upon me. Perhaps it heightened my pleasures as pain sometimes does, but pain was there and increased with my increasing awareness of failure to make others share a recognition of its cause. I began to feel that *New Hopes for a Changing World* needed fresh and deeper examination and I attempted to make this in my book *Human Society in Ethics and Politics,* the end of which, for a time, satisfied my craving to express my fears in an effective form.

What led me to write about ethics was the accusation frequently brought against me that, while I had made a more or less sceptical inquiry into other branches of knowledge, I had avoided the subject of ethics except in an early essay expounding Moore's *Principia Ethica.* My reply is that ethics is not a branch of knowledge. I now, therefore, set about the task in a different way. In the first half of the book, I dealt with the fundamental concepts of ethics; in the second part, I dealt with the application of these concepts in practical politics. The first part analyses such concepts as moral codes: good and bad, sin, superstitious ethics, and ethical sanctions. In all these I seek for an ethical element in subjects which are traditionally labelled ethical. The conclusion that I reach is that ethics is never an independent constituent, but is reducible to politics in the last analysis. What are we to say, for example, about a war in which the parties are evenly matched? In such a context each side may claim that it is obviously in the right and that its defeat would be a disaster to mankind. There would be no way of proving this assertion except by appealing to other ethical concepts such as hatred of cruelty or love of knowledge or art. You may admire the Renaissance because they built St Peter's, but somebody may perplex you by saying that he prefers St Paul's. Or, again, the war may have sprung from lies told by one party which may seem an admirable foundation to the contest until it appears that there was equal mendacity on the other side. To arguments of this sort there is no purely rational conclusion. If one man believes that the earth is round and another believes that it is flat, they can set off on a joint voyage and decide the matter reasonably. But if one believes in Protestantism and the other in Catholicism, there is no known method of reaching a rational conclusion. For such reasons, I had come to agree with Santayana that there is no such thing as ethical *knowledge*. Nevertheless, ethical concepts have been of enormous importance in history, and I could not but feel that a survey of human affairs which omits ethics is inadequate and partial.

I adopted as my guiding thought the principle that ethics is derived from passions and that there is no valid method of travelling from passion to what ought to be done. I adopted David Hume's maxim that 'Reason is, and ought only to be, the slave of the passions'. I am not satisfied with this, but it is the best that I can do. Critics are fond of charging me with being wholly rational and this, at least, proves that I am not entirely so. The practical distinction among passions comes as regards their success: some passions lead to success in what is desired; others, to failure. If you pursue the former, you will be happy; if the latter, unhappy. Such, at least, will be the broad general rule. This may seem a poor and tawdry result of researches into such sublime concepts as 'duty', 'self-denial', 'ought', and so forth, but I am persuaded that it is the total of the valid outcome, except in one particular: we feel that the man who brings widespread happiness at the expense of misery to himself is a better man than the man who brings unhappiness to others and happiness to himself. I do not know any rational ground for this view or, perhaps, for the somewhat more rational view that whatever the majority desires is preferable to what the minority desires. These are truly ethical problems, but I do not know of any way in which they can be solved except by politics or war. All that I can find to say on this subject is that an ethical opinion can only be defended by an ethical axiom, but, if the axiom is not accepted, there is no way of reaching a rational conclusion.

There is one approximately rational approach to ethical conclusions which has a certain validity. It may be called the doctrine of compossibility. This doctrine is as follows: among the desires that a man finds himself to possess, there are various groups, each consisting of desires which may be gratified together and others which conflict. You may, for example, be a passionate adherent of the Democratic Party, but it may happen that you hate the presidential candidate. In that case, your love of the Party and your dislike of the individual are not compossible. Or you may hate a man and love his son. In that case, if they always travel about together, you will find them, as a pair, not compossible. The art of politics consists very largely in finding as numerous a group of compossible people as you can. The man who wishes to be happy will endeavour to make as large groups as he can of compossible desires the rulers of his life. Viewed theoretically, such a doctrine affords no ultimate solution. It assumes that happiness is better than unhappiness. This is an ethical principle incapable of proof. For that reason, I did not consider compossibility a basis for ethics.

I do not wish to be thought coldly indifferent to ethical considerations. Man, like the lower animals, is supplied by nature with passions and has a difficulty in fitting these passions together, especially if he lives in a close-knit community. The art required for this is the art of politics. A man totally destitute of this art would be a savage and incapable of living in civilized society. That is why I have called my book *Human Society in Ethics and Politics*.

Though the reviews of the book were all that could be hoped, nobody paid much attention to what I considered most important about it, the impossibility of reconciling ethical feelings with ethical doctrines. In the depths of my mind this dark frustration brooded constantly. I tried to intersperse lighter matters into my thoughts, especially by writing stories which contained an element of fantasy. Many people found these stories amusing, though some found them too stylized for their taste. Hardly anyone seems to have found them prophetic.

Long before this, in the beginning of the century, I had composed various stories and, later, I made up stories for my children to while away the tedious climb from the beach to our house in Cornwall. Some of the latter have since been written down, though never published. In about 1912, I had written a novel, in the manner of Mallock's New Republic, called *The Perplexities of John Forstice*. Though the first half of it I still think is not bad, the latter half seems very dull to me, and I have never made any attempt to publish it. I also invented a story that I never published.

From the time when Rutherford first discovered the structure of the atom, it had been obvious that sooner or later atomic force would become available in war. This had caused me to foresee the possibility of the complete destruction of man through his own folly. In my story a pure scientist makes up a little machine which can destroy matter throughout the universe. He has known hitherto only his own laboratory and so he decides that, before using his machine, he must find out whether the world deserves to be destroyed. He keeps his little machine in his waistcoat pocket and if he presses the knob the world will cease to exist. He goes round the world examining whatever seems to him evil, but everything leaves him in doubt until he finds himself at a Lord Mayor's Banquet and finds the nonsense talked by politicians unbearable. He leaps up and announces that he is about to destroy the world. The other diners rush at him to stop him. He puts his thumb in his waistcoat pocket—and finds that in changing for dinner he forgot to move the little machine.

I did not publish this story at the time as it seemed too remote from reality. But, with the coming of the atom bomb, its remoteness from reality vanished, so I wrote other stories with a similar moral, some of which ended in atomic destruction, while others, which I called 'nightmares', exemplified the hidden fears of eminent men.

The writing of these stories was a great release of my hitherto unexpressed feelings and of thoughts which could not be stated without mention of fears that had no rational basis. Gradually their scope widened. I found it possible to express in this fictional form dangers that would have been deemed silly while only a few men recognized them. I could state in fiction ideas which I half believed in but had no good solid grounds for believing. In this way it was possible to warn of dangers which might or might not occur in the near future.

My first book of stories was *Satan in the Suburbs*. The title story was in part suggested to me by a stranger whom I met in Mortlake and who, when he saw me, crossed the road and made the sign of the Cross as he went. It was partly, also, suggested by a poor mad lady who I used to meet on my walks. In this story there was a wicked scientist who by subtle means caused people, after one lapse from virtue, to plunge into irretrievable ruin. One of these people was a photographer who made photography an opportunity for blackmail. I modelled him upon a fashionable photographer who had come to make a picture of me. He died shortly afterwards, and I then learnt that he practised all the sins of which I had accused him in the story. In one of the other stories, the hero proclaims a curse in which he mentions Zoroaster and the Beard of The Prophet. I got an indignant letter from a Zoroastrian saying how dare I make fun of Zoroaster. This story I had written, as a warning of what might befall her, for my secretary (a completely innocent young woman) who was about to go to Corsica on a holiday. It was published anonymously in a magazine with a prize offered for guessing the authorship. Nobody guessed right. One of the characters in the story is General Prz to whose name there is a footnote saying, 'pronounced Pish', and the prize was given to a man who wrote to the magazine: 'This is Trz (pronounced Tosh).' Another story portrayed a fight to the death between human beings and Martians. In this there is an eloquent appeal in the style of Churchill, calling upon all human beings to forget their differences and rise in defence of MAN. I had great fun proclaiming this speech, as nearly as possible in Churchill's manner, for a gramophone record.

A year later, I wrote another series of stories which I called *Nightmares of Eminent Persons*. These were intended to illustrate the secret fears that beset the Great while they sleep. A long short story that I published with *Nightmares* is called 'Zahatopolk' and concerns the hardening of what begins as a career of freedom of thought into a hard persecuting orthodoxy. This has hitherto been the fate of all the great religions; and how it is to be avoided in the future I do not know. When my secretary was typing the story she reached the point where the semi-divine king makes a sacrificial breakfast of a lovely lady. I went in to see how she was getting on and found her gibbering in terror. Various people have dramatized this story both for film and theatre production, as they have others that occur in my writings, but, when it has come to the point, no one has been willing to produce them or I have been unwilling to have them produced because of the particular dramatization, sometimes offensively frivolous. I regret this and regret especially that none of the *Nightmares* have been made into ballets. Various of the stories pose, and occasionally answer, various questions that I should like to call to people's attention.

I had an amusing experience with one of the *Nightmares* while I was composing it. The hero was a Frenchman who lamented his sad fate in French verse. One evening at dinner in the Ecu de France I started to declaim his last words in what I hoped was the best French classical style. The restaurant, being French, had a clientele mainly composed of Frenchmen. Most of them turned round and gazed at me in astonishment, then whispered together, wondering whether I was an unknown French poet whom they had hit upon by accident. I do not know how long they went on wondering.

Another *Nightmare* was inspired by a psycho-analytic doctor in America who was somewhat dissatisfied by the use commonly made of psycho-analysis. He felt that everyone might be brought to humdrum normality, so I tried portraying Shakespeare's more interesting heroes after they had undergone a course of psycho-analysis. In the dream, a head of Shakespeare speaks, ending with the words, 'Lord, what fools these mortals be'. I had an approving letter from the American doctor.

I found a reluctance on the part of both editors and readers to accept me in the rôle of a writer of fiction. They seemed, just on the face of it, to resent the fact that I was trying my hand at something they had not grown used to my doing. Everybody wanted me to continue as a writer of doom, prophesying dreadful things. I was reminded of what the learned men of China said when I asked what I should lecture on and they replied: 'Oh, just what you say in your last book.' Authors are not allowed by their public to change their style or to part widely from their previous subjects.

My defence for writing stories, if defence were needed, is that I have often found fables the best way of making a point. When I returned from America in 1944, I found British philosophy in a very odd state, and, it seemed to me, occupied solely with trivialities. Everybody in the philosophical world was babbling about 'common usage'. I did not like this philosophy. Every section of learning has its own vocabulary and I did not see why philosophy should be deprived of this pleasure. I therefore wrote a short piece containing various fables making fun of this cult of 'common usage', remarking that what the philosophers really meant by the term was 'common-room usage'. I received a letter when this was published from the arch offender saying that he approved, but that he could not think against whom it was directed as he knew of no such cult. However, I noticed that from that time on very little was said about 'common usage'.

Most of my books, I find on looking back over them, have myths to enforce the points. For instance, I turned up the following paragraph recently in *The Impact of Science on Society*: 'What I do want to stress is that the kind of lethargic despair which is now not uncommon is irrational. Mankind is in the position of a man climbing a difficult and dangerous precipice, at the summit of which there is a plateau of delicious mountain meadows. With every step that he climbs, his fall, if he does fall, becomes more terrible; with every step his weariness increases and the ascent grows more difficult. At last, there is only one more step to be taken, but the climber does not know this, because he cannot see beyond the jutting rocks at his head. His exhaustion is so complete that he wants nothing but rest. If he lets go, he will find rest in death. Hope calls: "one more effort—perhaps it will be the last effort needed." Irony retorts: "Silly fellow! Haven't you been listening to hope all this time, and see where it has landed you." Optimism says: "While there is life, there is hope." Pessimism growls: "While there is life, there is pain." Does the exhausted climber make one more effort, or does he let himself sink into the abyss? In a few years, those of us who are still alive will know the answer.'

Others of my stories, nightmares and dreams and so forth, later formed the fiction part of my book *Fact and Fiction*. I had expected reviewers to make witticisms at my expense in regard to the title and contents of this book, but this did not occur. My 'Maxims of La Rochefoucauld' contained in it afforded me considerable amusement and

I have added to them periodically. The making of my *Good Citizens'* *Alphabet* entertained me greatly. It was published at their Gabberbochus (which, I am told, is Polish for Jabberwocky) Press by my friends the Themersons with exceedingly clever and beautifully executed illustrations by Franciszka Themerson which heighten all the points that I most wanted made. They also published my *jeu d'esprit* on the end of the world, a short *History of the World*, for my ninetieth birthday in a little gold volume. My only venture into verse was published by the Humanists of America and is called—with apologies to Lewis Carroll— 'The Prelate and The Commissar'.

LETTERS

To and from Lucy Donnelly

212 Loring Avenue
Los Angeles, Cal.
Dec. 22, 1939

My dear Lucy

Ever since I got your nice letter I have been meaning to write to you, but have been terribly busy. It is the custom of this country to keep all intelligent people so harassed & hustled that they cease to be intelligent, and I have been suffering from this custom. The summer at Santa Barbara, it is true, was peaceful, but unluckily I injured my back & was laid up for a long time, which caused me to get behind hand with my lectures.—John & Kate, who came for the summer holidays, stayed when war broke out; it is a comfort to have them here, but John does not find the university of California a satisfactory substitute for Cambridge. I think of sending them both East to some less recent university, but last September there was no time for that. Apart from home sickness & war misery, we all flourish.

I am, when I can find time, writing a book on 'Words & Facts', or 'semantics' as it is vulgarly called. The only thing to be done in these times, it seems to me, is to salvage what one can of civilization, personally as well as politically. But I feel rather like a strayed ghost from a dead world.

The visit to you was delightful. As time goes on, one values old friends more & more.

Remember me to Miss Finch. With love to yourself,

> *yours aff*
> *Bertrand Russell*

New Place
Bryn Mawr
Pennsylvania
29 April 1940

My dear Bertie

Week by week I have sympathized with you & regretted bitterly that you

38

have not been allowed to live and work in peace in America. Then, after all the muddlement & disgusting publicity, came your admirable letter in the *New York Times*—so wise, so right in feeling & so to the point at the close. Something was needed from you personally in reply to the Editorial distributing blame judiciously all round & very suspiciously avoiding the issue. Too bad of the *Times*: Your article in the *American Mercury* I also rejoiced in as just right & very useful. But this cause célèbre which scores for academic freedom for our country, I fear will have cost you yourself dear in many ways & have seriously upset your plans for the next year. I am very sorry.

I think of you always & hope to see you when you come to the East again— and perhaps your family with you. They look one & all of them delightful in their pictures. In these bad times your children must be a joy & hope. Your letter at Christmas was a happiness to me, when I remember all the people in the world to whom you have given happiness & enlightenment I marvel the more over this last confusion.

> *Ever yours with love*
> *Lucy Donnelly*

P.S. The cutting I enclose from the *College News*, our student paper, is Bryn Mawr's modest testimony to the cause in your name.

> Fallen Leaf lodge
> Lake Tahoe, Cal.
> August 25, 1940

My dear Lucy

Peter is terribly busy, & I have finished my book, so I am answering your very nice letter to her.

We are leaving here in about a fortnight, & expect to get to Philadelphia about the 12th of September, except John & Kate, who go back to Los Angeles. I expect to be in Philadelphia only a few days, & then to go to Harvard, but Peter, with Conrad & the governess (Miss Campbell), means to stay somewhere near Philadelphia & hunt for a house. I have accepted the Barnes Institute; there was no other prospect of any post, however humble. No university dare contemplate employing me.

You once offered to put us up if we were in Philadelphia, & it would be very pleasant for us if you could have us for a few days from about the 12th, but I don't know if you have two spare rooms, one for Peter & me & one for Conrad & Miss Campbell. Still less do I know whether you would want a boy of three, whose behaviour might not always be impeccable. Please be *quite* frank about this.

Yes, I know Newman of John's. I have found him, on occasion, a very valuable critic.

I am sorry you will have to put up with us as a feeble substitute for the Renoirs. Perhaps in time I shall be able to soften Barnes's heart.

With Peter's thanks & my love,

> *Yours affectionately*
> *Bertrand Russell*

April 15, 1941

My dear Lucy

I blush with shame in the middle of the night every time I think of my outrageous behaviour at your dinner, when I deafened you by shouting at your ear. Please forgive me. Since the New York row I have been prickly, especially when I encounter the facile optimism which won't realize that, but for Barnes, it would have meant literal starvation for us all—But that is no excuse for abominable behaviour. I used, when excited, to calm myself by reciting the three factors of $a^3 + b^3 + c^3 - 3abc$; I must revert to this practice. I find it more effective than thoughts of the Ice Age or the goodness of God.

Yours affectionately
Bertrand Russell

Peacock Inn
Twenty Bayard Lane
Princeton, N.J.
May 14, 1944

My dear Lucy

This is a goodbye letter, with great regret that I can't bid you goodbye in person. After months of waiting, we are being suddenly shipped off at a moment's notice—Peter and Conrad are already gone & I go in 2 or 3 days. It was nice being your neighbours, & your house seemed almost a bit of England. Please tell Helen[1] I am very sorry not to write to her too—& give my love (or whatever she would like better) to Edith.

Ever yours aff
B.R.

Trinity College
Cambridge
Oct. 7, 1944

My dear Lucy

It was nice to get your letter written in August. Coming to your house always seemed almost like coming home; it & its contents, animate & inanimate, were so much more English than one could find elsewhere in U.S.A.

D. S. Robertson is a man I know only slightly, but he has a considerable reputation. How Keynes has expanded since he used to come & stay at Tilford! Last time I saw him he had an enormous paunch—but this was not the sort of expansion I had in mind!

John is still in London, learning Japanese forms of politeness. One would have thought forms of rudeness more useful. He will go to the East before the end of this year, & probably be there a long time. Kate has been home about a month. She ended in a blaze of glory, with a $250 prize, an offer from

[1] Helen Thomas Flexner.

Radcliffe to go on their staff, & from a Southern University to become a Professor, though not yet of age. Now the British Government pays her to read Goebbels.

The Robot bombs have been trying, & have not quite ceased, but they are no longer very serious. We all flourish. Love to Edith. Much love and friendship to yourself.

> *Ever yours*
> *Bertrand Russell*

New Place
Bryn Mawr, Penna.
February 20th 45

My dear Bertie

Edith's great pleasure in your two letters I have shared. I am especially glad that you thought well of her book—whatever of M.C.T. [M. Carey Thomas] herself. After living under the two presidents who have succeeded at the College, I confess that my opinion of her has risen a good deal. The new ways on the Campus make it strange and *unheimlich* to me. O, for 'the Culture' of the '90's! . . .

The world all round now is a very grim one, as you say, and bitter to those of us who once lived in a happier time. Here in America of course we are among the fortunate ones, well fed, well housed & all the rest, but we do not grow wiser, more gruesome minded I fear. Everywhere it seems we can depend only on old affections and tried loyalties.

I turn to you, who have for so long added to my life so much interest and pleasure, & to my happiness in hearing that you are planning to write your autobiography. You will make a great and important book. I hope from my very heart that I may live to read it. Your letters of course I will look up and send along for any help they can give you. Notes & reminders are useful. . .

I have long wanted to write and to hear from you again but seem away here to have nothing worth saying. Edith and I and other friends of course often talk of you and wish you back. Our neighborhood fell into dullness when you left. We drove out, Edith & I, one day in the autumn in a *pietas* to Little Datchett, now alas painted up in all colours and newly named 'Stone Walls' on a sign at the gate. But the wide Jeffersonian view was the same and very delightful. Are either of your elder children still in America? Conrad of course will have grown beyond my recognition. Will you not send me some word of them and of Peter. I hope that she is better in health and able to get proper food.

Even the London where you are living is almost unknown to me, though I remember once walking up and down Gloucester Place, looking out the house where Lady Louisa Stuart lived in old age: and you must be near Portman Square and Mrs Montagu's grand mansion there. The late eighteenth Century in England is a safe retreat in these days for one lost in the America of Bob Taft and Henry Wallace and the rest of all you know from the papers.

Alas, that Edith and I are too poor to go to England this summer to breathe its air again and to see our friends. How I wish it were not so.

Affectionately yours
Lucy Donnelly

P.S. Barnes has been as quiet as a mouse these last years.

Hotel Bellerive au Lac
Zurich
June 23, 1946

My dear Lucy

Thank you for your letter. I had not heard of Simon Flexner's death, which is sad. I don't know Helen's address; if I did, I would write to her. Will you please give her my very sincere sympathy, & tell her how greatly I admired & respected Simon.

What you say about my History of Philosophy is very pleasant reading. I am glad you like my Chap. on Plotinus, as I rather fancied it myself!

I am at the moment doing a short lecture tour in Switzerland; I return to Peter & Conrad in N. Wales in a week for the long vacation, after which I shall be back in Trinity, where I have been inhabiting Newton's rooms. I go about with feeling that within 20 years England will have ceased to exist. It makes everything hectic, like the approach of closing time at a party in a hotel—'We are for the night.' A few bombs will destroy all our cities, & the rest will slowly die of hunger.

In America, large sections of the rural middle west & the desert southwest will probably survive. But not much of your America. Three cheers for Patagonia, the future centre of world culture.

Meanwhile Rabbis & Muftis, Jinnah & Nehru, Tito & the Italians, etc., play their silly games. I am ashamed of belonging to the species Homo Sapiens.

The Swiss are passionately Anglophile, & very glad to be liberated from Nazi encirclement. I try not to depress them.

You & I may be thankful to have lived in happier times—you more than I, because you have no children.

Ever yours affectionately
Bertrand Russell

Penralltgoch
Llan Ffestiniog
Merioneth
March 17, 1948

My dear Lucy

Thank you for your good letter. It was a great pleasure to get it.

I enclose a letter to Helen, as I am not sure whether I have deciphered correctly the address you gave me. If not, will you please alter it as may be necessary. I have started on my autobiography, & find it an immense task. I shall be infinitely grateful for your batch of letters. It doesn't matter whether you send them to above address or to London.

My daughter Kate has just married an American named Charles Tait. She still lives in Cambridge Mass. I don't know him, but all I hear of him sounds nice.

I am terribly busy with international affairs, & have not time to write proper letters. Give nice messages to Edith. With love,

Yours aff
B.R.

> New Place
> Bryn Mawr College
> Bryn Mawr
> Pennsylvania
> May 8, 1948

My dear Bertie

I am sorry to have been so long in complying with any request of yours. This has been a bad and busy year here in Bryn Mawr and though I keep very well for my age, I am so easily tired and do everything so slowly, I accomplish little in a day.

In a word, I have only been able in the last fortnight to go through the papers & letters stored in the attic. The task was formidable and painful as well as happy. Many letters from you I found, dating from 1902 on, and have put aside to send you if you still want them. From your letter some time ago, I was uncertain whether you ask for all letters, or particularly for the one written to Helen on the last day of the Nineteenth Century.

All that you wrote to me I seem to have treasured down to the merest notes. They are wonderfully friendly, wise, kind letters, sympathetic almost beyond belief with my personal concerns and small Bryn Mawr affairs, while bringing in an invigorating breath from a larger freer world. I well remember the vivid pleasure of their coming, one after another, and the strength & interest they were to me.—A lifetime of gratitude I send back to you for them.—Whether they would be useful to you I cannot tell, possibly for dates, plans places & whatnot, and as a record of your own friendliness. Your memory is extraordinarily good & you have written so much that is wise & witty & important. Will you say whether you want the packet, & they really shall go off to you at once. In that case I should like to have them back when you are done with the letters. They are a precious record of a long friendship to me, though as I understand, your property. . . .

All is well I hope with you, as well as may be with the world in desperate confusion. Here we are in the midst of strikes, Presidential primaries, indecisions about Palestine, [indecipherable] bills & all that you can guess.

Edith asks me to give you her love with mine. & all good wishes for the Summer. We plan to go to Canada,[1] the nearest we are able to get to the British flag.

Affectionately yours
Lucy

---

[1] Where she died in the Summer of 1948.

From the 12th. Duke of Bedford

Froxfield House
Woburn
Bletchley
April 16th. 1945

Dear Lord Russell

Many thanks for your kind letter. I should have been very pleased for you to see Woburn but unluckily the abbey is infested by a government War Department of a very 'hush-hush' description and I am not allowed to enter the sacred precincts myself without a permit & suitable escort! Most of the pictures etc. are stored away, so I am afraid you will have to postpone your visit until the brief interlude between this war & world-war no 3.—if there *is* an interlude!! I am so sorry.

Yours sincerely
Bedford

From H. G. Wells

13, Hanover Terrace
Regent's Park, N.W.1
May. 20th '45

My dear Russell

I was delighted to get your friendly letter. In these days of revolutionary crisis it is incumbent upon all of us who are in any measure influential in left thought to dispel the tendency to waste energy in minor dissentions & particularly to counter the *systematic & ingenious* work that is being done to sabotage left thought under the cloak of critical reasonableness. I get a vast amount of that sort of propaganda in my letter box. I get more & more anarchistic & ultra left as I grow older. I enclose a little article 'Orders is Orders' that the *New Leader* has had the guts, rather squeamish guts, to print at last. What do you think of it?

We must certainly get together to talk (& perhaps conspire) & that soon. What are your times & seasons? My daughter in law Marjorie fixes most of my engagements and you & Madame must come to tea one day & see what we can do.

I have been ill & I keep ill. I am President of the Diabetic Soc'y & diabetes keeps one in & out, in & out of bed every two hours or so. This exhausts, and this vast return to chaos which is called the peace, the infinite meanness of great masses of my fellow creatures, the wickedness of organized religion give me a longing for a sleep that will have no awakening. There is a long history of heart failure on my paternal side but modern palliatives are very effective holding back that moment of release. Sodium bicarbonate keeps me in a grunting state of protesting endurance. But while I live I *have* to live and I owe a lot to a decaying civilization which has anyhow kept alive enough of the spirit of scientific devotion to stimulate my curiosity [and] make me its debtor.

Forgive this desolation. I hope to see you both before very long & am yours most gratefully.

H. G. Wells

From Clement Attlee

10, Downing Street
Whitehall
11 October, 1945

My dear Russell

Many thanks for your letter of October 9 and for sending me your article—
'What America could do with the Atomic Bomb'. I have read this with interest
and I am grateful to you for bringing it to my notice. I need hardly tell you
that this is one of the most difficult and perplexing problems with which
statesmen have ever been faced and I can assure you that all the points you
have made are present in my mind.

Yours sincerely
C. R. Attlee

*The following is the account that I wrote to my wife Peter immediately after the
plane accident in which I was involved. It is dated October 1948.*

You will no doubt have learnt that I was in an accident to-day—luckily one
in which I suffered no damage beyond loss of suit-case etc. I was sure the
newspapers would exaggerate so I telegraphed to you at once. I came from
Oslo in a sea-plane, and just as it touched the water on arrival here a sudden
wind blew it onto its side and let the water in. Boats were sent out instantly,
and we had to jump from a window and swim till they reached us, which was
only about a minute. I did not know till later that some who could not swim
were drowned. It did me no harm whatever. My writing is queer because my
pen is lost. I went to bed because I had no dry clothes. The Consul has now
brought me some and the Vice-Consul has lent me a suit till mine is dry.
Everybody has made far more fuss of me than the occasion warranted. I was
struck by the good behaviour of the passengers—all did exactly as they were
told without any fuss.

I will try to relate everything.

The weather was stormy, heavy rain and a gale of wind. The sea-plane had
just touched the water of the fjord when there was a violent jerk and I found
myself on the floor with some inches of water in which hats, coats, etc. were
floating. I exclaimed 'well, well!' and started looking for my hat, which I failed
to find. At first I thought a wave had broken in at a window; it didn't occur
to me it was serious.

I was in the very back of the plane, the only part where one could smoke;
this turned out to be the best place to be. After a few minutes the crew opened
a door and got the passengers from the back through to an open window, and
shoved us one by one into the sea. By this time their haste had made me
realize that things were serious. I jumped, clutching my attache case, but had
to let go of it to swim. When I got into the water I saw there was a boat close
by. We swam to it and were pulled on board. When I looked round, nothing
was visible of the plane except the tip of a wing. The swim was about 20 yards.
I saw nothing of what happened at the other end of the plane; I imagine they

jumped through another window. I gather the people killed were stunned when the accident happened. One of them was a Professor concerned in arrangements about my lecture. I pointed out my floating attache case to the people on the boat, and last night a policeman brought it. The things in it were all right, except that the silly books were somewhat damaged. No other piece of luggage was rescued.

The people who had come to the airport to meet me were very solicitous, and drove me at breakneck speed to the hotel, where I got my wet clothes off, went to bed, and consumed large quantities of brandy and coffee, after which I went to sleep. The Consul brought me socks, shirt, etc., and the Vice-Consul lent me a suit. My own will be wearable to-morrow. Then came an avalanche of journalists. One from Copenhagen asked what I thought while in the water. I said I thought the water was cold. 'You didn't think about mysticism and logic?' 'No' I said, and rang off.

I was not brave, only stupid. I had always thought a sea-plane would float. I did not realize there was danger, and was mainly concerned to save my attache case. My watch goes as well as ever, and even my matches strike. But the suitcase, with a suit, shirts, etc. is gone for ever. I am writing with a beastly pen, because mine is lost.

To Willard V. Quine

18 Dorset House
Gloucester Place, N.W.1
Feb. 4, 1949

Dear Dr Quine

Thank you for your kind letter, and for your paper on 'What There is'—a somewhat important subject. When I first sent my theory of description to *Mind* in 1905, Stout thought it such rubbish that he almost refused to print it.

I am glad you noticed the allusion to yourself on p. 140.

I was lucky in the aeroplane accident, as nearly half those on the plane ceased to be among 'what there is'.

Yours sincerely
Bertrand Russell

After my return to England I paid several visits to my first wife at her invitation, and received the following letters from her. The friendly correspondence lasted till her death very early in 1951.

25 Wellington Square
Chelsea, S.W.3
June 9. 1949

Dearest Bertie

I feel I must break the silence of all these years by sending thee a line of congratulation on thy o m. No one can rejoice in it more heartily than I do, just as no one was more sorry for the prison sentence and thy difficulties in America. Now I hope thee will have a peaceful old age, just as I am doing at

81, after a stormy time with Logan. I miss dear Lucy Donnelly's letters very much, but am glad they have raised over $50,000.00 to endow a Scholarship in English in her memory.

As ever, affectionately thine
Alys

25 Wellington Square
Chelsea, S.W.3
Sept. 30 1949

Dearest Bertie

I found these letters and this article of thine among my papers, and think thee may like to have them. I think I must have destroyed all thy other letters. Our scrapbook about the Sozial-Demokrats in Berlin in 1895 I presented to the London School of Economics, but have borrowed it back now as the BBC may want a Talk on it. I have told them thee could give it much better than I.

I have been told thee is writing thy Autobiography, which ought to be deeply interesting. (I don't care for B. B. [Bernard Berenson]'s but like George Trevelyan's.) I am also writing some Memoirs, and enclose a copy of what I think of saying about our marriage. But if thee thinks it incorrect, or wounding to thee, I could make it much shorter.

Thine ever
Alys

I hope thee will be interested in these recently published Letters of Mother's.

What Alys wrote of our marriage:

Bertie was an ideal companion, & he taught me more than I can ever repay. But I was never clever enough for him, & perhaps he was too sophisticated for me. I was ideally happy for several years, almost deliriously happy, until a change of feeling made our mutual life very difficult. A final separation led to a divorce, when he married again. But that was accomplished without bitterness, or quarrels, or recriminations, & later with great rejoicing on my part when he was awarded the O M. But my life was completely changed, & I was never able to meet him again for fear of the renewal of my awful misery, & heartsick longing for the past. I only caught glimpses of him at lectures or concerts occasionally, & thro' the uncurtained windows of his Chelsea house, where I used to watch him sometimes reading to his children. Unfortunately, I was neither wise enough nor courageous enough to prevent this one disaster from shattering my capacity for happiness & my zest for life.

25 Wellington Square
Chelsea, S.W.3
Jan. 13. 1950

Dearest Bertie

In September I sent thee a book of Mother's Letters, *A Religious Rebel*, with a 1909 packet of thy own letters to me, and a note from myself. I could not

47

understand why I had no reply, but now the packet has been returned to me—my name was on the outside and it was addressed to the Hon. Bertrand Russell, o m, Penralltgoch, Llan Ffestiniog, Merioneth but marked 'not known'. I should like it to reach thee if I knew thy address.

Thine ever
Alys

25 Wellington Square
Chelsea, S.W.3
Feb. 14. '50

Dearest Bertie

I enjoyed thy visit immensely, & hope we can be friends & see each other soon again. I wrote to B. B. about thy coming here, & he sends thee a warm invitation to go & stay with him at any time. He says there is no man alive whom he would rather be seeing and talking with than thee, & that he practically always agrees with everything thee writes. He has asked me to lend thee his book on Aesthetics, which I will do, tho' I do not think thee will care for it. The Autobiography is better, tho' not well written.

I should like to know thy opinion of Bob Gathorne-Hardy's *Recollections of Logan*, & will send thee my extra copy, if thee has not already seen it. It has been very well reviewed, & B. B. calls it 'a masterpiece'.

Ever thine
Alys

25 Wellington Square
Chelsea, S.W.3
Mar. 9. 1950

Dearest Bertie

Thanks for thy letter. I was not surprised at thy not answering mine of Sept. 30th. as I thought thee probably preferred not to have any intimate talk of the past, but I am thankful that thee did not feel unduly censured, nor that my radiant memories of our life together should be marred. Please do come & have lunch with me again as soon as thee can possibly spare time. I shall count the days till then, as I have so many questions I want to discuss with thee, & I hope it will be soon. Ring up before 9.30 or after 12.

I don't think I want thy letters from Paris, nor the German volumes, as the b b c decline a talk on Germany in 1895.

Thine ever
Alys

25 Wellington Square
Chelsea, S.W.3
April 14. 1950

Dearest Bertie

I have so enjoyed our two meetings & thee has been so friendly, that I feel I must be honest & just say once (but once only) that I am utterly devoted to

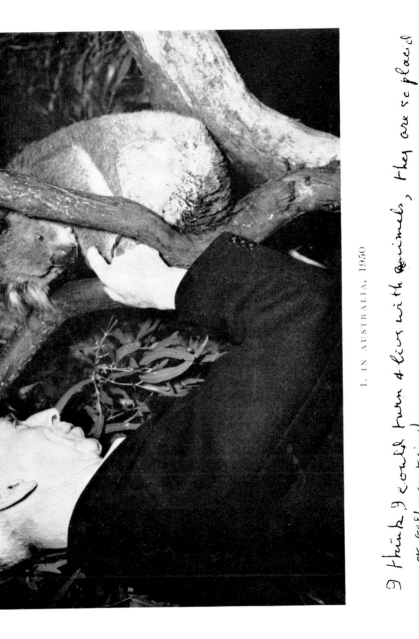

I. IN AUSTRALIA, 1950

I think I could turn & live with animals, they are so placid & self-contained ....
Not one is respects left or unhappy over the whole earth

2. Bertrand Russell with Madame Joliot-Curie in Stockholm, 1950

thee, & have been for over 50 years. My friends have always known that I loved thee more than anyone else in the world, & they now rejoice with me that I am now able to see thee again.

But my devotion makes no claim, and involves no burden on thy part, nor any obligation, not even to answer this letter.

But I shall still hope thee can spare time to come to lunch or dinner before very long, & that thee will not forget May 18th.

Thine ever
Alys

25 Wellington Square
Chelsea, S.W.3
June 8. 1950

Dearest Bertie

Thanks for my book returned, with the address I wanted on a very small slip of paper, & now for thy two volumes. I am immensely pleased to have them from thee (tho' I hope thee doesn't think I was hinting!) & shall enjoy them very much, & send my warmest thanks. Florence Halévy is delighted thee should have my copy of Elie's posthumous book, & sends thee her kindest remembrances & regards.

If thee can spare a minute before the 18th., do telephone about breakfast time any day to give me thy address in Australia. I should like to write to thee on my b. day in July.

Ever thine
Alys

25 Wellington Square
Chelsea, S.W.3
July 21. 1950

Dearest Bertie

I have had a nice 83rd. birthday with many callers with flowers & books & fruits & telegrams, & it would have been perfect if there had been a letter from thee. But I know thee must be desperately busy, & worse still desperately worried over Korea & this awful drift to War. We can hardly think or talk of anything else, but I try to keep serene & to distract my visitors from too much worry, when there seems nothing we can any of us do, & I think I have been successful today. This little poem was a help, by Helen Arbuthnot & the friend she lives with: 'Alys Russell, hail to thee! Angel of the Square, where would Wellontonia be If thou were not there.' (The rest too fulsome to quote. I tried to write a poem to thee on May 18th. but got no further than 'Bertrand Russell, hail to thee! Darling of the B B C'.—but cld. get no further.) I have only just read thy *Conquest of Happiness* & some of the chapters would have helped me very much in my talk on 'Being over 80'. But nothing thee says cld. equal my concluding paragraph, wh. I think thee missed, literally taken from *The Times*, my wished-for epitaph 'In loving memory of John & Mary Williams who lived such beautiful lives on Bromley Common'.

This letter will be full of happy events, as my last was full of woes, & I hope it will distract thee for a few minutes.

1. My kind Irish housekeeper, of 30 years service, is better from a bad heart attack, & will be back soon.

2. My Tennyson Talk was a great success, with much approval from the 3rd Prog. Producers, & Bob G. H. [Gathorne-Hardy] wrote to me: 'Your Broadcast was absolutely delicious, like an enchanting, exquisite, complete little short story, with a perfect twist at the end "How we must have bored him!".'

3. Karin seems quite well again, & is writing a book on 'Despair'. Desmond is speaking, I hear, on the despair of old age, which is a pity and not good news, & Hugh Trevor-Roper writes that the Berlin Congress (on Cultural Freedom?) would not have been sponsored by thee if thee had known how it would turn out, being a political demonstration, which the Eng. representatives (following the now classical tradition of Oxford Dons) did their best to disrupt. I am surprised at his criticism, as he is himself a narrow Oxford Don.

I could write on forever, but must walk up to the King's Rd. & post this letter. I have said nothing about thy cruel private grief in not seeing Conrad, & perhaps thy fear that John may have to go back to the Navy. I do feel for thee, but hope thee is somehow managing to conquer happiness.

Thine ever
Alys

25 Wellington Square
Chelsea, S.W.3
July 24. 1950

Dearest Bertie

Thy letter of the 16th arrived too late for my b. day, but is most welcome. I am glad the Australians are friendly & appreciative, but wish I cld. hear the details of the Cath. B. Control invigorating fight. I remember Cath. trouble at the Wimbledon Election, but think it was over Education. Thee may not remember my little Cardiff friend, Maud Rees Jones, who helped us at Wimbledon. She only remembers wanting to pick up the windblown stamps in thy room, & thy begging her not to, saying 'If you scrounge for them I shall have to scrounge too, but if we leave them, Alys will pick them up', wh. I did presently,—I can't find Chas. Wood's name in Edith Finch's book, only on p. 35 'He (Blunt) saw much of the 2 younger Stanley sisters, Kate & Rosalind. Beautiful & vivid they whirled him away in an orgy of lively talk with all the piquancy of enthusiastic prejudice. Nothing in heaven & earth passed unquestioned or undiscussed. They stimulated in him an intellectual activity that had much to do with the later individuality of his views, & that, more immediately proved disconcerting during his life in Germany', where in 1861 he became very intimate with Lady Malet who troubled him by her constant speculation on religious troubles.

Here is an amusing extract from one of my honeymoon letters from The Hague: 'I have sewed 2 buttons on Bertie's shirts & he doesn't mind my sewing as much as he thought he would.'

I envy thee seeing a Coral Island. Did we read together Curzon's *Monasteries of the East*? Robt. Byron, that clever yng. writer killed in the War, has had republished his excellent book on Mt Athos, beautifully written & deeply interesting.—Another b. day poem ends with:

'So here's a toast & drink it up
In lemonade or cyder cup
(For Auntie's Temperance)
That decades on we still shall be
Blessed by her merry company
Her lovely countenance.'

But not 'merry' now with the attack on Formosa, & defeats in Korea, alas!
Thine ever
Alys

25 Wellington Square
Chelsea, S.W.3
Nov. 19. 1950

Dearest Nobel Lord

I am enchanted with thy new Honour, & am only sorry I was not sure enough of thy address to cable my congratulations. I knew of it on the 7th., when a Swedish journalist friend came here for information about thee. (I lent him Leggatt's book, tho' it has been trans^d into Swedish I believe.) He told me incidentally that Churchill & Croce were thy runners-up, but thee won. The papers here have been very enthusiastic, including a BBC Talk to children, calling thee 'an apostle of humanity & of free speech'. The American papers must have gone wild over thee. I hope thee will not share the Prize with the Amer. dentist's wife, tho' she must be feeling rather flat.

Thanks for thy letter from Swarthmore. I am shocked at thy account of poor Evelyn [Whitehead]! & feel most sorry for her without her angelic Alfred to care for her. I hope her children are some comfort. I look forward to seeing thee before or after Stockholm, but agree that Scandinavia is unhealthy for philosophers. But anyhow the present King will not get thee up at 5 a.m., nor force thee to sit on or in a stove for warmth. (He is a *'connustur'* friend of B.B.'s bye the way, & has paid a fairly recent visit to I Tatti. B. B. telegraphed his congratulations to thee thro' me, & I hope thee remembered to send him thy Essays.) I send on some cuttings thee may have missed, & also a letter from Florence Halévy. Also Desmond on Shaw. Has thy article on Shaw appeared yet?

I am glad thee doesn't mean to travel again, as I feel thee shd. not have the strain of it, & that thee can better serve the cause of Internationalism, for which I have worked passionately for 30 years, by broadcasting at home, & writing.

Also it will save me from buying thee a new sponge bag for Xmas, which I felt sure thee must need!

Thine devotedly
Alys

From and to T. S. Eliot

24 Russell Square, W.C.1
10 June 1949

Dear Bertie

Permit me to add my sincere felicitations to your others; on the occasion of your joining this small and odd miscellaneous order. It is a fitting though belated tribute to the author of *The Philosophy of Leibnitz*, the *Principia* and the other works on which I fed thirty-five years ago. And also to the author of the Reith Lectures—who is one of the few living authors who can write English prose.

Yours ever
T. S. Eliot

The Master of Trinity recommends safety pins in the ribbon: but a neat tuck on each side is much better.

Ffestiniog, N. Wales
13.6.49

Dear Tom

Thank you very much for your nice letter. In old days when we were huddled together in Russell Chambers, we could hardly have expected that lapse of time would make us so respectable.

I will test your opinion against George Trevy's as soon as I get the chance.

Yours ever
B.R.

Faber and Faber Ltd.
24 Russell Square
London W.C.1
20th May, 1964

The Rt. Hon. The Earl Russell, o m
Plas Penrhyn
Penrhyndeudraeth
Merionethshire

Dear Bertie

My wife and I listened the other night to your broadcast interview and thought it went over extremely well.

As you may know, I disagree with your views on most subjects, but I thought that you put your beliefs over in a most dignified and even persuasive way. I wanted you to know this as you are getting on so far, and as I myself am, I hope, somewhat mellowed by age.

With grateful and affectionate memories,

Yours ever
Tom

Plas Penrhyn
23 May, 1964

Dear Tom

Many thanks for your letter of May 20. I am glad that you found my broadcast remarks 'dignified and even persuasive'. It was nice to hear from you again.

Yours ever
Bertie

From N. B. Foot
General Secretary of the New Commonwealth Society

(President British Section:
The Rt. Hon. Winston S.
Churchill, OM, CH, MP)
25 Victoria Street
London S.W.1
September 25th, 1947

Dear Lord Russell

I am sending you this letter on the eve of your departure for the Continent in the hope that it may provide you with a little information about the New Commonwealth which you may find useful. In the first place, however, I should like to reiterate our thanks to you for having taken on this journey. We are deeply appreciative of the honour you are doing us in acting as our representative, and we feel confident that your visit will be quite invaluable in arousing interest in the Society's proposals. I hope the arrangements which Miss Sibthorp has made for you will prove satisfactory in every way.

It was very kind of you to provide us with a precis of your address. I have read it with the greatest admiration and, if I may venture to say so without presumption, it seems to me to provide a masterly analysis of the problems that confront us and of the solution which it is our purpose to offer. As you know, we have always laid stress on the urgent need for the internationalisation of the major weapons of war and the creation of machinery for the peaceful settlement of all disputes, political as well as judicial. We believe, as you do, that the establishment of a full-fledged World Parliament is likely to prove a distant goal, and probably the most distinctive feature of our programme is the proposal that until such a development becomes feasible, the legislative function to which you refer in your address should be entrusted to a completely impartial Tribunal. We fully admit that this Tribunal would not be a perfect

53

instrument, but we are convinced that it would be infinitely more suitable for the just settlement of non-judicial issues than either the Security Council or the Permanent Court, bearing in mind that the former is made up of politicians whose first job is to further the interests of their own countries and the latter of lawyers who have little knowledge or experience outside the purely legal field.

With regard to the Society itself, we differ from UNA and other such organisations in that we have always endeavoured to function as an international Movement in the sense that our activities have never been confined to Great Britain. Before the war we had managed to build up embryonic national sections of the Movement in most of the European countries, and these were linked together in what we called our International Section. We are now faced with the task of rebuilding this machinery, and there can be no doubt that your visit to the Low Countries will be of the greatest value in helping us to carry that task a stage further.

In Holland the foundations of a New Commonwealth Committee have already been laid with Dr van de Coppello as its President and Dr Fortuin as its Honorary Secretary. You will, of course, be meeting these gentlemen during your visit, and it occurred to me that you might wish to be informed of their special connection with the Movement. I should also like to mention the names of Dr Peter de Kanter and his wife Mrs de Kanter van Hettinga Tromp who are members of our Committee and who have always played a leading part in New Commonwealth activity.

In Belgium we have not as yet been able to establish any sort of organism though we hope to be able to do so in the near future.

In apologising for bothering you with this letter, may I say again how deeply grateful we are to you for having consented to undertake this journey on our behalf.

Yours sincerely
N. B. Foot

From the Netherlands Section of the New Commonwealth Society

Amsterdam, October 7th 1947
Beursgebouw, Damrak 62A

Dear Lord Russell

Now that your tour through the continent of Western Europe has come to an end and you are back again in England, we want to express you once more our great thankfulness for the lectures you delivered to the Netherlands Section of The New Commonwealth in Amsterdam and The Hague. It was an unforgettable event to hear you—whom many of us already knew by your numerous important writings—speak about the question which occupies and oppresses our mind: the centuries-old problem of war or peace. We cannot say that your words have removed all our concern; on the contrary, to whatever we may have got used since the thirties, your supreme analysis of the present situation has considerably increased our anxiety. But we know now that you also joined those who are anxious to construct a state of international justice which will aim at the establishment of rules of law and in which the transgressor will be called to order by force, if necessary.

You will have learnt from the number of your auditors and the many conversations you had that your visit to our country has been a great success. There is no Dutch newspaper nor weekly that failed to mention your visit and your lectures.

Thank you for coming, Lord Russell; we shall not forget your words!

Yours very truly
Dr van de Coppello
President
Dr Fortuin
Secretary

From Gilbert Murray

Yatscombe
Boar's Hill Oxford
Sep. 12 1951

Dear Bertie

I was greatly touched by that letter you wrote to the Philosophic Society Dinner about our fifty years of close friendship. It is, I think, quite true about the fundamental agreement; I always feel it—and am proud of it.

I had explained that I preferred you to other philosophers because, while they mostly tried to prove some horrible conclusion—like Hobbes, Hegel, Marx etc, you were, I believe, content if you could really prove that $2 + 2 = 4$, and that conclusion, though sad, was at least bearable ('To think that two and two are four, and never five or three The heart of man has long been sore And long is like to be.')

Have you read the life of Jos Wedgwood (*The Last of the Radicals*) by his niece? He sent a questionnaire to a great list of people in which one question was: 'To what cause do you attribute your failure?' The only one who said he had not failed was Ld Beaverbrook! Interesting and quite natural.

Providence has thought fit to make me lame by giving me blisters on my feet so that I can not wear shoes; a great nuisance.

Yours ever, and with real thanks for your letter, which made me for a moment feel that I was not completely a failure.

G.M.

From General Sir Frank E. W. Simpson, KCB, KBE, DSO

Imperial Defence College
Seaford House
37, Belgrave Square
S.W.1
16th July, 1952

Dear Lord Russell

May I introduce myself to you as the present Commandant of this College, having taken over from Admiral Sir Charles Daniel at the beginning of this year.

I am writing to ask whether you could possibly spare the time to visit us again this year in December and give your excellent talk on 'The Future of Mankind'. Admiral Daniel has told me how valuable and stimulating your talks to this College have been in recent years.

The date I have in mind is Thursday, 4th December next, and the time 10.15 a.m. You know our usual procedure.

I much hope that you will agree to come and that the above date will be convenient for you.

Yours sincerely
F. E. W. Simpson

From the *Manchester Guardian*, 22nd April 1954

ATOMIC WEAPONS

Sir

In a leading article of your issue of April 20 you say: 'The United States is not so foolish or wicked as to fire the first shot in a war with atomic weapons.' This statement as it stands is ambiguous. If you mean that the United States would not fire the first shot, the statement may be correct. But if you mean that the United States would not be the first to use atomic weapons, you are almost certainly mistaken. The United States authorities have declared that any aggression anywhere by Russia or China will be met by all-out retaliation, which certainly means the bomb. It is apparently the opinion of experts that in a world war the Western Powers will be defeated if they do not use the bomb, but victorious if they use it. If this is the view of the Russian authorities, they will abstain at the beginning of a war from using the bomb and leave to our side the odium of its first employment. Can anybody seriously suggest that the Western Powers will prefer defeat? There is only one way to prevent the necessity for this choice, and that is to prevent a world war.

Yours &c.
Bertrand Russell

[Our point was simply that China, knowing the scruples which limit American action, could disregard an American threat to retaliate with atomic weapons if China did not desist from intervening in Indo-China. With Lord Russell's general point we are in agreement.—Ed. *Guard.*]

From my cousin, Sir Claud Russell

Trematon Castle
Saltash, Cornwall
12 July '52

Dear Bertie

I was given to read (in *Vogue*) by Flora your childhood's Memories, which I did with interest, and the more so, no doubt, as they evoked memories of my own. There must be few survivors of the Pembroke Lodge days. I think my parents went there fairly frequently on a Sunday, driving from London in a hired one-horse brougham (they never owned a carriage in London) and took one or two children with 'em. But I remember better an occasional weekend there, and no doubt your grandmother and my parents thought, with reason, that our association would be pleasant, and beneficial, to both. Your grandfather was dead before those days. I never saw him, but I remember my father telling my mother at breakfast in Audley Square 'Uncle John is dead'; and also that it fell to my father to return his KG to the Queen, and that some important part of the insignia—the Star or the Garter—could not be found, which my father had to tell the Queen, who said: 'that doesn't matter.' I would like to see Pembroke Lodge again, and walk about the grounds. I believe it is in a dilapidated state, and no longer the home of a deserving servant of the State. I remember Windsor Castle, and that Henry VIII saw from Richmond Hill the gun fired that told him Anne Boleyn was executed. I recall the family prayers, and my embarrassment at having to sing the hymn audibly. I wonder in how many houses are family prayers now the rule? The last I recall were at Sir Ernest Satow's. He was my Chief in Peking, and I went to see him in his retirement. He was a bachelor, an intellectual, who had read all there is, and a man of encyclopaedic knowledge. Yet, I believe an undoubting Christian. I formed this impression of him from his demeanour in the Legation Chapel at Peking, and the family prayers confirmed it. His Japanese butler, cook and housemaid, appeared after dinner, and he led the prayers. My only unpleasant memory of Pembroke Lodge arises from two boy friends of yours of the name of Logan. They conceived, I suppose, a measure of contempt for me, and made no secret of it. Perhaps they thought me a 'milk-sop', or 'softy'. However, I didn't see them often. *Per contra*, like you, I have a happy memory of Annabel (Clara we called her)[1] and I was often at York House. When her parents were in India, she came to us for her holidays (she was at school) and I was much in love with her—I being then about 15–16 years old. I wonder what became of the furniture and pictures etc. at Pembroke Lodge. I suppose Agatha had them at Haslemere. I remember particularly a statue, a life-size marble of a female nude, in the hall.[2] I think a gift from the Italian people to your grandfather, in gratitude for his contribution to the liberation and union of Italy. Like you, I owe to the Russells shyness, and sensitiveness—great handicaps in life, but no metaphysics, tho' I have tried to feebly—my father and elder brother had the latter, but not professionally, like you. What I owe to my French progenitors I leave others to judge. I noted lately in a volume of Lord Beaconsfield's letters one written from Woburn, in 1865, to Queen Victoria, in which he says: 'The predominant feature and organic deficiency of the Russell family is shyness. Even Hastings is not free from it, though he tries to cover it with an air of uneasy gaiety.' *I* am much too shy for that.

I am happy to know of my family link with the heroic defender of Gibraltar— my great aunt's great uncle. Athenais and I have taken to spending the winter

---

[1] A daughter of Sir Mounstuart Grant Duff.
[2] This statue had an inscription on the pedestal:
A Ld *John Russell*
Italia riconoscente.

at Gib. If ever, with advancing years, you want to escape the English winter, I recommend it. A better climate than the Riviera, and in a sterling area.

Excuse this long letter. One thing led to another.

Yours ever
Claud

Trematon Castle
Saltash, Cornwall
9 Aug. '52

Dear Bertie

Thank you for your letter, and I fully share your indignation at the fate of Pembroke Lodge. Can it be that what you call 'Bumbledom' is now the Crown? All the same, I hope when I'm in London to go and see the old place again, and may:

'Fond memory bring the light'
'Of other days around me',

or will I (more probably):

'Feel like one'
'Who treads alone'
'Some banquet hall deserted'
'Whose lights are fled' etc.

But did not Agatha wisely leave the Italia that I remember, to Newnham, where such a work of art could excite admiration, but never, I trust, an unruly thought.

I hope we may see you at Gib. next winter, if you want to escape the English one. The climate is more equable and healthy than that of the Riviera, and being British soil, if you have a bank balance at home, you can draw on it—or overdraw, for that matter. The Gibraltarians, tho' not typical Englishmen, are amiable and loyal. They know which side their bread is buttered, and there is no irredentism among them. O si sic omnes!

The Rock Hotel is the place to stay—well run, but not exactly cheap.

Yours ever
Claud

To and from Albert Einstein

41 Queen's Road
Richmond
Surrey
20 June, 1953

Dear Einstein

I am in whole-hearted agreement with your contention that teachers called before McCarthy's inquisitors should refuse to testify. When *The New York Times* had a leading article disagreeing with you about this, I wrote a letter to it supporting you. But I am afraid they are not going to print it. I enclose a copy, of which, if you feel so disposed, you may make use in any way you like.

Yours very sincerely
Bertrand Russell

Translation

Princeton
28.vi.53

Dear Bertrand Russell

Your fine letter to *The New York Times* is a great contribution to a good cause. All the intellectuals in this country, down to the youngest student, have become completely intimidated. Virtually no one of 'prominence' besides yourself has actually challenged these absurdities in which the politicians have become engaged. Because they have succeeded in convincing the masses that the Russians and the American Communists endanger the safety of the country, these politicians consider themselves so powerful. The cruder the tales they spread, the more assured they feel of their reelection by the misguided population. This also explains why Eisenhower did not dare to commute the death sentence of the two Rosenbergs, although he well knew how much their execution would injure the name of the United States abroad.

I have read your latest publications, 'Impact' and 'Satan . . .', with great care and real enjoyment. You should be given much credit for having used your unique literary talent in the service of public enlightenment and education. I am convinced that your literary work will exercise a great and lasting influence particularly since you have resisted the temptation to gain some short lived effects through paradoxes and exaggerations.

With cordial greetings and wishes,

Yours
A. Einstein

41 Queen's Road
Richmond
Surrey
5 July, 1953

Dear Einstein

Thank you very much for your letter, which I found most encouraging. Rather to my surprise *The New York Times* did at last print my letter about you. I hope you will be able to have an influence upon liberal-minded academic people in America. With warmest good wishes,

Yours very sincerely
Bertrand Russell

Albert Einstein on Russell—1940 (time of College of the City of New York row)

Es wiederholt sich immer wieder
In dieser Welt so fein und bieder
Der Pfaff den Poebel alarmiert
Der Genius wird executiert.

Translation

It keeps repeating itself
In this world, so fine and honest:
The Parson alarms the populace,
The genius is executed.

Albert Einstein on Russell's *History of Western Philosophy*, 1946

Bertrand Russell's 'Geschichte der Philosophie' ist eine koestliche Lektuere. Ich weiss nicht, ob man die koestliche Frische und Originalitaet oder die Sensitivitaet der Einfuehlung in ferne Zeiten und fremde Mentalitaet bei diesem grossen Denker mehr bewundern soll. Ich betrachte es als ein Glueck, dass unsere so trockene und zugleich brutale Generation einen so weisen, ehrlichen, tapferen und dabei humorvollen Mann aufzuweisen hat. Es ist ein in hoechstem Sinne paedagogisches Werk, das ueber dem Streite der Parteien und Meinungen steht.

Translation

Bertrand Russell's 'History of Philosophy' is a precious book. I don't know whether one should more admire the delightful freshness and originality or the sensitivity of the sympathy with distant times and remote mentalities on the part of this great thinker. I regard it as fortunate that our so dry and also brutal generation can point to such a wise, honourable, bold and at the same time humorous man. It is a work that is in the highest degree pedagogical which stands above the conflicts of parties and opinions.

'A LIBERAL DECALOGUE'[1]

by

Bertrand Russell

Perhaps the essence of the Liberal outlook could be summed up in a new decalogue, not intended to replace the old one but only to supplement it. The Ten Commandments that, as a teacher, I should wish to promulgate, might be set forth as follows:

1. Do not feel absolutely certain of anything.
2. Do not think it worth while to proceed by concealing evidence, for the evidence is sure to come to light.
3. Never try to discourage thinking for you are sure to succeed.

[1] This first appeared at the end of my article 'The Best Answer to Fanaticism—Liberalism', in *The New York Times Magazine*, December 16, 1951.

4. When you meet with opposition, even if it should be from your husband or your children, endeavor to overcome it by argument and not by authority, for a victory dependent upon authority is unreal and illusory.

5. Have no respect for the authority of others, for there are always contrary authorities to be found.

6. Do not use power to suppress opinions you think pernicious, for if you do the opinions will suppress you.

7. Do not fear to be eccentric in opinion, for every opinion now accepted was once eccentric.

8. Find more pleasure in intelligent dissent than in passive agreement, for, if you value intelligence as you should, the former implies a deeper agreement than the latter.

9. Be scrupulously truthful, even if the truth is inconvenient, for it is more inconvenient when you try to conceal it.

10. Do not feel envious of the happiness of those who live in a fool's paradise, for only a fool will think that it is happiness.

From the *News Chronicle*, 1st April, 1954

HE FORETOLD IT

In November, 1945, in a speech in the House of Lords on the atomic bomb, Bertrand Russell said:

It is possible that some mechanism, analogous to the present atomic bomb, could be used to set off a much more violent explosion which would be obtained if one could synthesise heavier elements out of hydrogen. All that must take place if our scientific civilisation goes on, if it does not bring itself to destruction: all that is bound to happen.

From the *News Chronicle*, 1st April 1954

THE BOMB:
WHERE DO WE GO FROM HERE?

Bertrand Russell, mathematician, philosopher, answers the questions that everyone is asking (in an interview with Robert Waithman).

Bertrand Russell sat very upright in his armchair, smoking a curved pipe and talking gently about the hydrogen bomb. But there was nothing gentle about his conclusions.

Britain's greatest living philosopher, whose mind and intellectual courage have moved the twentieth century since its beginning, is now 81. His hair is white and his voice is soft; and his opinions, as always, are expressed with a memorable clarity. I put a succession of questions to him and he answered them thus:

Is there any justification for alarm at the thought that some disastrous miscalculation may occur in the H-bomb tests?

61

Though, obviously, there will come a time when these experiments are too dangerous, I don't think we have reached that point yet.

If there were a hydrogen-bomb war it is quite clear that practically everybody in London would perish. A shower of hydrogen bombs would almost certainly sterilise large agricultural areas, and the resulting famine would be fearful.

But we are talking of the current tests, in peace-time. I do not expect disaster from them. I think those who may have been showered with radioactive ash, whose fishing catches have been damaged or destroyed, undoubtedly have every right to complain.

But I do not foresee a rain of radio-active ash comparable with the phenomena we saw after the explosion of the Krakatoa Volcano in 1883 (which I remember well), I do not think that, so long as the explosions are few, marine life will be grievously affected.

It is affected now by oil pollution, isn't it—though that is much less dramatic a story?

Do you think that a feeling of dread and uncertainty at the back of people's minds might have an evil social effect?

Well, you know, it isn't an effect that lasts long. As with the atom bomb at first, people get into a state; but after a little while they forget it.

If you have perpetually mounting crises, of course, it will be different. The truth is, though, that the thought of an old peril, however great, will not distract people from their daily jobs.

You will have observed that since the first atom bombs were exploded the birth rate has continued to go up. That is a reliable test.

I should say that the fear of unemployment, which is something everyone understands, has a much greater social effect than the fear of atom bombs.

And the international effects? Do we seem to you to have reached a strategic stalemate? Is there now a new basis for discussion between Russia and the West?

I think the existence of the hydrogen bomb presents a perfectly clear alternative to all the Governments of the world. Will they submit to an international authority, or shall the human race die out?

I am afraid that most Governments and most individuals will refuse to face that alternative. They so dislike the idea of international government that they dodge the issue whenever they can.

Ask the man in the street if he is prepared to have the British Navy partly under the orders of Russians. His hair will stand on end.

Yet that is what we must think about.

You see no virtue in any proposal that the experiments should be stopped?

None whatever, unless we have found a way of causing the Russian experiments to be stopped, too.

In my opinion, there is only one way. It is to convince the Russians beyond doubt that they can win no victory: that they cannot ever Communise the world with the hydrogen bomb.

Perhaps they are beginning to feel that. It seems to me to be significant that the Russian leaders are now allowing the Russian people to know of the devastation to be expected from an atomic war.

But I would hasten the process. I would invite all the Governments of the world, and particularly the Russians, to send observers to see the results of the American tests. It ought to be made as plain as it can be made.

There is one more thing we should do. We should diminish the anti-Communist tirades that are now so freely indulged in. We should try hard to bring about a return to international good manners. That would be a great help.

And if—or when—the Russians are convinced?

I think it ought to be possible to lessen the tension and to satisfy the Russians that there is no promise for them in atomic war. Then the first, vital step will have to be taken.

We shall have to set up an arrangement under which all fissionable raw material is owned by an international authority, and is only mined and processed by that authority. No nation or individual must have access to fissionable raw material.

And there would have to be an international inspectorate to ensure that this law is maintained.

The Russians have a morbid fear of being inspected. We shall have to help them to overcome it. For until they are agreeable to it nothing can be effectively done.

The H-bomb tests must be helping to persuade them. Hence to put off the tests would simply be to put off the day of agreement. It goes without saying that we, too, must always be ready to negotiate and to agree.

Once this first, vital agreement has been reached it should be possible, gradually, to extend international control.

That is the only answer I can see.

CHAPTER II

AT HOME AND ABROAD

MORE IMPORTANT than anything in pulling me through the dark apprehensions and premonitions of these last two decades is the fact that I had fallen in love with Edith Finch and she with me. She had been a close friend of Lucy Donnelly whom I had known well at the turn of the century and had seen something of during my various American visits as I had of Edith during my years in the United States in the 'thirties and 'forties. Lucy was a Professor at Bryn Mawr, where Edith also taught. I had had friendly relations with Bryn Mawr ever since I married a cousin of the President of that College. It was the first institution to break the boycott imposed on me in America after my dismissal from the City College of New York. Paul Weiss of its Department of Philosophy wrote asking me to give a series of lectures there, an invitation which I gladly accepted. And when I was writing my *History of Western Philosophy*, the Bryn Mawr authorities very kindly allowed me to make use of their excellent library. Lucy had died and Edith had moved to New York where I met her again during my Columbia lectures there in 1950.

Our friendship ripened quickly, and soon we could no longer bear to be parted by the Atlantic. She settled in London, and, as I lived at Richmond, we met frequently. The resulting time was infinitely delightful. Richmond Park was full of reminiscences, many going back to early childhood. Relating them revived their freshness, and it seemed to me that I was living the past all over again with a fresh and happier alleviation from it. I almost forgot the nuclear peril in the joys of recollection. As we walked about the grounds of Pembroke Lodge and through Richmond Park and Kew Gardens, I recalled all sorts of things that had happened to me there. There is a fountain outside Pembroke Lodge at which the footman, employed to make me not afraid of water, held me by the heels with my head under water. Contrary to all modern views, this method was entirely successful: after the first application, I never feared water again.

Edith and I each had family myths to relate. Mine began with Henry VIII, of whom the founder of my family had been a protégé,

3. Edith Russell by Lotte Meitner-Graf

4. Oil painting of Bertrand Russell by Hans Erni

watching on his Mount for the signal of Anne Boleyn's death at the Tower. It continued to my grandfather's speech in 1815, urging (before Waterloo) that Napoleon should not be opposed. Next came his visit to Elba, in which Napoleon was affable and tweaked his ear. After this, there was a considerable gap in the saga, until the occasion when the Shah, on a State visit, was caught in the rain in Richmond Park and was compelled to take refuge in Pembroke Lodge. My grandfather (so I was told) apologized for its being such a small house, to which the Shah replied: 'Yes, but it contains a great man.' There was a very wide view of the Thames valley from Pembroke Lodge marred, in my grandmother's opinion, by a prominent factory chimney. When she was asked about this chimney, she used to reply, smiling: 'Oh, that's not a factory chimney, that's the monument to the Middlesex Martyr.'

Edith's family myths, as I came to know them, seemed to me far more romantic: an ancestor who in 1640 or thereabouts was either hanged or carried off by the Red Indians; the adventures of her father among the Indians when he was a little boy and his family for a short time lived a pioneering life in Colorado; attics full of pillions and saddles on which members of her family had ridden from New England to the Congress at Philadelphia; tales of canoeing and of swimming in rocky streams near where Eunice Williams, stolen away by the Indians in the great massacre at Deerfield, Massachusetts, was killed. It might have been a chapter from Fennimore Cooper. In the Civil War, Edith's people were divided between North and South. Among them were two brothers, one of them (a Southern General) at the end had to surrender his sword to his brother, who was a Northern General. She herself had been born and brought up in New York City, which, as she remembered it, seemed very like the New York of my youth of cobbled streets and hansom cabs and no motor cars.

All these reminiscences, however entertaining, were only some of the arabesques upon the cake's icing. Very soon we had our own myths to add to the collection. As we were strolling in Kew Gardens one morning, we saw two people sitting on a bench, so far away that they seemed tiny figures. Suddenly, one of them jumped up and ran fast towards us and, when he reached us, fell to his knees and kissed my hand. I was horrified, and so abashed that I could think of nothing whatsoever to say or do; but I was touched, too, by his emotion, as was Edith, who pulled herself together enough to learn that he was a German, living in England, and was grateful to me for something; we never knew for what.

We not only took long walks in the neighbourhood of Richmond and in London, along the River and in the Parks and in the City of

65

a Sunday, but we sometimes drove farther afield for a walk. Once on the Portsmouth Road we met with an accident. Through no fault of ours we were run into by a farm lorry and our car was smashed to bits. Luckily, at the time there were plenty of observers of our guiltlessness. Though shaken up, we accepted a lift from some kind passers-by into Guildford where we took a taxi to Blackdown to have our intended walk. There I recalled my infant exploits. My people had taken Tennyson's house during a summer's holiday when I was two years old, and I was made by my elders to stand on the moor and recite in a heart-rending pipe,

> O my cousin, shallow-hearted! O my Amy, mine no more!
> O the dreary, dreary moorland! O the barren, barren shore!

We went to plays, new and old. I remember particularly *Cymbeline*, acted in Regent's Park, Ustinov's *Five Colonels*, and *The Little Hut*. My cousin Maud Russell invited us to a party celebrating the achievement of the mosaic floor designed by Boris Anrep in the National Gallery. My portrait summoning Truth from a well occurs there with portraits of some of my contemporaries. I enjoyed sittings to Jacob Epstein for a bust that he asked to make of me which I now have.

These small adventures sound trivial in retrospect, but everything at that time was bathed in the radiant light of mutual discovery and of joy in each other. Happiness caused us for the moment to forget the dreadful outer world, and to think only about ourselves and each other. We found that we not only loved each other entirely, but, equally important, we learned gradually that our tastes and feelings were deeply sympathetic and our interests for the most part marched together. Edith had no knowledge of philosophy or mathematics; there were things that she knew of which I was ignorant. But our attitude towards people and the world is similar. The satisfaction that we felt then in our companionship has grown, and grows seemingly without limit, into an abiding and secure happiness and is the basis of our lives. Most that I have to relate henceforth may be taken, therefore, to include her participation.

Our first long expedition was to Fontainebleau when the only reminder of public squabbles was owing to Mussadeq's attempt to secure a monopoly of Persian oil. Apart from this, our happiness was almost as serene as it could have been in a quiet world. The weather was sunny and warm. We consumed enormous quantities of *fraises du bois* and *creme fraiche*. We made an expedition into Paris where, for past services, the French radio poured unexpected cash upon me that financed an epic luncheon in the Bois, as well as solemner things, and where we walked in the Tuilleries Gardens and visited Notre Dame. We never visited the Chateau at Fontainebleau. And we laughed consumedly—sometimes about nothing at all.

We have had other holidays in Paris since then, notably one in 1954 which we determined should be devoted to sight-seeing. We had each lived in Paris for fairly long periods, but I had never visited any of the things that one should see. It was pleasant to travel up and down the river in the *bateaux mouches*, and to visit various churches and galleries and the flower and bird markets. But we had set-backs: we went to the Ste. Chapelle one day and found it full of Icelanders being lectured to on its beauties. Upon seeing me, they abandoned the lecture and crowded about me as the 'sight' of most importance. My remembrance of the Ste. Chapelle is somewhat garbled. We retreated to the terrace of our favourite restaurant opposite the Palais de Justice. The next day we went to Chartres which we both love. But, alas, we found it turned—so far as it could be—into a tourists' Mecca full of post-cards and souvenirs.

In the spring of 'fifty-two we visited Greece where we spent some time in Athens and then ten days or so driving through the Peloponesus. As everyone does, we at once set off for the Acropolis. By mistake and thinking to take a short cut, we approached it from the back. We had to scramble up a cliff by goat paths and through barbed wire to get there. We arrived scratched and breathless, but triumphant. We returned again often by more orthodox routes. It was very beautiful by moonlight. And very quiet; till suddenly, at my elbow, I heard a voice say: 'Mis-ter Russ-ell, is it not?', with the accent portentous upon each syllable. It was a fellow tourist from America.

The mountains were still snow-capped, but the valleys were full of blossoming fruit trees. Kids gambolled in the fields, and the people seemed happy. Even the donkeys looked contented. The only dark spot was Sparta which was sullen and brooding beneath Taygetus from which emanated a spirit of frightening evil. I was thankful to reach Arcadia. It was as Arcadian and lovely as if born of Sidney's imagination. At Tiryns, the guardian of the ancient citadel bemoaned the fact that it had been very badly restored. Upon being asked when this distressing renovation had taken place, he replied, 'During the Mycenaean times'. Delphi left me quite unmoved, but Epidaurus was gentle and lovely. Oddly enough its peace was not broken by a bus-load of Germans who arrived there shortly after us. Suddenly, as we were sitting up in the theatre dreaming, a beautiful clear voice soared up and over us. One of the Germans was an operatic Diva and, as we were, was enchanted by the magic of the place. On the whole, our fellow tourists did not trouble us. But the United States army did. Their lorries were everywhere, especially in Athens, and the towns were noisy with the boisterous, cock-sure, shoutings and demands of their men. On the other hand, the Greeks whom we met or observed in passing, seemed gentle and gay and intelligent. We were impressed by the happy way in which they played with their children in the Gardens at Athens.

I had never before been in Greece and I found what I saw exceedingly interesting. In one respect, however, I was surprised. After being impressed by the great solid achievements which everybody admires, I found myself in a little church belonging to the days when Greece was part of the Byzantine Empire. To my astonishment, I felt more at home in this little church than I did in the Parthenon or in any of the other Greek buildings of Pagan times. I realized then that the Christian outlook had a firmer hold upon me than I had imagined. The hold was not upon my beliefs, but upon my feelings. It seemed to me that where the Greeks differed from the modern world it was chiefly through the absence of a sense of sin, and I realized with some astonishment that I, myself, am powerfully affected by this sense in my feelings though not in my beliefs. Some ancient Greek things, however, did touch me deeply. Among these, I was most impressed by the beautiful and compassionate Hermes at Olympia.

In 1953, Edith and I spent three weeks in Scotland. On the way we visited the house where I was born on the hills above the Wye valley. It had been called Ravenscroft, but is now called Cleddon Hall. The house itself was kept up, but during the war the grounds had got into a sorry condition. My parents had, at their own instructions, been buried in the adjoining wood, but were later at the family's wish, transported to the family vault at Chenies. On the way, too, we visited Seatoller in Borrowdale, where I had spent five weeks as a member of a reading party in 1893. The party was still remembered, and the visitors' book contained proof of a story that I had told Edith without obtaining belief, namely that Miss Pepper, who had waited on us, subsequently married a Mr Honey. On arriving at St Fillans (our destination) I told the receptionist that I had not been there since 1878. She stared, and then said: 'But you must have been quite a little boy.' I had remembered from this previous visit various landmarks at St Fillans such as the wooden bridge across the river, the house next to the hotel which was called 'Neish', and a stony bay which I had imagined to be one of the 'sun-dry places' mentioned in the Prayer Book. As I had not been there since 1878, the accuracy of my memories was considered established. We had many drives, sometimes along no more than cart tracks, and walks over the moors that remain memorable to us. One afternoon, as we climbed to the crest of a hill, a doe and her fawn appeared over the top trotting towards us and, on our way down, on the shore of a wild little tarn, a proud and very tame hoopoe alighted and looked us over. We drove home to St Fillans through the gloomy valley of Glencoe, as dark and dreadful as if the massacre had just taken place.

Two years later we went again to St Fillans. This time, however, we had a far less care-free time. We had to stop on the way in Glasgow for me to make a speech in favour of the Labour candidate for Rotherglen, a tireless worker for World Government. Our spirits were somewhat damped by the fact that I had gradually developed trouble with my throat which prevented me from swallowing properly, a trouble which I take pleasure in saying, resulted from my efforts to swallow the pronouncements of politicians. But much more distressing than any of this was the fact that my elder son had fallen seriously ill. We were beset by worry about him during the whole of this so-called 'holiday'. We were worried, too, about his three young children who were at that time more or less, and later almost wholly, in our care.

When Peter left me I had continued to live at Ffestiniog, happily working there in a house on the brow of the hill with a celestial view down the valley, like an old apocalyptic engraving of Paradise. I went up to London only occasionally, and when I did, I sometimes visited my son and his family at Richmond. They were living near the Park in a tiny house, much too small for their family of three little children. My son told me that he wanted to give up his job and devote himself to writing. Though I regretted this, I had some sympathy with him. I did not know how to help them as I had not enough money to stake them to an establishment of their own in London while I lived in North Wales. Finally I hit upon the scheme of moving from Ffestiniog and taking a house to share with my son and his family in Richmond.

Returning to Richmond, where I spent my childhood, produced a slightly ghostly feeling, and I sometimes found it difficult to believe that I still existed in the flesh. Pembroke Lodge, which used to be a nice house, was being ruined by order of the Civil Service. When they discovered, what they did not know until they were told, that it had been the home of famous people, they decided that everything possible must be done to destroy its historic interest. Half of it was turned into flats for park-keepers, and the other half into a tea shop. The garden was cut up by a complicated system of barbed wire, with a view, so I thought at the time, to minimizing the pleasure to be derived from it.[1]

---

[1] Later, I changed my opinion of their proceedings and thought that they had done the adaptation very well if it had to be done.

I had hoped vaguely that I might somehow rent Pembroke Lodge and install myself and my family there. As this proved impossible, I took a largish house near Richmond Park, turning over the two lower floors to my son's family and keeping the top two for myself. This had worked more or less well for a time in spite of the difficulties that almost always occur when two families live at close quarters. We had a pleasant life there, living separately, each having our own guests, and coming together when we wished. But it made a very full life, with the family coming and going, my work, and the constant stream of visitors.

Among the visitors were Alan and Mary Wood who came to see me about a book that he wished to write on my philosophical work. He soon decided to do a life of me first. In the course of its preparation we saw much of both him and his wife and came to be very fond of them and to rely upon them. Some of the encounters with visitors, however, were odd. One gentleman from America who had suggested coming to tea, turned up accompanied by a mistress of the American McCarthy whose virtues she extolled. I was angry. Another was an Indian who came with his daughter. He insisted that she must dance for me while he played her accompaniment. I had only a short time before, returned from hospital and did not welcome having all the furniture of our sitting-room pushed back and the whole house shake as she cavorted in what, under other circumstances, I might have thought lovely gyrations.

That visit to the hospital became one of the myths to which I have already referred. My wife and I had gone on a long walk in Richmond Park one morning and, after lunch, she had gone up to her sitting-room which was above mine. Suddenly I appeared, announcing that I felt ill. Not unnaturally, she was frightened. It was the fine sunny Sunday before the Queen's coronation. Though my wife tried to get hold of a neighbour and of our own doctors in Richmond and London, she could get hold of no one. Finally, she rang 999 and the Richmond police, with great kindness and much effort, came to the rescue. They sent a doctor who was unknown to me, the only one whom they could find. By the time the police had managed to get hold of our own doctors, I had turned blue. My wife was told by a well-known specialist, one of the five doctors who had by then congregated, that I might live for two hours. I was packed into an ambulance and whisked to hospital where they dosed me with oxygen and I survived.

The pleasant life at Richmond had other dark moments. At Christmas, 1953, I was waiting to go into hospital again for a serious operation and my wife and household were all down with flu. My son and his wife decided that, as she said, they were 'tired of children'. After

Christmas dinner with the children and me, they left, taking the remainder of the food, but leaving the children, and did not return. We were fond of the children, but were appalled by this fresh responsibility which posed so many harassing questions in the midst of our happy and already very full life. For some time we hoped that their parents would return to take up their rôle, but when my son became ill we had to abandon that hope and make long-term arrangements for the children's education and holidays. Moreover, the financial burden was heavy and rather disturbing: I had given £10,000 of my Nobel Prize cheque for a little more than £11,000 to my third wife, and I was now paying alimony to her and to my second wife as well as paying for the education and holidays of my younger son. Added to this, there were heavy expenses in connection with my elder son's illness; and the income taxes which for many years he had neglected to pay now fell to me to pay. The prospect of supporting and educating his three children, however pleasant it might be, presented problems.

For a time when I came out of the hospital I was not up to much, but by May I felt that I had recovered. I gave the Herman Ould Memorial Lecture to the PEN Club called 'History as an Art'. We were asked to supper afterwards by the Secretary of the Club and I enjoyed indulging my literary hates and loves. In particular, my great hate is Wordsworth. I have to admit the excellence of some of his work—to admire and love it, in fact—but much of it is too dull, too pompous and silly to be borne. Unfortunately, I have a knack of remembering bad verse with ease, so I can puzzle almost anyone who upholds Wordsworth.

A short time later, on our way home to Richmond from Scotland, we stopped in North Wales where our friends Rupert and Elizabeth Crawshay-Williams had found a house, Plas Penrhyn, that they thought would make a pleasant holiday house for us and the children. It was small and unpretentious, but had a delightful garden and little orchard and a number of fine beech trees. Above all, it had a most lovely view, south to the sea, west to Portmadoc and the Caernarvon hills, and north up the valley of the Glaslyn to Snowdon. I was captivated by it, and particularly pleased that across the valley could be seen the house where Shelley had lived. The owner of Plas Penrhyn agreed to let it to us largely, I think, because he, too, is a lover of Shelley and was much taken by my desire to write an essay on 'Shelley the Tough' (as opposed to the 'ineffectual angel'). Later, I met a man at Tan-y-Ralt, Shelley's house, who said he had been a cannibal—the first and only cannibal I have met. It seemed appropriate to meet him at the house of Shelley the Tough. Plas Penryhn seemed to us as if it would be an ideal place for the children's holidays, especially as there were friends of their parents living nearby whom they already knew and who had children of their own ages. It would be a happy alternative, we thought, to cinemas in Richmond and 'camps'. We rented it as soon as possible.

But all this was the daily background and the relief from the dark world of international affairs in which my chief interest lay. Though the reception accorded *Human Society in Ethics and Politics* was so amiable, its publication had failed to quiet my uneasiness. I felt I *must* find some way of making the world understand the dangers into which it was running blindly, head-on. I thought that perhaps if I repeated parts of *Human Society* on the BBC it would make more impression than it had hitherto made. In this, however, I was thwarted by the refusal of the BBC to repeat anything that had already been published. I therefore set to work to compose a new dirge for the human race.

Even then, in the relatively early days of the struggle against nuclear destruction, it seemed to me almost impossible to find a fresh way of putting what I had already, I felt, said in so many different ways. My first draft of the broadcast was an anaemic product, pulling all the punches. I threw it away at once, girded myself up and determined to say exactly how dreadful the prospect was unless measures were taken. The result was a distilled version of all that I had said theretofore. It was so tight packed that anything that I have since said on the subject can be found in it at least in essence. But the BBC still made difficulties, fearing that I should bore and frighten many listeners. They asked me to hold a debate, instead, with a young and cheerful footballer who could offset my grim forebodings. This seemed to me utterly frivolous and showed so clearly that the BBC Authorities understood nothing of what it was all about that I felt desperate. I refused to accede to their pleadings. At last, it was agreed that I should do a broadcast in December by myself. In it, as I have said, I stated all my fears and the reasons for them. The broadcast, now called 'Man's Peril', ended with the following words: 'There lies before us, if we choose, continual progress in happiness, knowledge, and wisdom. Shall we, instead, choose death, because we cannot forget our quarrels? I appeal, as a human being to human beings: remember your humanity, and forget the rest. If you can do so, the way lies open to a new Paradise; if you cannot, nothing lies before you but universal death.'

The broadcast had both a private and a public effect. The private effect was to allay my personal anxiety for a time, and to give me a feeling that I had found words adequate to the subject. The public effect was more important. I received innumerable letters and requests for speeches and articles, far more than I could well deal with. And I learned a great many facts that I had not known before, some of them rather desolating: a Battersea County Councillor came to see me and told me of the provisions that the Battersea Council had promulgated that were to be followed by all the inhabitants of that district in case of nuclear attack. Upon hearing the warning siren, they were to rush to Battersea Park and pile into buses. These, it was hoped, would whisk them to safety in the country.

Almost all the response to the broadcast of which I was aware was serious and encouraging. But some of my speeches had farcical interludes. One of them I remember with some smug pleasure: a man rose in fury, remarking that I looked like a monkey; to which I replied, 'Then you will have the pleasure of hearing the voice of your ancestors'.

I received the prize given by Pears' Cyclopaedia for some outstanding work done during the past year. The year before, the prize had been given to a young man who ran a mile in under four minutes. The prize cup which I now have says 'Bertrand Russell illuminating a path to Peace 1955'.

One of the most impressive meetings at which I spoke was held in April, 1955, in memory of the Jews who died at Warsaw in February, 1943. The music was tragic and beautiful, and the emotion of the assembled company so deep and sincere as to make the meeting very moving. There were records made of my speech and of the music.

Among the first organizations to show a pronounced interest in my views were the World Parliamentarians and, more seriously perhaps, the Parliamentary World Government Association with whom I had many meetings. They were to hold joint meetings in Rome in April, 1955, at which they invited me to speak. We were put up, oddly enough, in the hotel in which I had stayed with my Aunt Maude on my first trip to Rome over a half century before. It was a cold barracks that had ceased to provide meals for its guests, but was in a pleasant part of the old city. It was Spring and warm. It was a great pleasure to wander about the city and along the Tiber and up the Pincio for the otherwise unprovided meals. I found the Roman meetings very moving and interesting. I was happy that my speeches seemed to affect people, both at the meeting in the Chamber of Deputies and elsewhere. At all of them there were very mixed audiences. After one, I was held up by a man almost in tears because he had not been able to understand what had been said because he spoke no English. He besought me to translate what I had said into Esperanto. Alas, I could not. I enjoyed, too, meeting a number of friendly and notable literary and political figures in whose work I had been interested but with whom I had never before had a chance to discuss matters.

I had hoped, on the way north from Rome, to pay a visit to Bernard Berenson at Settignano. In this I was prevented by the pressure of work. Later, I learned that he took my defection very ill, especially as he had felt me, he said, to be arrogant and unfriendly at our last meeting. I was extremely sorry for this since my feelings towards him were, as they had always been, most friendly and I felt anything but arrogant towards him. But the last meeting to which he alluded had been a somewhat trying occasion to me. His wife Mary had asked me to lunch with them and I had gone. At the time of my separation from her sister Alys, she had written me a cutting letter saying that they did not wish to have anything further to do with me. Her invitation to lunch came many years later. I was glad to accept as I had never wished any break in our friendship, but I felt a little awkward and shy as I could not forget entirely her previous letter. Bernard Berenson had evidently never known of the letter or had forgotten it. I myself had felt that the luncheon had healed the breach and had been glad when he begged me to come to I Tatti again as I should have liked to do.

Meantime, as I assessed the response that my broadcast had achieved and considered what should be done next, I had realized that the point that I must concentrate upon was the need of co-operation among nations. It had occurred to me that it might be possible to formulate a statement that a number of very well-known and respected scientists of both capitalist and communist ideologies would be willing to sign calling for further joint action. Before taking any measures, however, I had written to Einstein to learn what he thought of such a plan. He had replied with enthusiasm, but had said that, because he was not well and could hardly keep up with present commitments, he himself could do nothing to help beyond sending me the names of various scientists who, he thought, would be sympathetic. He had begged me, nevertheless, to carry out my idea and to formulate the statement myself. This I had done, basing the statement upon my Christmas broadcast, 'Man's Peril'. I had drawn up a list of scientists of both East and West and had written to them, enclosing the statement, shortly before I went to Rome with the Parliamentarians. I had, of course, sent the statement to Einstein for his approval, but had not yet heard what he thought of it and whether he would be willing to sign it. As we flew from Rome to Paris, where the World Government Association were to hold further meetings, the pilot announced the news of Einstein's death. I felt shattered, not only for the obvious reasons, but because I saw my plan falling through without his support. But, on my arrival at my Paris hotel, I found a letter from him agreeing to sign. This was one of the last acts of his public life.

While I was in Paris I had a long discussion about my plan with Frederic Joliot-Curie. He warmly welcomed the plan and approved of the statement except for one phrase: I had written, 'It is feared that if many bombs are used there will be universal death—sudden only for a fortunate minority, but for the majority a slow torture of disease and disintegration'. He did not like my calling the minority 'fortunate'. 'To die is *not* fortunate', he said. Perhaps he was right. Irony, taken internationally, is tricky. In any case, I agreed to delete it. For some time after I returned to England, I heard nothing from him. He was ill, I learned later. Nor could I induce an answer from various other important scientists. I never did hear from the Chinese scientist to whom I had written. I think the letter to him was probably misaddressed. Einstein had advised me to enlist the help of Niels Bohr who, he thought, would certainly be in favour of my plan and my statement. But I could achieve no reply from him for many weeks in spite of repeated letters and telegrams. Then came a short letter saying that he wished to have nothing to do with either plan or statement. The Russian Academicians, still suspicious of the West, also refused to sign, although they wrote commending the plan with some warmth. After some correspondence, Professor Otto Hahn refused to sign, because, I understood, he was working for the forthcoming 'Mainau Declaration' of scientists. This declaration was already in preparation, but seemed to me to be somewhat emasculated by the fact that it was intended to include among its signatories only scientists of the West. Fortunately, others who signed the Mainau Declaration agreed with me and signed both. My most personal disappointment was that I could not obtain the signature of Lord Adrian, the President of the Royal Society and Master of my College, Trinity. I knew that he agreed with the principles in my broadcast, which were those of the manifesto that I hoped he would sign. He had himself spoken publicly in similar vein. And I had been pleased when I learned that Trinity wished to have in its Library a manuscript of 'Man's Peril'. But when I discussed my statement or manifesto with him I thought I understood why he was reluctant to sign. 'It is because it is too eloquent, isn't it?' I asked. 'Yes', he said. Many of the scientists to whom I wrote, however, at once warmly agreed to sign, and one, Linus Pauling, who had heard of the plan only at second hand, offered his signature. I was glad to accept the offer.

When I look back upon this time I do not see how the days and nights provided time to get through all that I did. Journeys to Rome and Paris and again to Scotland, family troubles, arrangements to settle in North Wales for the holidays, letters, discussions, visitors, and speeches. I wrote innumerable articles. I had frequent interviews and much correspondence with an American, R. C. Marsh, who was collecting and editing various early essays of mine which appeared the following year under the title *Logic and Knowledge*. And I was also preparing my book *Portraits from Memory* for publication in 1956. In January, 1955, I gave a lecture at the British Academy on J. S. Mill, which I had considerable difficulty in composing. I had already spoken so often about Mill. But the speech had one phrase that I cherish: in speaking about the fact that propositions have a subject and a predicate, I said it had led to 'three thousand years of important error'. And the speech was acclaimed in a most gratifying manner. The audience rose, thumped and clapped.

June came and still all the replies to my letters to the scientists had not been received. I felt that in any case some concrete plan must be made as to how the manifesto should be publicized. It seemed to me that it should be given a dramatic launching in order to call attention to it, to what it said and to the eminence of those who upheld it. After discarding many plans, I decided to get expert advice. I knew the editor of the *Observer* slightly and believed him to be liberal and sympathetic. He proved at that time to be both. He called in colleagues to discuss the matter. They agreed that something more was needed than merely publishing the fact that the manifesto had been written and signed by a number of eminent scientists of varying ideologies. They suggested that a press conference should be held at which I should read the document and answer questions about it. They did far more than this. They offered to arrange and finance the conference with the proviso that it not become, until later, public knowledge that they had done so. It was decided finally that the conference should take place on July 9th (1955). A room was engaged in Caxton Hall a week before. Invitations were sent to the editors of all the journals and to the representatives of foreign journals as well as to the BBC and representatives of foreign radio and TV in London. This invitation was merely to a conference at which something important of world-wide interest was to be published. The response was heartening and the room had to be changed to the largest in the Hall.

It was a dreadful week. All day long the telephone rang and the door-bell pealed. Journalists and wireless directors wanted to be told what this important piece of news was to be. Each hoped, apparently, for a scoop. Three times daily someone from the *Daily Worker* rang to say that their paper had not been sent an invitation. Daily, three times, they were told that they had been invited. But they seemed to be so used to being cold-shouldered that they could not believe it. After all, though they could not be told this, one purpose of the manifesto was to encourage co-operation between the communist and the non-communist world. The burden of all this flurry fell upon my wife and my housekeeper. I was not permitted to appear or to speak on the telephone except to members of the family. None of us could leave the house. I spent the week sitting in a chair in my study trying to read. At intervals, I was told later, I muttered dismally, 'This is going to be a damp squib'. My memory is that it rained during the entire week and was very cold.

The worst aspect of the affair was that not long before this I had received a letter from Joliot-Curie saying that he feared that, after all, he could not sign the manifesto. I could not make out why he had changed. I begged him to come to London to discuss the matter, but he was too ill. I had been in constant touch with Dr E. H. S. Burhop in order that the manifesto should not in any way offend those of communist ideology. It was largely due to his efforts that the night before the conference was scheduled to take place Monsieur Biquard came from Paris to discuss with Burhop and myself Joliot-Curie's objections. Monsieur Biquard has since taken Joliot-Curie's place in the World Federation of Scientific Workers. They arrived at 11.30 p.m. Sometime after midnight we came to an agreement. The manifesto could not be changed from the form it had had when Einstein had signed it and, in any case, it was too late to obtain the agreement of the other signatories to a change. I suggested, therefore, that Joliot-Curie's objections be added in footnotes where necessary and be included in my reading of the text the following morning. I had hit upon this scheme in dealing with an objection of one of the Americans. Joliot-Curie's emissary at last agreed to this and signed the manifesto for him, as he had been empowered to do if an agreement could be reached.

Another difficulty that had beset me was the finding of a chairman for the meeting who would not only add lustre to the occasion but would be equipped to help me in the technical questions that would surely be asked. For one reason or another everyone whom I approached refused the job. I confess that I suspected their refusal to have been the result of pusillanimity. Whoever took part in this manifesto or its launching ran the risk of disapproval that might, for a time at any rate, injure them or expose them to ridicule, which they would probably mind even more. Or perhaps their refusal was the result of their dislike of the intentional dramatic quality of the occasion. Finally, I learned that Professor Josef Rotblat was sympathetic. He was, and still is, an eminent physicist at the Medical College of St Bartholomew's Hospital and Executive vice-President of the Atomic Scientists' Association. He bravely and without hesitation agreed to act as Chairman and did so when the time came with much skill. From the time of that fortunate meeting I have often worked closely with Professor Rotblat and I have come to admire him greatly. He can have few rivals in the courage and integrity and complete self-abnegation with which he has given up his own career (in which, however, he still remains eminent) to devote himself to combatting the nuclear peril as well as other, allied evils. If ever these evils are eradicated and international affairs are straightened out, his name should stand very high indeed among the heroes.

Amongst others who encouraged me at this meeting were Alan Wood and Mary Wood who, with Kenneth Harris of the *Observer*, executed a variety of burdensome and vexatious drudgeries to make the occasion go off well. And in the event it did go well. The hall was packed, not only with men, but with recording and television machines. I read the manifesto and the list of signatories and explained how and why it had come into being. I then, with Rotblat's help, replied to questions from the floor. The journalistic mind, naturally, was impressed by the dramatic way in which Einstein's signature had arrived. Henceforth, the manifesto was called the Einstein–Russell (or *vice versa*) manifesto. At the beginning of the meeting a good deal of scepticism and indifference and some out and out hostility was shown by the press. As the meeting continued, the journalists appeared to become sympathetic and even approving, with the exception of one American journalist who felt affronted for his country by something I said in reply to a question. The meeting ended after two and a half hours with enthusiasm and high hope of the outcome of the call to scientists to hold a conference.

When it was all over, however, and we had returned to our flat at Millbank where we were spending the weekend, reaction set in. I recalled the horrid fact that in making various remarks about the signatories I had said that Professor Rotblat came from Liverpool. Although he himself had not seemed to notice the slip, I felt ashamed. The incident swelled to immense proportions in my mind. The disgrace of it prevented me from even speaking of it. When we walked to the news hoardings outside of Parliament to see if the evening papers had noted the meeting and found it heralded in banner headlines, I still could not feel happy. But worse was to come. I learned that I had omitted Professor Max Born's name from the list of signatories, had, even, said that he had refused to sign. The exact opposite was the truth. He had not only signed but had been most warm and helpful. This was a serious blunder on my part, and one that I have never stopped regretting. By the time that I had learned of my mistake it was too late to rectify the error, though I at once took, and have since taken, every means that I could think of to set the matter straight. Professor Born himself was magnanimous and has continued his friendly correspondence with me. As in the case of most of the other signatories the attempt and achievement of the manifesto took precedence over personal feelings.

78

Word continued to pour in of the wide news coverage all over the world of the proclamation of the manifesto. Most of it was favourable. My spirits rose. But for the moment I could do nothing more to forward the next step in opposition to nuclear armament. I had to devote the next few weeks to family matters. During the dreadful week before the proclamation when the telephone was not ringing about that subject it was ringing to give me most distressing news about my elder son's illness. I now had to devote all my mind to that and to moving my family for the summer to our new house in North Wales. The latter had been painted and refurbished during our absence under the kind auspices of Rupert and Elizabeth Crawshay-Williams. The necessary new furnishing to augment what we had bought from the estate of the former tenant had been bought in London during five afternoons at the end of June. So all was more or less ready for us. We went there to prepare for the coming of the three grandchildren as soon as possible. I was glad to escape from London. Most people seem to think of me as an urban individual, but I have, in fact, spent most of my life in the country and am far happier there than in any city known to me. But, having settled the children with the nurse who had for some years taken care of them at Richmond, I had to journey to Paris again for another World Government Conference. It was held in the Cité Universitaire and the meetings proved interesting. There were various parties in connection with it, some official and some less so. One was at the Quai d'Orsay. At one, a cocktail party held in the house of the great couturière Schiaparelli, I went out into the garden where I was quickly surrounded by a group of women who thought that women should do something special to combat nuclear warfare. They wished me to support their plans. I am entirely in favour of anyone doing what they can to combat nuclear warfare, but I have never been able to understand why the sexes should not combat it together. In my experience, fathers, quite as much as mothers, are concerned for the welfare of their young. My wife was standing on a balcony above the garden. Suddenly she heard my voice rise in anguished tones: 'But, you see, I am not a mother!' Someone was dispatched at once to rescue me.

After this Paris conference at the end of July, we returned to Richmond for another congress. The Association of Parliamentarians for World Government had planned in June to hold a congress for both Eastern and Western scientists and others if they could manage it during the first days of August. They, as I did, believed that the time had come for communists and non-communists to work together. I had taken part in their deliberations and was to speak at the first meeting. Three Russians came from the Moscow Academy as well as other people, particularly scientists, from many parts of the world. The

Russians were led by Academician Topchiev of whom I was later to see much and whom I grew to respect and greatly like. This was the first time since the war that any Russian Communists had attended a conference in the West and we were all exceedingly anxious to have the meetings go well. In the main they did so. But there was a short time when, at a committee meeting towards the end of the second day, the Russians could not come to agreement with their Western colleagues. The organizers telephoned me and asked if I could do anything to soothe matters. Fortunately agreement was managed. And at the final meeting I was able to read the resolutions of the conference as having been reached unanimously. Altogether, the conference augured well for co-operation. I could return to Wales for a few weeks of real holiday with the happy feeling that things were at last moving as one would wish.

Naturally, all work did not stop even during the holiday. I had already been considering with Professors Rotblat and Powell how we could implement the scientists' manifesto which had called for a conference of scientists to consider all the matters concerning and allied to the nuclear dangers. Professor Joliot-Curie, who was himself too ill to take active part in our plans, encouraged us at long distance. We were fairly sure by this time of being able to get together a good group of scientists of both East and West.

In the early days of preparing the manifesto, I had hoped that I might be supported in it by the Indian scientists and Government. At the beginning of Nehru's visit to London in February, 1955, my hope of it soared. Nehru himself had seemed most sympathetic. I lunched with him and talked with him at various meetings and receptions. He had been exceedingly friendly. But when I met Dr Bahba, India's leading official scientist, towards the end of Nehru's visit, I received a cold douche. He had profound doubts about any such manifesto, let alone any such conference as I had in mind for the future. It became evident that I should receive no encouragement from Indian official scientific quarters. After the successful promulgation of the manifesto, however, Nehru's more friendly attitude prevailed. With the approval and help of the Indian Government, it was proposed that the first conference between Western and Eastern scientists be held in New Delhi in January, 1957.

Throughout the early part of 1956, we perfected, so far as we could, our plans for the conference. By the middle of the year we had sent off invitations over my name to about sixty scientists. But 1956 was a year of bits and pieces for me, taken up chiefly by broadcasts and articles. An endless and pleasant stream of old friends and new acquaintances came and went. We decided to sell our Richmond house and move permanently to North Wales. We kept, however, as a *pied à terre* in London, our flat in Millbank, with its wonderful view of the river in which I delighted. Later, we were turned out of this flat for the modernization of Millbank. Politically, I took part in numberless meetings concerned with a variety of affairs, some to do with the troubles in Cyprus, some to do with World Government. (The World Government Association gave a dinner in my honour in February at the House of Commons. I have never felt sure how many of the people at the dinner knew that it had been announced as a dinner in my honour. At any rate, some of the speeches might have turned my head happily if only I could have believed them.) I was especially concerned with a campaign about the imprisonment of Morton Sobell in the United States.

At the time of the Rosenberg's trial and death (one is tempted to say assassination) in 1951, I had paid, I am ashamed to say, only cursory attention to what was going on. Now, in 1956, in March, my cousin Margaret Lloyd brought Mrs Sobell, Morton Sobell's mother, to see me. Sobell had been kidnapped by the United States Government from Mexico to be brought to trial in connection with the Rosenberg case. He had been condemned, on the evidence of a known perjurer, to thirty years' imprisonment, of which he had already served five. His family was trying to obtain support for him, and his mother had come to England for help. Several eminent people in America had already taken up cudgels on his behalf, but to no avail. People both here and in the United States appeared to be ignorant of his plight and what had led up to it. I remember talking of the case with a well-known and much admired Federal Court Judge. He professed complete ignorance of the case of Morton Sobell and was profoundly shocked by what I told him of it. But I noted that he afterwards made no effort to get at the facts, much less to do anything to remedy them. The case seemed to me a monstrous one and I agreed to do all I could to call people's attention to it. A small society had already been formed in London to do this, and they agreed to help me. I wrote letters to the papers and articles on the matter. One of my letters contained the phrase 'a posse of terrified perjurers', which pleased me and annoyed those who did not agree with me. I was inundated by angry letters from Americans and others denying my charges and asking irately how I could be so bold as to call American justice into question. A few letters came from people, including members of the above-mentioned London group, who agreed with me, though no one in England, so far as I know, upheld my point of view publicly. I was generally and often venomously charged with being anti-American, as I often have been when I have criticized adversely any Americans or anything American. I do not

F
81

know why, since I have spent long periods in that country and have many friends there and have often expressed my admiration of various Americans and American doings. Moreover, I have married two Americans. However—ten years later it had come to be generally agreed that the case against Morton Sobell did not hold water. The Court of Appeals pronounced publicly on the case in 1962–63. On reading the judges' verdict, I understood them to say that it was not worth granting Sobell a new trial. On appealing for advice from Sobell's defence lawyers on my interpretation of the verdict, I was informed: 'It was terrible, though not quite as crude as you'd imagined.' The defence lawyers had argued that 'Ethel Rosenberg's constitutional Fifth-Amendment rights had been violated during the trial, and that this had been fully established in a subsequent Supreme Court decision, known as the "Grunewald" decision. This decision indicated that Ethel Rosenberg had been entitled to a new trial; and since her innocence would have established her husband's and Sobell's, they too were entitled to new trials . . . The Rosenbergs, alas, were no longer around, but Sobell should have his day in court.' Although his family continue their long, brave fight to obtain freedom for him, Morton Sobell remains in prison.

Early in 1947 I had said in the House of Lords that in America 'any person who favours the United Nations is labelled as a dangerous "Red" '. I was alarmed by such uncritical anti-communism, especially as it was adopted increasingly by organizations purporting to be liberal. For this reason I felt obliged, early in 1953, to resign from the American Committee for Cultural Freedom. I remained Honorary President of the International Congress for Cultural Freedom. Three years later I was sent the proof of a book called *Was Justice Done? The Rosenberg–Sobell Case* by Malcolm Sharp, Professor of Law at the University of Chicago. It made it quite clear to me, and I should have thought to anyone, that there had been a miscarriage of justice. I denounced in the press the hysteria and police-state techniques which had been used against the Rosenbergs and Sobell. The response of the American Committee for Cultural Freedom seems even more absurd in the light of the evidence which has mounted during the intervening years than it seemed at the time. 'There is no evidence whatsoever', the American Committee pronounced, 'that the Federal Bureau of Investigation committed atrocities or employed thugs in the Rosenberg case. There is no support whatever for your charge that Sobell, an innocent man, was the victim of political hysteria. There is no ground whatever for your contention that either Sobell or the Rosenbergs were condemned on the word of perjurers, terrified or unterrified. . . . Your remarks on American judicial procedure, the analogy you draw between the technique of the Federal Bureau of Investigation and the policy [*sic*] methods of Nazi Germany or Stalin's Russia, constitute a major disservice to the cause of freedom and democracy.' Having learned that the American branch approved of cultural freedom in Communist countries but not elsewhere, I resigned from the Congress for Cultural Freedom.

But in the summer of 1956 things seemed to be moving in our direction so far as the proposed conference of scientists was concerned. Then, in October, two misfortunes overtook the world: the first was the Hungarian Revolt and its suppression;[1] the second was the Suez affair. In relation to the latter I felt shocked, as I said publicly, and sickened by our Government's machinations, military and other. I welcomed Gaitskell's speech, dry and late in coming though it was, because it said more or less officially a number of things that should have been said. But the loss of influence in international affairs which Great Britain must suffer in consequence of this ill-advised Suez exploit seemed to me well-nigh irreparable. In any case, it was obviously impossible to take the Western participants in the conference by the round-about route then necessary to arrive in India in January, 1957. So we had to re-plan our next move.

The problem was how the work was to be carried out and where such a conference should be held and, above all, how it could be financed. I felt very sure that the conference should not be bound by the tenets of any established body and that it should be entirely neutral and independent; and the other planners thought likewise. But we could find no individual or organization in England willing, if able, to finance it and certainly none willing to do so with no strings attached. Sometime before, I had received a warm letter of approbation for what I was doing from Cyrus Eaton in America. He had offered to help with money. Aristotle Onassis, the Greek shipping magnate, had also offered to help if the conference were to take place at Monte Carlo. Cyrus Eaton now confirmed his offer if the conference were to be held at his birthplace, Pugwash in Nova Scotia. He had held other sorts of conferences there of a not wholly dissimilar character. We agreed to the condition. Plans went ahead fast under the guidance of Professors Rotblat and Powell. They were greatly helped by Dr Burhop and, then and later, by Dr Patricia Lindop, a physicist of St Bartholomew's Medical College. Her informed and dedicated devotion to the causes of peace and co-operation among scientists was, I found, comparable

---

[1] I am sometimes asked why I did not at the time fulminate against the Russian suppression of the Hungarian Revolt. I did not because there was no need. Most of the so-called Western World was fulminating. Some people spoke out strongly against the Suez exploit, but most people were acquiescent.

even to Professor Rotblat's. She managed her work, her children and household and the scientists with apparently carefree grace and tact. And the first conference took place in early July, 1957, at Pugwash.

I was unable to go to this first conference because of my age and ill health. A large part of my time in 1957 was devoted to various medical tests to determine what was the trouble with my throat. In February, I had to go into hospital for a short time to find out whether or not I had cancer of the throat. The evening that I went in I had a debate over the BBC with Abbot Butler of Downside which I much enjoyed, and I think he did also. The incident went off as pleasantly as such a trying performance could do and it was discovered conclusively that I did not have cancer. But what did I have? And so the tests continued and I continued to have to live on baby's food and other such pabulum.

Since that time I have made several journeys abroad, though none so long as that to Pugwash. I fight shy of longer journeys partly because I fear if I go to one country people in other countries who have pressed me to go there will be affronted. The only way around this, for one who is not an official personage, is to renounce distant travels. In 1958, however, I journeyed to a Pugwash conference in Austria. I stayed on after the meetings and, with my wife, made a journey by motor car. We drove along the Danube to Durnstein which I had wished to see ever since my boyhood delight in Richard Coeur de Lion. I was greatly impressed by the magnificent bleak grandeur of Melk on its bluff about the river and by the beauty of its library. Then we drove in a large circle through the mountains back to Vienna. The air was delicious and spicy. It seemed like a journey into the story books of my youth, both in the countryside, which is that of fairy books, and in the kindness and simplicity and gaiety of the people. Above one little village there was a great lime tree where the villagers gathered to gossip of an evening and on Sunday. It was a magical tree in a magical meadow, calm and sweet and full of peace. Once, as we drove along a narrow lane beside a dashing stream at the foot of a mountain, we were held up by a landslide. Great trunks of fir trees were piled up across the road. We stopped, wondering how to turn or to pass it. Suddenly, men and women appeared, as if sprung from the ground, from the nearby farms and set to work, laughing and joking, to move the obstruction. In a trice, it seemed to me, the road was free and we were being waved on by smiling people.

But to return to Pugwash—I was kept in close touch by letter and telephone with the proceedings of the first conference and was pleased with what I heard. We had decided that not only physicists but biological and social scientists should be invited to attend. There were twenty-two participants in all—from the United States, the Soviet

Union, China, Poland, Australia, Austria, Canada, France, Great Britain, and Japan. The meetings were carried on in both English and Russian. It pleased me especially that it showed that real co-operation such as we had hoped, could be achieved among scientists of extremely divergent 'ideologies' and apparently opposing scientific as well as other views.

The conference was called the Pugwash Conference of Scientists and for the sake of continuity the movement has continued to be identified by the name Pugwash. It established among other things a 'Continuing Committee' of five members of which I was the Chairman to organize further conferences. More important, it established a form that future conferences followed. A number of plenary meetings were held at which important papers were read. There were a greater number of meetings of the small committees set up at the start, at which particular aspects of the general subjects were discussed and decided. Most important of all, it was held in an atmosphere of friendliness. Perhaps the unique characteristic of this and subsequent Pugwash Conferences was the fact that the members consorted with each other in their spare time as well as during the scheduled meetings and grew to know each other as human beings rather than merely as scientists of this or that potentially inimical belief or nation. This most important characteristic was in large part made possible by the astute understanding by Cyrus Eaton of the situation and what we wished to accomplish and by his tactful hospitality.

As I was not present, I shall not attempt to describe in detail the action or findings of this or any of the other conferences. Professor Rotblat compiled an excellent and comprehensive history of this and the following seven conferences that were held up to the time of its publication in 1962. Suffice it to say here, that there were three committees at the first conference: (1) on the hazards arising from the use of atomic energy; (2) on the control of nuclear weapons, which outlined the general objectives of disarmament which subsequent conferences discussed in detail; and (3) on the social responsibilities of scientists. The findings of the first, as Professor Rotblat points out, probably comprise the first agreement reached between scientists of East and West on the effects of nuclear tests. The third committee summarized its findings in eleven items of common belief which became, little more than a year later, the basis of what is known as the 'Vienna Declaration'. This first Pugwash conference published a statement that was formally endorsed by the Soviet Academy of Sciences and warmly welcomed in China, but less publicized and more slowly in the West.

The Continuing Committee first met in London in December, 1957 and a further and similar conference, again made possible by Cyrus

Eaton, was held at Lac Beauport in Canada in the spring of 1958. Then came a more ambitious endeavour: a large conference in September, 1958, at Kitzbühel in Austria. It was made possible through the good offices of Professor Hans Thirring, under the auspices of the Theodor–Koerner Foundation. It was followed by meetings held in Vienna. At the former conferences no press or observers had been permitted to attend. At this third conference not only were observers present but they included members of the families of the participants. At the great meetings at Vienna the press was in evidence. At the meeting in the Austrian Academy of Sciences on the morning of September 20th the Vienna Declaration was promulgated. It was a statement that had been accepted with only one abstention by all the members of the conference at Kitzbühel and it forms, as Professor Rotblat has said, the *credo* of the Pugwash movement. It is too long to be included here, but may be found in his history. The meeting was opened by the President of Austria, Dr Adolf Schaef, for the conference had been given a very generous welcome by the Austrian State. Amongst others of both East and West I spoke in my capacity of president of the movement and chairman of the Continuing Committee. It seemed to me an impressive and unforgettable formal occasion. In my speech I recalled my grand-father's speech at a Congress (also in Vienna) during the Crimean War in which he spoke in favour of peace, but was over-ruled. Following the great meeting, we attended the President's lunch in the Alter Hof. Then came an important meeting when ten of the participants in the conference addressed ten thousand people at the Wiener Stadhalle— but this I could not attend.

The most obvious achievement of the Pugwash movement has been the conclusion, for which it was largely responsible, of the partial Test-ban Treaty which forbade nuclear tests above ground in peace time. I, personally, was not and am not happy about this partial ban. It seems to me to be, as I should expect it to be, a soother of consciences and fears that should not be soothed. At the same time, it is only a slight mitigation of the dangers to which we are all exposed. It seemed to me more likely to be a hindrance than a help towards obtaining the desired total ban. Nevertheless, it showed that East and West could work together to obtain what they wished to obtain and that the Pugwash movement could be effective when and where it desired to be. It was rather a give-away of the *bona fides* of the various 'Disarmament Conferences' whose doings we have watched with some scepticism for a good many years.

The Pugwash movement now seems to be firmly established and part of the respectable progress of scientific relations with international affairs. I myself have had little to do directly with its progress in the last years. My interest turned to new plans towards persuading peoples and Governments to banish war and in particular weapons of mass extermination, first of all nuclear weapons. In the course of these fresh endeavours, I felt that I had become rather disreputable in the eyes of the more conservative scientists. The Pugwash movement held a great meeting of scientists from all over the world in London in September, 1962. I was to speak about the founding of the movement and I warned my friends that I might be hissed—as I was fully convinced that I should be. I was deeply touched by being given a standing ovation when I rose to speak which included, I was told, all the participants, all, that is, save Lord Hailsham. He was present in his capacity as the Queen's Minister of Science. He was personally, I think, friendly enough to me, but, weighed down by office, he sat tight. That was the last occasion on which I have taken public part in a Pugwash conference.

LETTERS

From Bernard Berenson

I Tatti
Settignano
Florence
March 29, 1945

Dear Bertie

Mary died the 23d, & as I know that she remained very fond of you to the end, I wish you to hear of her end. It was a liberation, for she suffered distressingly, & increasingly in recent years.

Not many months ago, I read out to her yr. article in *Horizon* about America. It delighted her & me as well.

Of other publications of yours we have seen nothing in years. We have been cut off from the Western World for a good five years. I learned with pleasure that you had returned to your Cambridge & to Trinity. It makes me believe that we may meet again some day. It will have to be here, as I doubt whether I shall get to England soon.

You must have a grown up son by now. What of him?

With affectionate remembrance.

Sincerely yours
B.B.

Hotel Europa e Britannia
Venezia
June 1, 54 till July

Dear Bertie

I hear from Mrs Sprigge that you would like to revisit I Tatti. It would give me real pleasure to see you again, and your wife whom I remember. I

87

propose your coming for ten days or a fortnight at any time between Dec. 1 and April 1. The other months we are either away or too crowded & I want you to myself. For many years I have been reading what you published about things human, feeling as if nobody else spoke for me as you do.

Do not delay, for in these weeks I shall be reaching my 90th year & *le Grand Peut-être* may want me any day.

With affectionate remembrance.

> *Ever yrs*
> *B.B.*

I Tatti
Settignano
Florence
July 12 '54

Dear Bertie

Thank you for *Nightmares*. I have enjoyed yr. wit, your evocation, your *Galgenhumors. Continuez!*

Yes, any time between Jan. 10 & March 1 would suit me best. I should be happy if you could stay a fortnight.

> *Sincerely yours*
> *B.B.*

P.S. Later, you will give me precise dates. B.B.

I Tatti
Settignano
Florence
Nov. 16, '54

Dear Bertie

Your note of the 12th grieves me. I looked forward to seeing you, the last of my near-contemporaries, & one with whom I have so much in common.

Unless work chains you to London you could carry it on at least as well here as at home. I never see guests except at meals, or if they want to join me in my now so short walks.

If Jan. 15–March 15 are impossible is there another time that would suit you better.

Could you come in the summer? We three are at Vallombrosa in a paradise but rustic, & far less roomy & comfy.

Incline yr. heart toward my proposal.

> *Sincerely*
> *B.B.*

P.S. I never shall cross the Alps again. London, Paris, New York etc. are far, far too tiring for me now.

Saniet Volpi-Tripoli
May 8, 55

Dear Bertie

Of course I knew you were in Rome, & I had a faint hope that you might find time to spend a day or two with me in Florence. I was disappointed that you could not make it.

Let me urge you again to come for a fortnight or so any time between Nov. 15 & March 15, preferably Jan. 15 to March 15. You could work as well as at home for I never see guests except at meals & evenings—if they care to keep me company after dinner.

It would be a joy to live over the remembered days of so long ago. Of your wife too I retain pleasant remembrance & should be happy to renew our acquaintance.

Do you really hope that disaster can be averted? I fear experiments can not be avoided, & damn the consequences.

Sincerely yrs.
B. B.

I wrote the following soon after going to live in Richmond in the house which I shared with my son and his family.

May 12th, 1950

I have been walking alone in the garden of Pembroke Lodge, and it has produced a mood of almost unbearable melancholy. The Government is doing great works, all bad. Half the garden is incredibly lovely: a mass of azaleas and bluebells and narcissus and blossoming may trees. This half they have carefully fenced in with barbed wire (I crawled through it), for fear the public should enjoy it. It was incredibly like Blake's Garden of Love, except that the 'priests' were bureaucrats.

I suffer also from entering into the lives of John and Susan. They were born after 1914, and are therefore incapable of happiness. Their three children are lovely: I love them and they like me. But the parents live their separate lives, in separate prisons of nightmare and despair. Not on the surface; on the surface they are happy. But beneath the surface John lives in suspicious solitude, unable to believe that any one can be trusted, and Susan is driven beyond endurance by sharp stabs of sudden agony from contemplation of this dreadful world. She finds relief in writing poetry, but he has no relief. I see that their marriage will break up, and that neither will ever find happiness or peace. At moments I can shut out this terrifying intuitive knowledge, but I love them both too much to keep on thinking about them on a level of mundane common sense. If I had not the horrible Cassandra gift of foreseeing tragedy, I could be happy here, on a surface level. But as it is, I suffer. And what is wrong with them is wrong with all the young throughout the world. My heart aches with compassion for the lost generation—lost by the folly and greed of the generation to which I belong. It is a heavy burden, but one must rise above it. Perhaps, by suffering to the limit, some word of comfort may be revealed.

89

To Charles W. Stewart, the illustrator of my Nightmares of Eminent Persons. *I longed to find a Daumier or, better still, a Goya to point up the savage irony of this book as well as the warning contained in my* Human Society in Ethics and Politics.

20 Nov. 1953

Dear Mr Stewart

Thank you for the roughs. I like them very much and shall be glad to have you do the pictures. I note what you say about Stalin and am assuming that the picture will be somewhat different from the rough. I particularly like the existentialist's nightmare and the one in Zahatopolk where the lady is being burnt. In the other Zahatopolk picture I like it all except that I think the valley ought to be more smiling and full of flowers, but perhaps it will be so when you have finished the picture. In the picture of Dr Southport Vulpes I suppose the things in the sky are aeroplanes, and I think it might be a good thing if they were somewhat larger and more emphatic. I quite agree to your suggestion of a single heading for every other nightmare, and I have no objection to having Vulpes put between Eisenhower and Acheson as you suggest. I am looking forward with pleasure to a picture of the quarrel between the two ladies in Faith and Mountains. As this story is at the printers, I am sending you a spare typescript which, however, I should like to have back when you have finished with it.

I am engaged on another book, not of stories, but on ethics and politics, to be called *Human Society: Diagnosis & Prognosis.* I want in this book to have three pictures, or one picture in three parts, like a triptych, illustrating the uses of intelligence in the past, present and future. If you feel inclined to undertake this and if Stanley Unwin is agreeable, I shall be very glad. Any time within the next four months would do. I should like all three as savage and bitter as possible.

I return the roughs herewith.

Yours sincerely
Bertrand Russell

From Ion Braby about *The Good Citizen's Alphabet*

Queensland
St Nicholas-at-Wade
near Birchington, Kent
March 31 1953

Dear Lord Russell

Thank you so much for the book. It is delightful. I am not sure whether the drawings are worthy of the text or the text worthy of the drawings. In either event they could hardly be better. I think FOOLISH, GREEDY and JOLLY are my favourites, but I am very fond of UNFAIR, ERRONEOUS and DIABOLIC and many more. And, also, of the opening address (I feel that is the word) and its illustrations. I am sure you and the artist will be due for a triple dose of hemlock, for you will be accused of corrupting not only the young but the middle-aged and elderly too—and corrupting the latter two is very wrong, as they have less time to recover. Anyway, I am very glad to be subverted by it; thank you again.

I sent my book off to The Bodley Head at the end of the week before last, and hope to get an answer soon. I need hardly say once more how much I appreciate your interest and help.

With best wishes
Yours sincerely
Ion

From Rupert Crawshay-Williams

Castle Yard
Portmeirion
Penrhyndeudraeth
Merioneth
August 1, 1953

Dear Bertie

I was so delighted by your story—and especially as I read most of it in a remarkably dingy cubicle in a Divinity students' hostel in Dublin—that I determined to write you a letter long enough for comment on the particular bits I liked; and I've been putting this off—largely because my holiday in Ireland did not do as a holiday is supposed to, but somehow put me into a state of mind in which all my work was worse—and much slower—than it had been before. (But this may have been a bit because revising, and particularly cutting down, is so much more boring than the actual working out of ideas.)

Anyway *Faith and Mountains* is certainly my favourite of all your stories so far. I suppose this is partly because its theme is a cup of tea just up my street. But I think you have worked it out beautifully, with just the right amount—not too much—of pastiche and exaggeration. The pseudo-scientific plausibility of the two opposing doctrines is delightful, especially in the light of Mr Wagthorne's later point about man's ability to believe what afterwards appears to have been nonsense. Incidentally, that whole paragraph on p. 43 builds up with beautifully timed comic effect to all the names beginning with M. The timing of your effects in general—for instance, the moments you choose for understatement or for sharp statement—is now technically most efficient. (The Professor's opening speech at the grand meeting; the conciseness of the paragraph at the beginning of Chapter VII in which his future is outlined— nice bit about Tensing!; 'And with that they fell into each other's arms'.)

Also there are a nice lot of sly digs put over with a straight face (which is one of your finger-prints, of course): The Magnets dismissal of *mere* brawn; the believers finally remaining in out of the way suburbs. And I liked the conceits about the very narrow valley and about Mr Thorney's use of a sextant. And the T.L.S. pastiche, with its 'shallow certainty' and 'deeper sources of wisdom' and 'the coldly critical intellect'.

Your 'message' of course is highly commendable; and as a matter of fact Zachary's answer to his father at the end is most concise and decisive. But,

91

for me, even more decisive—because it made me laugh out loud (and also Elizabeth, who sends her love and entire agreement)—is the last paragraph. You have caught so neatly and ludicrously the dingy commonplaceness of so many hymns. (Now I come to think of it, part of the effect comes from the slight confusion of thought between third and fourth lines: diseases of *the* chest and Makes *our* muscles grow.) And then comes—perfectly correctly—the word 'Sublimities' in the last line.

I was glad to see, by the way, your emphasis, in a review in the *Sunday Times* some weeks ago, upon the role of power politics rather than ideologies— and also your re-emphasis upon the way in which science and scientific method have conditioned (all that is 'best' in) Western Values. It is maddening the way in which the opposite 'soupy' belief is accepted even by most unsoupy people.

My word 'soupy' was used the other day—in exactly my sense—by a novelist called Angus Wilson when reviewing a book on Georges Sand in the *Observer*. I very much hope this is a sign that it is spreading; Angus Wilson is I believe a friend of Cyril Connolly's to whom I did once introduce the word.

The names Tomkins and Merrow (together) ring a faint bell in my mind. Should it be a loud bell, and should I recognize it?

Yours ever
Rupert

It's now Sunday, and I've just remembered that the local post office box won't take large envelopes. So I'll send the MS back to-morrow.

From J. B. S. Haldane

University College London
Department of Biometry
5th November, 1953

Dear Russell

Thank you very much for your information. I have, of course, altered the passage to bring it into line with the facts. In my old age I am getting rather interested in animal behaviour, and have even done something to 'decode' the bees' language (of which a fair account is to be found in Ribbands *The Behaviour and Social Life of Honeybees*). As you know, bees returning from a rich source of food dance. The class of all dances is a propositional function with four variables, which may be rendered

'There is a source of food smelling of A, requiring B workers, at a distance C in direction D.'

A is indicated by demonstration, B, C, and D symbolically. I have brought a little precision into the translation of the symbols for C. The paper will be sent you in due course. If, however, bees are given honey vertically above them they cannot communicate this fact, though they dance in an irregular manner. There are undanceable truths, like the ineffable name of God.

The political system of bees, discovered by Lindauer, is even more surprising. He has records of a debate as to a nest site which lasted for five days.

You will perhaps correct me if I am incorrect in describing a propositional function as a class of propositions. If one comes to them 'from outside' as in the observation of bees, this seems a natural way of looking at the matter.

Meanwhile various Germans (not v. Frisch and Lindauer) are plugging the fixity of animal behaviour in a rather Nazi manner (v. reprint by my wife). The word 'imprinting', due to Thorpe, is used for long-lasting changes in conduct due to a juvenile experience (e.g. the following of Spalding by chickens).

Yours sincerely
J. B. S. *Haldane*

From H. McHaigh Esq.

87 Orewa Rd.
Auckland, N.Z.
17/viii/'51

Dear Sir

I had the pleasure of lecturing you last year: while you were in Sydney. But, one evening this week you were closer: here, in Auckland, I heard your voice—reproduced from I.Y.A. Auck. Radio broadcast.

Now I understand how, or why, the 'Bulletin' artist was able to depict so terribly the vile personality shewn in that weekly's columns—labelled with your name: as well as seeing you in the flesh, he must have heard you speak.

Frequently, while the radio is turned on, I have wondered whether members of Broadcasting Boards have ears; or, whether, having ears, they have a grain of good taste amongst them. But, as soon as the announcer named you as the person emitting those dreadfully disgusting sounds, I knew that, ears or no ears, those men are utterly careless about inflicting pain—and about disclosing the shocking ruin that (as in your case) a human being can make of himself. For, unless thoroughly bestialized, no man could possibly give out such sounds from his mouth.

When, or if, you ever entertain shame and self-disgust (and I pray it may be soon), I suggest that you gather and destroy every sound-record of your voice: you owe that reparation at least.

God help you.

Yours truly
H. *McHaigh*

From and to H. N. Brailsford

37 Belsize Park Gardens
London
N.W.3
19 May 1952

My Dear Russell

You have been overwhelmed, I'm sure, with congratulations, and yet I would like to add mine, for few can have come from friends who knew you in the last century. I recall vividly our first meeting at the Courtneys during the

Boer War. I welcome this birthday because it gives me a happy occasion to thank you for all I have gained from your writings. Best of all in these days were the courage and optimism of your recent broadcasts.

Evamaria joins me in sending you, with our gratitude, our warmest greetings.

> *Yours ever*
> *Noel Brailsford*

[undated] May 1952

My dear Brailsford

Thank you for your letter of May 19. I owe much to you. Your review of my *Social Reconstruction* encouraged me more than any other at a time when I very much needed encouragement. I caused fury in Cambridge by quoting from your *War of Steel and Gold* a passage showing how much parsons and such were making out of armaments. The fury was of a sort of which I was glad to cause. I am very glad you have liked my recent broadcasts. Please convey my thanks to Mrs Brailsford as well as to yourself.

> *Yours ever*
> *Bertrand Russell*

From Ernest Jones, the psycho-analyst

> The Plat
> Elsted, Nr. Midhurst, Sx.
> February 20, 1955

Dear Bertrand Russell

What pleasure you have given to a host of people by your characteristically courageous, forthright and penetrating observations in today's *Observer*. You and W. K. Clifford greatly resemble each other in these attributes. I wonder how much the study of mathematics conduced to them in both of you. Your concluding paragraph might be a paraphrase of the concluding one in his *Lectures and Essays*, a copy of which I enclose in case you have mislaid his book. Many of his Essays could very well be reprinted to-day. It is sad to think that the eighty years since he wrote them have shown such little progress in the apprehension of the clear principles he enunciated.

By the way, he quotes elsewhere Coleridge's pungent aphorism: 'He who begins by loving Christianity better than Truth, will proceed by loving his own sect or Church better than Christianity, and end in loving himself better than all.'

> *Yours very sincerely*
> *Ernest Jones*

> The Plat
> Elsted, Nr. Midhurst, Sx.
> April 25, 1955

Dear Bertrand Russell

In your luminous essay on Einstein in the *Observer* there is one sentence which I am a little inclined to question: it is about his being surprisingly indifferent to empirical confirmations. The following is a quotation from a letter he wrote to Freud in April 1936:

'Bis vor Kurzem war mir nur die spekulative Kraft Ohrer Gedankengänge sowie der gewaltige Einfluss auf die Weltanschauung der Gegenwart klar geworden, ohne mir über den Wahrheitswert Ihrer Theorien klar werden zu können. In letzter Zeit aber hatte ich Gelegenheit von einigen an sich geringfügigen Fällen zu hören, die jegliche abweichende Auslegung (von der Verdrängungslehre abweichend) ausschliessen. Dies empfand ich als beglückend; denn es ist stets beglückend, wenn eine grosse und schöne Idee sich als in der Wirklichkeit zutreffend erweist.' [1]

I had taken the concluding sentence to be based on his own experience, such as the 1919 bending of light, etc.

If a subscription or the use of my name could make any contribution to the magnificent campaign you inaugurated in Rome pray command me.

> *Yours sincerely*
> *Ernest Jones*

Miss Graves was a deeply religious lady who surprised me by her tolerance. I first came in contact with her over Chinese affairs. Afterwards she was chiefly concerned with Latin America.

From Anna Melissa Graves

> 921 Jahncke Ave.
> Covington, Louisiana
> USA
> February 24, 1957

Dear Lord Russell

I have not heard from Victor Haya de la Torre, that is I have not had a letter, but he sent me an account of himself which appeared in *The Observer*, and from that account or 'interview' he had evidently made the pilgrimage to see you. I am glad for I am sure that seeing you and meeting you was—or should have been—of real benefit to him. I hope you did not think the time you gave him wasted.

In this 'interview' he said you were so 'true' and 'hopeful'. He does not need the example of optimism, having always been a believer in a better time coming; but most Latin Americans—perhaps all politicians of every land need the example of anyone to whom Truth means as much as it does to you. I am very glad he recognized *that* first of all in you.

I wonder if you remember I asked you if you could to return his letter to me, asking me to ask you to receive him. It was enclosed in my second note

---

[1] 'Until recently I was only able to speculate over your trains of thought concerning the powerful influence of our present environment. I understood these without having to assess the validity of your theories.

'Of late however, I have had the opportunity to attend a colloquium on you, which laid out each divergent interpretation (of the Theories of Inhibition). This gave me great pleasure as it is always satisfying when a grand and wonderful idea is found to be practical.'

to you and you answered the first note. It would be very natural if you thought the second note did not need an answer; but if you have not destroyed or mislaid Victor's letter I should be grateful if you could return it; but if it is lost that would not be at all a serious matter.

I should also be grateful if you told me your impression of him. I think I am going to Los Angeles, California, to live with Anna Louise Strong. I think I can do more for the Negroes here after having lived here than I could if I stayed. If one does what one longs to do, one often gets them into trouble. I think the condition here is worse than it is (or rather worse than it was when Reginald Reynolds wrote his book) worse here than in South Africa, of course not worse than in Kenya, but in South Africa the non-Africans (British and Boers) who wish to treat the Africans justly seem freer to—seemed freer to— work for justice than one is here. Eastland is very determined to call all who are working for justice to the Negroes—'Communists', 'Agents of Moscow'. But it is not the Eastlands who are so dangerous, it is the cultured charming 'White-Southerners'. They could end all the injustice, but then they would not be themselves if they did. They can't open their eyes, because they don't dare.

Very sincerely yours, and gratefully for giving time to Victor
Anna Melissa Graves

From Clement Davies

31 Evelyn Mansions
Carlisle Place
London S.W.1
[Dec. 24, 54]

My dear Bertrand Russell
May I be allowed to say 'thank you' for your splendid Broadcast speech last night. I say my 'thank you' most sincerely. What memories you stirred!! and how my thoughts went speeding along with yours at a super-sonic rate. Yes, we have accomplished much that I longed to see done 50 and more years ago—and how one battled in those days against great odds, while, today, those very opponents not only are on our side but actually are so enthusiastic about the reforms that they claim they originated them.

The remembrance of those days and the changes that have been brought about and secured, hearten me with regard to the International Situation. The odds against your and my ideals and against adopting Reason instead of Force as the arbiter in human differences are so apparently strong that our struggles might seem hopeless. But here again, we shall see and see soon a great change and if our experience in home affairs is repeated in International affairs, then those who today oppose us and reject our remedies, will not only accept the remedies but claim that they and they alone were responsible for them and that they brought to suffering humanity the Peace which all men & women desire.

Well; I hope I am right, and I shall cheer them loud and long, just as I today cheer my opponents who long ago said they would not lick stamps.

5. Bertrand Russell sitting for Epstein, 1953

A handwritten retort
by Bertrand Russell

Lord Russell

All earthly knowledge finally explored,
 Man feels himself from doubt and dogma free.
There are more things in Heaven, though, my lord,
 Than are dreamed of in your philosophy.

6. Bertrand Russell by Ronald Searle, *Punch*, March 1957

Again my most grateful thanks. With our united warmest regards &
wishes to you both

Very sincerely yours
Clement Davies

31 Evelyn Mansions
Carlisle Place
London, S.W.1
Sept. 19, 55

My dear Bertrand Russell
You have tempted me into reminiscence by recalling your excursion into
the political arena against the redoubtable Joe Chamberlain and his raging
tearing propaganda in favour of tariffs and ultra nationalism.

My first effort was also against the formidable Joe. It was in November
1899 and I was of the very ripe experienced age of 15. I went on the platform
at a Tory meeting to denounce the South African War—my oratory was not
allowed to last long in spite of a strenuous effort, and I returned home with
black eyes (two) and a bloody nose. It was not so much an anti-war effort
as a Defence of the Boers. Little did I dream that they would misuse the
Freedom which we wanted them to have and which we restored to them in
1906—to the disadvantage of the Black and Coloured Africans.

With warmest regards & best wishes from us to you both

Ever yours sincerely
Clement Davies

PRESS CONFERENCE

by

THE EARL RUSSELL

at

Caxton Hall, Westminster

on

Saturday, 9th July, 1955

Professor J. ROTBLAT: Ladies and gentlemen, this conference was called by
Lord Bertrand Russell in order to make public a statement signed by a number
of scientists on the significance of nuclear warfare. I hope that each of you
received a copy of the statement. I am going to call on Lord Russell to give
you a short summary of this statement and afterwards it will be open to you
to ask questions relating to this topic. Lord Russell.

Earl RUSSELL: Ladies and gentlemen, the purpose of this conference is to
bring to your notice, and through you to the notice of the world, a statement
signed by eight of the most eminent scientists in the field cognate to nuclear

G   97

warfare, about the perils that are involved in nuclear warfare and the absolute necessity therefore of avoiding war.

I will just read you a brief abstract here which I think you already have:

'The accompanying statement, which has been signed by some of the most eminent scientific authorities in different parts of the world, deals with the perils of a nuclear war. It makes it clear that neither side can hope for victory in such a war, and that there is a very real danger of the extermination of the human race by dust and rain from radio-active clouds. It suggests that neither the public nor the governments of the world are adequately aware of the danger. It points out that an agreed prohibition of nuclear weapons, while it might be useful in lessening tension, would not afford a solution, since such weapons would certainly be manufactured and used in a great war in spite of previous agreements to the contrary. The only hope for mankind is the avoidance of war. To call for a way of thinking which shall make such avoidance possible is the purpose of this statement.

The first move came as a collaboration between Einstein and myself. Einstein's signature was given in the last week of his life. Since his death I have approached men of scientific competence both in the East and in the West, for political disagreements should not influence men of science in estimating what is probable, but some of those approached have not yet replied. I am bringing the warning pronounced by the signatories to the notice of all the powerful Governments of the world in the earnest hope that they may agree to allow their citizens to survive.'

Now I should like to say just a little about the genesis of this statement. I think it was an outcome of a broadcast which I gave on the 23rd December last year on the B B C on the perils of nuclear war. I had appreciative letters from various people, among others from Professor Joliot-Curie, the eminent French man of science, and I was particularly pleased at getting an appreciative letter from him because of his being a noted Communist.

I thought that one of the purposes that I had in view was to build a bridge between people of opposing political opinions. That is to say, to unite men of science on a statement of facts which would leave out all talk of what people thought in the matter of politics. I wrote to Einstein suggesting that eminent men of science should do something dramatic about nuclear war, and I got a reply from him saying that he agreed with every word. I therefore drew up a draft, after consultation with a certain number of people, which I sent to Einstein and he—being already not in very good health—suggested, I quote his own phrase, that I 'should regard myself as dictator of the enterprise' because I think chiefly his health was not equal to doing it. When I sent him the draft he replied, 'I am gladly willing to sign your excellent statement'. I received this letter on the very day of his death and after I had received news of his death, so that this was I suppose about the very last public act of his life.

The aims of drawing up the statement were to keep to what men of science as such can pronounce upon, to avoid politics and thus to get signatures both from the Right and from the Left. Science ought to be impartial, and I thought that one could get a body of agreement among men of differing politics on the importance of avoiding nuclear war, and I think that in that respect this document is fairly successful.

There are, apart from myself, eight signatories[1] of the document. All eight are exceedingly eminent in the scientific world. Most of them are nuclear physicists, some in a field which is very important in this connection, geneticists, and men who know about mutations caused by radiation, a very important subject which arises when you are considering nuclear warfare. But they were chosen solely and only for their scientific eminence and with no other view.

I applied to eighteen, I think, altogether and of these, half, or nearly half, eight[2] in fact, agreed. Some I have not yet heard from for various reasons. In particular, I applied to the most eminent of Chinese physicists, Dr Li Sze Kuang, and I have not yet had his answer. None of the answers I have received were unsympathetic. Those who did not sign had various good reasons, for instance, that they had official positions or were engaged in some official work which made it difficult, but nobody either of Right or of the Left replied in a manner that was unsympathetic.

I had one signature from Professor Infeld of the University of Warsaw, who was joint author with Einstein of two books. I had not a signature, but a very sympathetic letter, from Skobeltsyn of Moscow. Professor Joliot-Curie was, in the first-place, son-in-law of the discoverer of radium, but he does not depend on that for his fame, he is a Nobel prizewinner. He is the sixth of the eight who has got the Nobel Prize for work of scientific character; and the other two I think probably will get the Nobel Prize before very long! That is the order of eminence of these men.

Mr Joliot-Curie made two reservations, one of which was of some importance, the other not so important. I spoke of the necessity for limitations of sovereignty and he wants it added that these limitations are to be agreed by all and in the interests of all, and that is a statement which I entirely agreed to. Then there is another reservation that he made. I say, 'Shall we put an end to the human race: or shall mankind renounce war?' and he wants to say, 'Shall mankind renounce war as a means of settling differences between states?' With these limitations he agreed to sign the document.

Professor Muller also made a very small reservation that seemed only to be explaining what I had meant.

I will say just a few words about these men, some of whom possibly are not so well known in the journalistic world as they are in the scientific world. They consist of two British scientists, two Americans—Eistein himself, whom I do not reckon among Americans, because Einstein's nationality is somewhat universal—one Pole, one Frenchman and one Japanese. Professor Rotblat I am very happy to have here. He is, as you know, Director of Research in Nuclear Physics in Liverpool.[3] He did a very interesting piece of what you might almost call detective work about the Bikini bomb. Those of you who are old enough may possibly remember that in 1945 people were quite shocked

---

[1] Ten—Prof. Max Born and Prof. Linus Pauling to be added.
[2] Ten.   [3] Prof. of Physics in the University of London.

by the atom bomb. Well that seems now ancient history if you think of the atom bomb as something like bows and arrows.

We advanced from that to the H-bomb which was very much worse than the atom bomb and then it turned out, at first I think through the detective work of Professor Rotblat and afterwards by the admission of the American authorities, that the bomb exploded at Bikini was very much worse than an H-bomb. The H-bomb now is ancient history. You have a twofold trigger arrangement. You have first uranium 235 to set off the hydrogen. Then you have the hydrogen to set off uranium 238, of which there are vast slag heaps discarded in producing uranium 235. Now we use uranium 238 for the purpose, it is very much cheaper to make, the bombs are very much more destructive when they are made, and so you see science advances rapidly. So far the Bikini bomb is the latest thing, but we cannot tell where we are going to come to.

I think that this statement, as I conceive it, is only a first step. It will be necessary to go on to get the men of science to make authoritative pronouncements on the facts and I think that should be followed by an International Congress of men of science from all scientific countries at which the signatories would, I hope, propose some such resolution as I have suggested at the end of this statement. I think resolutions with something of those terms could be suggested at the various national congresses that take place in due time. I think that the men of science should make the public and the governments of the world aware of the facts by means of a widespread popular campaign. You know it is a very difficult thing to get men of science to embark on popular campaigns; they are not used to that sort of thing and it does not come readily to them, but it is their duty, I think, at this time to make the public aware of things; they have to persuade the world to avoid war, at first by whatever expedients may suggest themselves, but ultimately by some international machinery that shall make the avoidance of war not a matter of day-to-day expedients but of world organisation. I think they should emphasise that science, which has come to have a rather sinister meaning in the minds of the general public, I think, if once this question of war were out of the way, would be capable of conferring the most enormous benefits upon mankind and making the world a very much happier place than it has ever been before. I think they should emphasise that as well as the dangers that arise through war.

I am here to answer questions, and I should be very happy to do my best to answer any questions that any of you may wish to ask.

CHAPTER III

TRAFALGAR SQUARE

URING THE first five months of 1957 I made a great many broadcasts for the BBC. Almost the last of these was an interview between Alan Wood and myself and a representative of the BBC in connection with Alan's publication of his biography of me. Alan was bitterly disappointed by this interview. His experience of broadcasting was less than mine and so he was considerably surprised when the lady who represented the BBC asked us questions which she had not asked at our rehearsal, indeed which concerned subjects such as my private life. We were both somewhat disconcerted by her questions. However, the book itself had a good reception in spite of being rather tepidly advertised. It seems to me to be an excellent piece of work.

I very much hope that Alan was happy in the reviews given to the book. We launched it pleasantly among some of my old friends and relations at a small party at Millbank on my birthday. This was almost the last time that I saw Alan. He fell very ill shortly after this and died in October. A little over two months later, his wife, Mary, died. It was a heart-breaking loss. They were young and happy and clever and able, and full of plans for their future and that of their two small sons. Their loss to me was incalculable. I not only was very fond of them, but had come to depend upon their knowledge of everything to do with me and their sympathetic understanding, and I greatly enjoyed their companionship.

It must be said that there were limitations to Alan's understanding of the matters discussed in my books. This showed particularly in regard to political matters. I regarded him as rather conservative, and he regarded me as more radical than I was or am. When I argued that everybody ought to have a vote, he thought that I was maintaining that all men are equal in ability. I only disabused him of this belief by pointing out that I had supported eugenics, which is concerned with differences in natural ability. Such disagreements, however, never marred our friendship, and never intruded in purely philosophical conversations.

These sad happenings and the fact that my wife fell ill of a bad heart attack in early June dislocated and slowed up our activities for some months. I got through little that could be of any conceivable public interest for some time. By November, however, my concern with international affairs had boiled up. I felt that I must again do something to urge at least a modicum of common sense to break into the policies of the two Great Powers, Russia and America. They seemed to be blindly, but with determination, careering down a not very primrose-strewn path to destruction, a destruction that might—probably would—engulf us all. I wrote an open letter, to President Eisenhower and Premier Khrushchev, addressing them as 'Most Potent Sirs'. In it I tried to make clear the fact that the things which they held in common were far more numerous and far more important than their differences, and that they had much more to gain than to lose by co-operation. I believed then, as I still believe, in the necessity of co-operation between nations as the sole method of avoiding war; and avoidance of war is the only means of avoiding disaster. This, of course, involves rather disagreeable concessions by all nations. A decade later, Russia seemed to have recognized the need of co-operation—except, possibly, in relations to her co-Marxist State, China. The United States continued to confound co-operation with domination. But, in 1958, I had hope, though slight hope, of both Great Powers coming to their senses, and in this letter I tried to lay my case before them.

Almost at once a reply came from Premier Khrushchev. No answer came from President Eisenhower. Two months later John Foster Dulles replied for him. This reply stung Premier Khrushchev into writing to me again answering various points made by Mr Dulles. All these letters appeared in the *New Statesman*. They were soon published in book form with an introduction by that paper's editor, Kingsley Martin, and a final reply from me to Mr Dulles and Mr Khrushchev. The letters speak for themselves and my final reply gives my point of view on them. The righteously adamantine surface of Mr Dulles's mind as shown in his letter filled me with greater foreboding than did the fulminations and, sometimes, contradictions of Mr Khrushchev. The latter seemed to me to show some underlying understanding of alternatives and realities; the former, none.

During that autumn, George Kennan had been giving the Reith Lectures over the BBC and saying some excellent things drawn with acumen from his wide and first-hand knowledge of American and Russian policies. Early in December a group of us met with Kingsley Martin at his invitation to talk things over. As far as I remember it was at this meeting that the first glimmerings flickered of what was to become the Campaign for Nuclear Disarmament. A meeting of the sponsors of the National Council for the Abolition of Nuclear Weapons Tests was held at the house of Canon John Collins in Amen Court and the CND was formally started early in January, 1958. The officers were to be: Canon Collins, the Chairman; Mrs Peggy Duff, the Secretary; and myself, the President. An Executive Committee was formed comprising some of those leaders already established in anti-nuclear movements and a certain number of other interested notables. There had been for some time various associations working to overcome the dangers with which the international scene was fraught. The CND proposed to take them all in—or at least almost all.

The CND was publicly launched at a large meeting at the Central Hall, Westminster, on February 17, 1958. So many people attended this meeting that there had to be overflow meetings. It seems now to many people as if the CND has been part of the national scene from the beginning of time, and it has lost its lustre and energy through familiarity. But in its early days its information and reasoning were not only sincere but were fresh and commanded considerable attention among a variety of individuals and circles important in the nation. And the first meeting went off with great éclat and success. Moreover, interest in the CND quickly spread. Soon there were committees formed in different parts of the country and then Regional Committees. Many meetings were held, at some of which I spoke. I remember, in particular, one at Manchester in 1959 at which Lord Simon of Wythenshawe was in the chair.

I saw much of Lord Simon in those days and until his death in October, 1960, as he was greatly concerned by the nuclear peril and worked hard to make the dangers known. He arranged a debate on the subject in the House of Lords and held a great number of meetings and press conferences at his London flat. He was a member of the executive committee of the CND and we saw eye to eye in most matters to do with it. He became, as I already was, an upholder of the activities of the Direct Action Committee. We both believed that the dangers must be called to the attention of the public in as many ways as possible and that if we stuck to merely meetings and even marches, no matter how admirable they might be, we should end by preaching only to the already converted. The chairman of the CND did not approve of civil disobedience and so, though nominally the Direct Action Committee was to be tolerated, it could not be aided openly by the CND. The latter did not, for instance, take part in the Aldermaston March, as it was staged by the Direct Action Committee in 1958. The march proved a success, and the CND took it over lock, stock and barrel the following year and made, of course, a much larger and more important thing of it. I was not able to attend the 1959 march or the subsequent meeting in

Trafalgar Square, but the following year I spoke in the Square at the end of the march. I wished, in these years, that I had been young enough to take part in the marches. Later, they seemed to me to be degenerating into something of a yearly picnic. Though individual marchers were as sincere as ever in their endeavours and as admirable, the march was quite ineffective in achieving their aim, which was to call serious attention to and spread the movement. For the most part, the march became a subject of boredom or distress or hilarity, and converted very few of those hitherto unconverted. It was useful, nevertheless, as I think it still is, in continuing, if not enlarging, the movement. New and fresh forms of opposition to dangerous nuclear policies must be sought constantly in order to obtain converts and to catch and hold the interest of people of very diverse outlook.

Shortly after this 1960 Aldermaston March, the Summit Meeting between Eisenhower and Khrushchev took place—and crashed. We had all had high hopes of it and its break-up following the U2 incident was a blow to us. The more we learned of the skulduggery behind it the greater its foreboding quality became. It augured ill for progress towards co-operation, let alone towards disarmament. It seemed more than ever as if new methods must be sought to impress upon the public the increasingly precarious state of international affairs before people relapsed into frustrated apathy. But what this new means could be I did not see.

The CND had been working for unilateral disarmament, believing that if Great Britain gave up her part in the nuclear race and even demanded the departure of United States bases from her soil, other nations might follow suit. It was a slim hope, and still is, but none-the-less it was, and is, a hope. As such, it seemed worth following up. The Campaign also hoped to persuade not only the general public to this way of thinking but also the Government. As most of its upholders were drawn from the Labour Party, it went to work upon the Parliamentary Labour Party. My own view was that the matter was one that transcends Party politics and even national boundaries. As this reasonable view, as it seemed to me, failed to grip the public imagination, I was willing to uphold the Campaign in its efforts. The means towards the end that we both desired mattered less than its achievement. Perhaps, I thought, if the Labour Party *could* be persuaded to support the Campaign, we might be a short step towards the goal.

I had put my point of view clearly in the introduction to my book *Common Sense and Nuclear Warfare* which I wrote during the summer of 1958 and published early in 1959. I had been encouraged during 1958 by receiving the Kalinga Prize, at Unesco in Paris as I could not travel to India. (To be sure the French physicist who was deputed to bear-lead me on that occasion remarked comfortingly to his wife after I had been expounding my views: 'Never mind, my dear, by next year France will be able to explode her own bomb.') And the continued and growing success of the Pugwash movement, as well as the interest shown in the open correspondence with Khrushchev and Eisenhower (Dulles) were encouraging. I continued my search, as I have done since, to find fresh approaches through which to try to sway public opinion, including governmental opinion. All that I had succeeded in doing in 1958 touched only this or that relatively small circle of people. The CND at that time gave hope that a more general public could be reached. It seemed to me then as it does today that governmental policies must be regarded in the light of common sense. They must be shorn of red tape and 'tradition' and general mystique. They would be seen then to be leading, as they are, only to probable general destruction.

The policies that were needed were those dictated by common sense. If the public could be shown this clearly, I had a faint hope that they might insist upon governmental policies being brought into accord with common sense. I wrote my *Common Sense and Nuclear Warfare* in this hope. The book was fairly widely read, I believe, and commended. But it did not tackle the question as to exactly how each individual could make his opinion known and influence policy-making, a fact that left some readers dissatisfied. I had one moment of high hope when the Minister of Defence, Duncan Sandys, wrote commending the book and saying that he would like to talk with me about it. He was a Conservative, and a policy-maker in a national Government, and had collaborated in a pamphlet on the subject himself. But when I went to see him, he said, 'It is a good book, but what is needed is not only nuclear disarmament but the banning of war itself'. In vain I pointed out the passage in my book in which I had said that the only way to ensure the world against nuclear war was to end war. He continued to believe that I could not have said anything so intelligent. He cast my other arguments aside. I came away discouraged. I realized that most of the already informed people who read my book would read it with a bias so strong that they would take in only what they wished to take in. For the following months, therefore, I returned to the piecemeal business of speaking at meetings, CND and other, and broadcasting, and to the pleasures of my own life.

To celebrate my eighty-seventh birthday, we drove down through Bath and Wells and Glastonbury to Dorset. We visited the swannery and gardens at Abbotsbury where, by chance, we witnessed a peacock's nuptial dance, precisely articulated, one of the most enchanting and beautiful ballets that I have ever seen. We made a sentimental pilgrimage to the small Italianate eighteenth century Kingston Russell House which I had not seen before. I thought it most perfect and most perfectly set in its garden and valley. I wished immensely that I could myself live in it. I seldom feel this kind of envy, but Kingston Russell House touched me deeply. And I was interested in hunting out the old farm buildings and the village where my family had begun its more notable career. It was an altogether satisfactory expedition, but for some reason that I have now forgotten had to be cut short. So, to complete our allotted holiday, we went another extended drive after my birthday, this time in the Peak District. This, however, from the point of view of enjoyment was a complete failure. Places that should have been lonely and quiet were teeming with holiday-makers like ourselves; places that should have seemed full of life even though quiet, like Jane Austen's Bakewell, were tarnished by convention meetings. Perhaps it all seemed dreary because we struck the wrong note in the beginning by visiting Alderley where my Stanley grandparents had had an estate. The house had been destroyed. Only the gardens remained, in derelict state. The Government had taken it over for some unholy project. I have a small table, made for my mother and a larger one made for my father by the estate carpenter, from the Alderley Doomsday Oak when it had to be cut down. But the whole place made me melancholy. It was very desolate.

Early in 1960 we went to Copenhagen for a short time for me to receive the Sonning Prize for contribution to European Culture, bestowed by the University of Copenhagen. The speech of acceptance gave me a chance to outline my attitude towards present cultural differences, based upon the history of past changes in cultures. If this were reflected upon and adopted as being valid, as I think it is, it would change for the better present co-operation between nations and would increase the possibility of further and effective co-operation. My speech was published later under the title 'Old and New Cultures' in my book *Fact and Fiction*.

The occasion of the prize-giving was a pleasant one with a reception and a fine State dinner following it. My wife was seated between the Minister of Education, who declared himself to be unable to speak English, and Professor Niels Bohr, upon whom the burden of conversation therefore fell. He took his duties seriously and talked steadily through the banquet. He was very difficult to understand, we were told, even when speaking his native Danish to Danes; and, in English, I had always found it extremely hard to follow him as he spoke very quickly. My wife found it impossible. That was exasperating enough, since he was clearly talking of things that she would have wished to hear about. But, far worse on such an occasion, as he talked, he leaned further and further towards her, absorbed in his own words. Finally, he was eating the delicious confections from her plate and drinking her wine whilst the notable company of diners looked on, smiling and entranced. It was a tribute to his charm that she continued to like him, as I did.

I have seldom enjoyed my many speeches and articles during these years as they usually concerned nuclear matters. But now and again I have made a pleasurable excursion into other matters as I did at Copenhagen. I even ventured, a little later, into Shakespearean exigesis in a letter to *The Times*. For some weeks there had raged a discreet and venomous correspondence concerning the probable person to whom the printed sonnets were dedicated. The initials W. H. were interpreted this way and that by great stretches of imagination and with much learning. It seemed to me that, like Melchisedek, Mr W. H. was a clerical error for Mr W. S. who was, in truth, 'the onlie begetter' of the sonnets. I ventured, hesitantly and half in fun, to put this view forward. No one took it up and no further letters appeared on the subject. I fear that I spoiled the scholarly fun.

One evening I broadcast over the Asian service in company with a number of Asian students. As I walked down the corridor in the hotel where the occasion took place, a small, bird-like lady leapt from one of the huge red plush thrones placed at intervals along the wall, stood before me and declaimed, 'And I saw Shelley plain', and sat down. I tottered on, shattered, but delighted.

I did a series of TV interviews with Woodrow Wyatt as interlocutor that came out in book form as *Bertrand Russell Speaks his Mind*. It gave me a chance to say a good deal that I wanted to say about international affairs as well as much else to a wide audience in various parts of the world. In February, 1960, I had a debate with the Indian scientist Bahba and Teller, the Father of the Bomb, at which Ed. Murrow was the interlocutor on CBS. I found it a most distressing occasion. The debate was difficult, since we were each speaking from our own country and could not follow the facial expression or reaction of each other as we talked. Still more disconcerting, I was inhibited by my intense dislike of Teller and by what I felt to be disingenuous flattery. I came away from the BBC studio feeling that I had let down all those who agreed with my point of view by not putting up the better show that the facts of our case warranted. Another disappointing TV occasion was a BBC discussion of nuclear matters by Mrs Roosevelt, Lord Boothby, Mr Gaitskell, and myself. I was horrified to hear Mrs Roosevelt enunciate the belief that it would be better, and that she would prefer, to have the human race destroyed than to have it succumb to Communism. I came away thinking that I could not have heard aright. Upon reading her remarks in the next morning's papers I had to face the fact that she really had expressed this dangerous view.

I had a controversy with an American philosopher named Sidney Hook at this time that was one which both of us found difficult to conduct on logical lines. He was a Menshevic who had become apprehensive of Russia ruling the world. He thought this so dreadful that it would be better the human race should cease to exist. I combated this view on the ground that we do not know the future, which, so long as Man survives, may be immensely better than the past. I instanced the times of Genghiz Khan and Kublai Khan, separated by only a generation, but one horrible, the other admirable. But there were plenty of contrary instances that he could have adduced, in view of which a definite decision was impossible. I maintained, however, that any chance of a better world depended upon hope, and was on this account to be preferred. This was not a *logical* argument, but I thought that most people would find it convincing. Several years later, Hook again attacked me publicly, but this time in such a manner that no comment from me was necessary. It amused me, however, that for his defence of 'freedom' and his attack on my views on Vietnam, he chose as his vehicle a journal later admitted to be financed by the Central Intelligence Agency.[1]

The attitude of most of humanity towards its own destruction surprised me. In December, 1959, I had read Neville Shute's *On the Beach* and I attended a private viewing of its film. I was cast down by the deliberate turning away it displayed from the horrible, harsh facts entailed by nuclear war—the disease and suffering caused by poisoned air and water and soil, the looting and murder likely among a population in anarchy with no means of communication, and all the probable evils and pain. It was like the prettified stories that were sometimes told about trench warfare during the First World War. Yet the film was put out and praised by people who meant to make the situation clear, not to belittle the horror. I was particularly distressed by the fact that I myself had praised the film directly after seeing it in what I came to think the mistaken opinion that a little was better than nothing. All that sort of thing does, I came to think, is to make familiar and

---

[1] The *New Leader* received 3,000 dollars from Chiang Kai-shek's treasury for publishing an article hostile to China. Later it prepared the book *The Strategy of Deception: A Study in World Wide Communist Tactics* and was secretly paid 12,000 dollars by the US Government. When the US Information Agency asked a House Appropriations Sub-Committee to increase its allowance for 'book development' from 90,000 dollars to 195,000 dollars, the Agency assured the legislators that the funds would go for books 'written to our own specifications' and having 'strong anti-communist content' (*The New York Times*, May 3, 1964).

rob of its true value what should carry a shock of revulsion. Irony such as that in *Dr Strangelove* or *Oh, What a Lovely War* is a different matter. That does cause people to think, at least for a short time.

By the summer of 1960 it seemed to me as if Pugwash and CND and the other methods that we had tried of informing the public had reached the limit of their effectiveness. It might be possible to so move the general public that it would demand *en masse*, and therefore irresistibly, the remaking of present governmental policies, here in Britain first and then elsewhere in the world. For a time, however, I had to put my bothers behind me, especially as they were so shapeless and amorphous, as my daughter and her husband and their children came to visit me. I had not seen them for a long time, not since I was last in the United States. Since that time my son-in-law had become a full fledged Minister in the Episcopal Church—he had been a layman and in the State Department—and he was taking his whole family to Uganda where he had been called as a missionary. My daughter had also become very religious and was whole-heartedly in sympathy with his aspirations. I myself, naturally, had little sympathy with either of them on this score. When I had wished to send a sum of money to them shortly before they came to England, and had to go to the Bank of England to arrange the transfer, my request was greeted with smiles and sometimes laughter at so old and confirmed an atheist wishing to help someone to become a Minister of the Gospel. But about many things we agreed, especially in liberal politics, and I loved my daughter dearly and was fond of her family. They were to stay in England for two years to prepare for their mission work, and each July they came to North Wales where they were put up in one of the Portmeirion Hotel cottages and we saw them daily. This, with other smaller happenings, absorbed most of my time during these two months.

Towards the end of July, 1960, I received my first visit from a young American called Ralph Schoenman. I had heard of some of his activities in relation to CND so I was rather curious to see him. I found him bursting with energy and teeming with ideas, and intelligent, if inexperienced and a little doctrinaire, about politics. Also, I liked in him, what I found lamentably lacking in many workers in the causes which I espoused, a sense of irony and the capability of seeing the humour in what was essentially very serious business. I saw that he was quickly sympathetic, and that he was impetuous. What I came only gradually to appreciate, what could only emerge with the passage of time, was his difficulty in putting up with opposition, and his astonishingly complete, untouchable self-confidence. I believed that intelligence working on experience would enforce the needed discipline.

I did not at first fully understand him but I happened to be approved of by him and, in turn, to approve of what he was then working for. And for his continued generosity towards me personally I was, and can still only be, deeply grateful. His mind moved very quickly and firmly and his energy appeared to be inexhaustible. It was a temptation to turn to him to get things done. At the particular time of our first meetings he acted as a catalyst for my gropings as to what could be done to give our work in the CND new life. He was very keen to start a movement of civil disobedience that might grow into a mass movement of general opposition to governmental nuclear policies so strong as to force its opinions upon the Government directly. It was to be a *mass* movement, no matter from how small beginnings. In this it was new, differing from the old Direct Action Committee's aspirations in that theirs were too often concerned with individual testimony by way of salving individual consciences.

The scheme seemed to me to have great possibilities and the more I talked with Schoenman the more favourable to it I became. I was aware that the chairman of the CND did not approve of civil disobedience and had little sympathy with even the Direct Action Committee. I also knew that the CND tolerated and was coming more and more to support in words if not in action its activities. I discussed the matter with the chairman. He did not dispute the possible efficiency of civil disobedience or oppose my upholding such a new movement. He only urged me not to make any announcement about this fresh effort till after the Conference of the Labour Party when he hoped that the Party might 'go unilateral' and take up at least some of our doctrines. To this I readily agreed.

Knowing that the chairman would neither oppose nor aid the new movement, it did not occur to me to consult him about our day to day preparations. I went to work with Schoenman to prepare a list of people who might be approached to uphold such a movement. Letters went out to them over my name. I was very insistent that letters should go to no one who was not known to us as being sympathetic, but, unfortunately, mistakes were made. One letter was sent to someone with a name similar to the intended recipient but with a different address and entirely, unhappily, different views. He at once sent our letter to the *Evening Standard* with a scathing letter of his own about our activities and intentions. This was published considerably before our plans were thoroughly formed or the participants gathered, and worse still, before the chairman thought the project should be revealed. There was a big meeting in Trafalgar Square on September 24th at which I spoke. Before it took place, I suggested to the chairman that I speak of the proposed new mass movement of civil disobedience within the CND. He replied that it might injure CND's chances of influencing the Labour Conference. I said that I would consult Frank Cousins, the head of the Transport Workers' Union, and if he felt it in any way dangerous to the desires of CND, I would not touch upon the subject. Frank Cousins replied to my letter briefly, saying that it did not matter one way or the other what I did or said. I informed the chairman of Cousins's letter and of my consequent intention to speak of the new movement. He accepted this, and I spoke of the new movement in Trafalgar Square.

After the announcement in the *Evening Standard* of the proposed mass movement of civil disobedience, it was necessary to hurry through our plans. But the event caused a great uproar. The chairman of CND made statements to his friends and to the Executive Committee and to the press which, in effect, charged me with starting a new movement behind his back and one not permissible within the rulings of CND. During the first week of October, I met with him daily for many hours at my house in Hasker Street to try to work out some *modus vivendi*. He brought with him to these meetings a friend who was not an upholder of methods of civil disobedience, to put it mildly, so I asked a member of the CND Executive Committee who professed then to be in sympathy with me, to come as balance. At my insistence, because there had been so many allegations as to what I had said and not said, a tape recording was taken of these meetings, a copy of which was sent to the CND offices for the chairman and the original of which I kept.

By October 7th we had come to an agreement which would permit us to continue to work together and gave a statement to that effect to the press. But within a short time it became evident to me that I could not continue in my position of president of the CND, which necessitated work with its chairman, and that, if only to preserve the harmonious working of the CND itself, I must resign. This I did in a letter to the press, following a letter to the chairman.

The result of all this was, for me, a shower—a storm—of letters and visits from upholders of the CND throughout the country, expostulating with me and, most of them, accusing me of causing a split in the CND. This surprised me, as I had no intention of doing so. Nor do I think that I did. Moreover, I observed no weakening in its work owing to my action. It seemed to me that the CND would get on better if it had officers who saw, at least broadly, eye to eye than it would do under the leadership of those who patently did not trust each other. I had no intention, as I said and continued repeatedly to say, of withdrawing my support of much CND work. I sent statements to the various branches of the CND explaining this and the reasons for my actions. So far as I know, these statements went unread. At the CND Executive Meeting on November 5th, my resignation was accepted. One member, I was told, wished me to be sued for libel because of something I had said or written. He was persuaded not to proceed—which was, perhaps for my personal reputation, a pity. I continued to speak at meetings of the CND at which I was asked to speak, and I remained at the head of the Welsh CND. I withdrew only my interest in CND policy-making and any responsibility that, as its president, I had for the actions of its officers.

Meantime, the new movement towards mass civil disobedience had come to be called the Committee of 100. I had been in frequent touch with the small company of young people who were its early upholders. Inspired largely by the enthusiasm of Ralph Schoenman, this company had grown into a fairly large and steadily expanding group. Early in September he had brought the Rev. Michael Scott to see me. Scott was an active member of the Direct Action Committee and became one of the most stalwart member of the Committee of 100. I saw him as well as Schoenman almost daily, and he and I published under our joint names a leaflet entitled 'Act or Perish' which presents the nucleus of the policy of the Committee.

The early members of the Committee of 100 were for the most part drawn from the CND and the ranks of the Direct Action Committee. There was much activity and there were daily meetings, most of which I could not, and was not expected to, attend. I spoke for the Committee, I think, only at a meeting in Friends House, Euston, in October, 1960, and, again, at a press conference held in Kingsway Hall in December. Gradually, adherents were drawn from outside the fold, a process greatly accelerated both by the opposition widely felt to the establishment of the US Polaris Base at Holy Loch, and especially, by the announcement of the first proposed demonstration of civil disobedience. This was to be a 'sit-down'—of at least two thousand people, it was hoped—outside the Ministry of Defence on February 18th, 1961. It was planned that each succeeding demonstration would demand the participation of more people, the number increasing at each fresh demonstration until a really mass movement was achieved. To ensure a good beginning it was decided to pledge as many as possible to take part in the first sit-down.

The activity of the Committee was intense during the days preceding February 18th. Posters went up (and were torn down), people were stopped in the street and approached in pubs and cafés and were argued with till they were converted to the need of the coming demonstration. But of all this I only heard. I took part only in endless discussions.

I hope that no one who reads these pages will think that I am attempt-

"ALL RIGHT! FOR THE LAST TIME. WHO'S THE BRAINS BEHIND THIS?"

7. Cartoon from *Evening Standard*, September 1961

8. Bertrand Russell with Professor Rotblatt, 1962

[*Sincroflash Ltd*]

90th Birthday Medallion by Christopher Ironside

ing to write a history of the Committee of 100 or of the CND or, indeed, of any other movement or public event. I am trying only to recount what I remember that affected my own life.

My enthusiasm was high for the work and preparations that were being made for February 18th, and I was in complete agreement with the plans and with the aspirations of the Committee. I have already written in this volume of my views of civil disobedience, and I stated them publicly in speeches and articles at this time, notably in an article in the *New Statesman* for February 17th. My sole misgivings were connected with the hurried and piece-meal way in which our policies had been worked out owing to their premature publication and with the dread lest it might be too difficult—impossible, perhaps—to avoid violence in such a crowd, considering the opposition that might be encountered. Passive resistance, it seemed to me, might be very difficult to inculcate amid such enthusiasm. In the event, it posed no difficulty.

The morning of February 18th was dark and drizzly and cold, and our spirits plummeted. If it rained, the numbers participating in the demonstration would undoubtedly dwindle in spite of the large nucleus already pledged to take part. But when we assembled in Trafalgar Square there was a great crowd. Precisely how great it was, it is impossible to say. The median number as reckoned by the press and the police and the Committee made it about 20,000. The speeches went well and quickly. Then began the march up Whitehall preceded by a large banner and managed with great skill by the Committee's marshals. It comprised a surging but calm and serious crowd of somewhat over 5,000 of those who had been in the Square. At one point we were held up by the police who tried to stop the march on the ground that it was obstructing traffic. The objection, however, manifestly did not hold, and the march proceeded. Finally, over 5,000 people were sitting or lying on the pavements surrounding the Ministry. And there we sat for about two hours till darkness had fallen, a very solid and quiet, if not entirely mute, protest against governmental nuclear policies. A good many people joined us during this time, and more came to have a look at us, and, of course, the press and TV people flocked about asking their questions. As soon as word came that the marchers had all become seated, Michael Scott and Schoenman and I took a notice that we had prepared and stuck it on the Ministry door. We learned that the Government had asked the Fire Department to use their hoses upon us. Luckily, the Fire Department refused. When six o'clock arrived, we called an end to the sit-down. A wave of exultation swept through the crowd. As we marched back towards Whitehall in the dusk and lamplight, past the cheering supporters, I felt very happy—we had accomplished what we set out to do that afternoon, and our serious purpose had been made manifest. I was moved, too, by the cheers that greeted me and by the burst of 'for he's a jolly good fellow' as I passed.

The demonstration was much more auspicious than we had any right to expect. During the next months the fortunes of the Committee prospered. Branch Committees were established about the country and in some foreign countries; and some countries developed their own Committees. All the correspondence entailed by this activity and by the necessary printing and dissemination of 'literature' (leaflets, statements, etc.) not to speak of the need to keep some kind of office, cost a good deal. This, of course, as it always does in any organization without fixed membership or dues, meant much time wasted in raising funds. Nevertheless, and owing to the generous and often self-sacrificing voluntary efforts of many people, the Committee grew in strength.

To show my continued support of the CND, I spoke to the Youth CND of Birmingham in mid-March and again in mid-April. One of these speeches caused turmoil because of a remark that I made about our then Prime Minister. The remark was widely quoted out of context by the press. In context, it is merely a Q.E.D. to the preceding argument. Unfortunately, by the time the uproar had broken, I had fallen ill and was unable to defend myself for some weeks, too late to cut any ice. I spoke, also at the meeting in Trafalgar Square at the end of the Aldermaston March.

Towards the end of March, I had arranged with Penguin Books, who, in turn, had arranged with my usual publisher, Sir Stanley Unwin, to write a further book for them on nuclear matters and disarmament, carrying on my *Common Sense and Nuclear Warfare* and expanding parts of it. The new book was to be called *Has Man a Future?* and I began work on it at once. But it was interrupted by a series of recordings that I made in London and by the two Birmingham meetings and then by a very bad bout of shingles which prevented my doing any work whatsoever for some time. But during my convalescence I wrote a good deal of the new book, and it was finished in time to meet its first deadline. It was published in the autumn.

On August 6th, 'Hiroshima Day', the Committee of 100 arranged to have two meetings: a ceremony in the morning of laying a wreath upon the Cenotaph in Whitehall and, in the afternoon, a meeting for speeches to be made at Marble Arch. The former was carried out with dignity. We wished to remind people of the circumstances of the nuclear bomb at Hiroshima. We also thought that, in commemorating the British dead, we might call attention to the fact that it was up to the living to prevent their deaths from going for nothing. We hoped in the afternoon's speeches to support this point of view. To many people, however, to bracket the deaths at Hiroshima and Nagasaki with the deaths of those who fought the Japanese in the Second War was blasphemous. It is doubtful if many of these same people object to the statue of General Washington or of General Smuts being given places of public honour.

The meeting in Hyde Park was a lively one. The police had forbidden us to use microphones as their use was prohibited by Park rules. This ruling had been overlooked in many previous cases, but was firmly held to in our case. We had determined to try to use microphones, partly because we knew that they would be necessary to make ourselves heard, and partly to expose the odd discrepancy in the enforcement of Park rules. We were, after all, an organization devoted to civil disobedience. I, therefore, started to speak through a microphone. A policeman quietly remonstrated. I persisted. And the microphone was removed by the police. We then adjourned the meeting, announcing that we would march to Trafalgar Square to continue it. All this we had planned, and the plan was carried out with some success. What we had not counted on was a thunderstorm of majestic proportions which broke as the crowd moved down Oxford Street and continued throughout most of the meeting in the Square.

A month later, as we returned from an afternoon's drive in North Wales, we found a pleasant, though much embarrassed, Police Sergeant astride his motorcycle at our front door. He delivered summonses to my wife and me to be at Bow Street on September 12th to be charged with inciting the public to civil disobedience. The summons was said to be delivered to all the leaders of the Committee but, in fact, it was delivered only to some of them. Very few who were summoned refused to appear.

We went up to London to take the advice of our solicitors and, even more important, to confer with our colleagues. I had no wish to become a martyr to the cause, but I felt that I should make the most of any chance to publicize our views. We were not so innocent as to fail to see that our imprisonment would cause a certain stir. We hoped that it might create enough sympathy for some, at least, of our reasons for doing as we had done to break through to minds hitherto untouched by them. We had obtained from our doctors statements of our recent serious illnesses which they thought would make long imprisonment disastrous. These we handed over to the barrister who was to watch our cases at Bow Street. No one we met seemed to believe that we should be condemned to gaol. They thought the Government would think that it would not pay them. But we, ourselves, did not see how they could fail to sentence us to gaol. For some time it had been evident that our doings irked the Government, and the police had been raiding the Committee office and doing a clumsy bit of spying upon various members who frequented it. The barrister thought that he could prevent my wife's and my incarceration entirely. But we did not wish either extreme. We instructed him to try to prevent our being let off scot-free, but, equally, to try to have us sentenced to not longer than a fortnight in prison. In the event, we were each sentenced to two months in gaol, a sentence which, because of the doctors' statements, was commuted to a week each.

Bow Street seemed like a stage set as we walked down it with our colleagues amid a mass of onlookers towards the Court at a little before 10.30 in the morning. People were crowded into most of the windows, some of which were bright with boxes of flowers. By contrast the scene in the courtroom looked like a Daumier etching. When the sentence of two months was pronounced upon me cries of 'Shame, shame, an old man of eighty-eight!' arose from the onlookers. It angered me. I knew that it was well meant, but I had deliberately incurred the punishment and, in any case, I could not see that age had anything to do with guilt. If anything, it made me the more guilty. The magistrate seemed to me nearer the mark in observing that, from his point of view, I was old enough to know better. But on the whole both the Court and the police behaved more gently to us all than I could have hoped. A policeman, before proceedings began, searched the building for a cushion for me to sit upon to mitigate the rigours of the narrow wooden bench upon which we perched. None could be found—for which I was thankful—but I took his effort kindly. I felt some of the sentences to be quite unduly harsh, but I was outraged only by the words of the magistrate to one of us who happened to be a Jewish refugee from Germany. The police witness appeared to me to cut a poor figure in giving evidence. Our people, I thought spoke well and with dignity and very tellingly. Neither of these observations surprised me. And I was pleased to be permitted to say most of what I had planned to say.

By the end of the morning all our cases had been heard and we were given an hour for lunch. My wife and I returned to Chelsea. We emerged from the Court into cheering crowds, and to my confusion one lady rushed up and embraced me. But from the morning's remarks of the Magistrate and his general aspect, we were not hopeful of getting off lightly when we returned to receive our sentences in the afternoon. As each person in alphabetical order was sentenced, he or she was taken out to the cells where we behaved like boys on holiday, singing and telling stories, the tension of incertitude relaxed, nothing more to try to do till we were carted away in our Black Marias.

It was my first trip in a Black Maria as the last time I had been gaoled I had been taken to Brixton in a taxi, but I was too tired to enjoy the novelty. I was popped into the hospital wing of the prison and spent most of my week in bed, visited daily by the doctor who saw that I got the kind of liquid food that I could consume. No one can pretend to a liking for being imprisoned, unless, possibly, for protective custody. It is a frightening experience. The dread of particular, severe or ill treatment and of physical discomfort is perhaps the least of it. The worst is the general atmosphere, the sense of being always under observation, the dead cold and gloom and the always noted, unmistakable, prison smell—and the eyes of some of the other prisoners. We had all this for only a week. We were very conscious of the continuing fact that many of our friends were undergoing it for many weeks and that we were spared only through special circumstances, not through less 'guilt', in so far as there was any guilt.

Meantime the Committee of 100 had put out a leaflet with my message from Brixton. On the back of the leaflet was its urgent appeal to all sympathizers to congregate in Trafalgar Square at 5 o'clock on Sunday, September 17th, for a march to Parliament Square where a public assembly was to be held and a sit-down. The Home Secretary had issued a Public Order against our use of Trafalgar Square on that occasion, but the Committee had determined that this would be no deterrent. Unfortunately for us, my wife and I were still in gaol and were not released till the following day. I say unfortunately because it must have been a memorable and exhilarating occasion.

We delighted in our reunion in freedom at home very early on Monday morning. But almost at once we were besieged by the press and radio and TV people who swarmed into Hasker Street. Our continued involvement with them prevented us from learning for some time all that had been happening since the Bow Street session of the previous week. From what we had learned from the papers that we had seen in prison, we knew that all sorts of meetings and sit-downs had been held, not only in Britain, but also in many other countries, protesting against our imprisonment. Moreover, my wife had gathered from some of the prisoners at Holloway that the demonstration of the 17th was a success. They had listened to the radio and stood on the balcony above their nets in the great hall of the prison making the sign of thumbs-up to her and shouting excitedly that the sit-down was going splendidly. We learned only gradually quite how unbelievably great a success it had been.

The full story of that demonstration I must leave to some historian or participant to tell. The important part is that unprecedented numbers took part. It augured well for an approach to the mass movement that we desired. By early evening the Square and the streets leading to it were packed with people sitting down and with people coming only to observe what was going on who tried to force themselves into possible observation points. There was no question of marching to Parliament Square. No one could get through, though attempts were made. There was no violence, no hullabaloo on the part of the sitters-down. They were serious. And some of them were making what was individually an heroic gesture. For instance, Augustus John, an old man, who had been, and was, very ill (it was a short time before his death) emerged from the National Gallery, walked into the Square and sat down. No one knew of his plan to do so and few recognized him. I learned of his action only much later, but I record it with admiration. There were other cases of what amounted to heroism in testifying to a profound belief. There were also a good many ludicrous happenings, particularly, I was told, later in the evening when various notabilities arrived to see how things were going and were mistaken by the police for ardent upholders of the Committee and were piled, protesting, into Black Marias. But the police could hardly be blamed for such mistakes. In the vast crowd individual identities could not be distinguished, even in a dogcollar. The police could, however, be very much blamed for their not infrequent brutality. This could not be disputed, since there were many pictures taken which sometimes caught instances of regrettable police action.

Television and press accounts and pictures of this demonstration and of the preceding gaolings appeared in countries throughout the world. They had an excellent effect in setting people everywhere thinking about what we were doing and attempting to do and why. That was what we had hoped would happen, but we had not prepared sufficiently for the overwhelming publicity and interest that would be generated. From the beginning we had been careful to arrange that only certain of our members would expose themselves to possible imprisonment at any particular demonstration. There was always to be a corps of leaders to carry on the work. But the Government, by sentencing a large number, not for any particular misdeed at any particular time, but for the general charge of incitement, had managed to disrupt this rota. Added to this, were the arrests made during the general scrum of the September 17th sit-down when track could hardly be kept of who might be arrested and who not. The result was that there were very few experienced members of the Committee left to deal with pressing matters and future plans. I was tired and kept busy by matters that only I could deal with arising chiefly from my imprisonment. All this was a grievous pity for we had been given a great chance which we were unable to avail ourselves of fully.

At the end of the week after gaol we returned to North Wales but the barrage of press and TV interviews continued wherever we were and, of course, there were daily visitors from all over—Italians, Japanese, French, Belgian, Singalese, Dutch, South and North Americans, etc., etc. It was all wearing, and when we could we drove off into the country by ourselves. We had a number of adventures. One afternoon we walked along a sandy beach and around a rocky point to a cove. The rocks of the point were covered by dried seaweed. At first we tested the solidity of the way, but we grew careless, and unexpectedly I, who was ahead, sank to my thighs. At each move, I sank further. My wife was only at the edge of the bad patch. She managed to crawl to a rock and finally to haul me out. On other occasions, our car got stuck in the sand or in the bog and had to be pulled out—once, to our amused annoyance, by a nuclear station's van.

When we returned to London, too, we had adventures. One morning two young men and a young woman appeared upon my doorstep and demanded to see me as, they said, they wished to discuss anti-nuclear work. I discussed matters with them for some time and then intimated that it was time for them to go. They refused to go. Nothing that I or my housekeeper—we were the only people in the house—could say would budge them, and we were far from being strong enough to move them. They proceeded to stage a sit-down in my drawing-room. With some misgivings, I sent for the police. Their behaviour was impeccable. They did not even smile, much less jeer. And they evicted the sitters-down. The latter were later discovered, I was told, to be a young actress who wanted publicity and two of her admirers wishing to help her. They got the publicity and provided me with a good story and much entertainment. Some of the Committee were rather annoyed by my having called in the police.

During the next months there were a number of Committee of 100 meetings, both public and private, at which I spoke, notably in Trafalgar Square on October 29th and in Cardiff on November 1st. Demonstrations had been announced for December 9th to be held at various us air and nuclear bases in the country. But in planning this the Committee, in its inexperience of holding large demonstrations not in London but in the country, were too optimistic, especially in matters relating to transportation. For instance, they felt sure that the buses that they hired to take demonstrators from London to one of the targets, Wethersfield, would turn up since the bus drivers themselves had professed themselves sympathetic to the Committee's views. But, as some of us had feared, the bus company refused its buses to the Committee at the last minute. Some hardy and determined demonstrators made their way to Wethersfield by other means, but the loss of the buses and the lack of any alternative arrangements meant that the numbers were very much less than had been expected. The further difficulties encountered were great: The machinations of the police who had raided the Committee rooms and harried its members, and the opposition of the Government, which employed a large number of its ground and air force, its guard dogs and fire hoses to protect the Committee's targets from unarmed people pledged to non-violence. Nevertheless, the demonstration made a good showing. The Committee had made a mistake, however, in announcing beforehand that it would make a better showing than it could possibly hope to do and in not planning thoroughly for alternatives in foreseeable difficulties.

The Committee had already begun to weaken itself in other ways. Long discussions were beginning to be held amongst its members as to whether the Committee should devote itself only to nuclear and disarmament matters or should begin to oppose all domestic, social and governmental injustice. This was a waste of time and a dispersal of energies. Such widespread opposition, if to be indulged in at all, was obviously a matter for the far future when the Committee's power and capabilities were consolidated. By such projects consolidation could only be delayed. Again, this unfortunate tendency was the outcome, largely, of the practical political and administrative inexperience of the Committee added to the over-estimation of the meaning of September 17th's success. The latter should have been regarded as very great encouragement but not as, by any means, the certain promise of a *mass* civil disobedience movement. In proportion to the population of the country, the movement was still small and too unproved to stand against determined opposition. Unfortunately, the comparative failure of December 9th was considered only as a discouragement, not as a lesson towards a period of consolidation. I tried in my public statements at the time to overcome the discouragement and, privately, to inculcate the lesson. But in both attempts I failed.

The immediate aftermath of the demonstration of December 9th was the charging of five leaders of the Committee under the Official Secrets Act of 1911. It was, from a layman's point of view, a curiously conducted trial. The prosecution was allowed to present its case in full, resting on the question as to whether it was prejudicial to the safety of the nation for unauthorized people to enter the Wethersfield air field with the intention of immobilizing and grounding the aircraft there. The defence's case was that such stations as Wethersfield, like all the stations engaged in nuclear 'defence' of the country, were in themselves prejudicial to the safety of the country. Professor Linus Pauling, the physicist, and Sir Robert Watson-Watt, the inventor of radar, who had come from the United States to give evidence as to the dangers of the present nuclear policy of which Wethersfield was a part, and I were kept hanging about for many hours. Then all our testimony, like that of other defence witnesses, of whom some, I believe, were not permitted to be called at all, was declared irrelevant to the charges and

ruled out. It was managed quite legally, but all loopholes were ruthlessly blocked against the defence and made feasible for the prosecution.
There were a few bright moments, to be sure: when Air Commander
MacGill, the prosecution's chief witness was asked how far it was from
London to Wethersfield, he replied, 'in a fast plane, about fifty miles'.
The jury returned the verdict guilty, though, and this is rather interesting, they were out for four and a half hours. No one had believed
any other verdict possible under the circumstances. The five convicted
men were given gaol sentences of eighteen months apiece; the one
woman, the welfare secretary of the Committee, was given a year.

I felt keenly that I, since I had encouraged the demonstration but had
not been able to take part, was as guilty as the condemned and I managed
when I was finally able to speak at the trial to say so. Many others
felt likewise, and, after the trial, we repaired to the Cannon Street police
station to declare ourselves guilty. As was to be expected, no notice was
taken of our declarations though they were received civilly by the police.
The Committee held a meeting in Trafalgar Square to state the
significance of the trial and its own attitude towards it. In snow and
gale, Sir Robert Watson-Watt and I and a number of others spoke to a
not inconsiderable audience.

For some time thereafter I had little to do in the way of public speaking
for the Committee. During that last week of July the Committee as well
as the C N D sent participants to the 'World Disarmament Conference'
held in Moscow. Just as it was about to start, I received a request from
Professor Bernal pressing me to send a representative with a message
to the conference. Christopher Farley, who had participated both in the
planning and in the action of the Committee, went on my behalf. While
he was there, he, in company with some other non-communists, held
a public meeting in Red Square and handed out leaflets. This was illegal,
and was vehemently opposed, by a variety of means, by the chairman
of the C N D who was there. It was also opposed by others, even some who
at home, indulged in civil disobedience. They felt that they were guests
of the Russians and should abide by the strict laws of hospitality. The
meeting was dispersed, but its holders were triumphant in the belief
that they had pointed out the international character of the civil disobedience movement and had been able to hold something of a debate
before being dispersed. At the time, I received only hot objections,
but no reasons were given for the objections. When Farley returned
and I heard what he had to say, I felt that he had done the right thing
in backing the meeting, and that it had helped to establish the fact
that we were neutral and should invoke civil disobedience wherever
we could in a cause which was international.

Towards the end of August the Committee began to put into effect its plan for a demonstration on September 9th. Taking warning from the previous December 9th, they decided to return to central London and to pledge people to take part. They announced that they would not hold the demonstration if they could not get 7,000 pledges. As September 9th drew near, it became evident that they could not procure this number of pledges in time. I felt very strongly that, in view of their public announcement, they should abandon the demonstration, especially as to hold to their promise those who had pledged would be to ask them to attend the demonstration unprotected by the promised number of co-participants. The secretary of the London Committee was very loath to give up and many members thought that it was unnecessary to do so. This flouting of a given promise disgusted me, and added itself to my growing belief that the Committee was disintegrating. In the end, the demonstration was called off.

During the time since the Secrets trial many things had been happening to me unconnected with the Committee—lunches such as the one given me by the foreign journalists in London, TV broadcasts such as the long one for United States consumption at which the interlocutor was named Susskind, visits from travelling dignitaries such as that of the five leading Russian journalists who spent an afternoon with me in Wales. We also went on a holiday drive for somewhat over a fortnight at the end of March, a holiday which was a total failure since the weather was cold, raw, and dreary and we were both ill throughout with raging colds. The most important events in relation to my own life were those centring about my ninetieth birthday on May 18th.

I looked forward to my birthday celebrations, I confess, with considerable trepidation, for I had been informed of their prospect though told nothing of the toil and anxiety that was going into their consummation. Only afterwards did I hear of the peculiar obstructions caused by impresarios and the managers of concert halls, or of the extreme kindness and generosity of conductors and orchestras and soloists. I only gradually learned of the immense amount of time and energy, thought and sheer determination to give me pleasure expended by my friends for many weeks. The most active of these was Ralph Schoenman who was chiefly responsible for all aspects of the concert, including the excellently arranged and, to me, most pleasing programme. When I did learn all this, I was deeply touched, as I was by the parties themselves. And to my surprise, I found that I enjoyed greatly being the centre of such unexpectedly friendly plaudits and encomiums.

On my birthday itself, we had a jolly family teaparty with two of my grandchildren and my London housekeeper Jean Redmond and, to celebrate, a fine cake topped appropriately by a small constable (donated by the baker) bearing one candle for good luck. In the evening, a dinner arranged by A. J. Ayer and Rupert Crawshay-Williams took place at the Café Royal. It seemed to me a happy occasion. Some of my friends made speeches: Ayer and Julian Huxley spoke most kindly of me and E. M. Forster recalled the early Cambridge days and spoke delightfully about my old friend Bob Trevelyan. And I met for the first time the Head of my family, the Duke of Bedford and his wife. I admired his determination to keep Woburn a private estate at however great cost to himself and against great odds. I also liked his unconventionality. I had been told that when asked to speak at the concert in my honour, he had accepted without hesitation. So I was prepared to like him—and I was not disappointed. The evening was not less enjoyable for me in re-establishing connection with a number of old friends such as Arthur Waley and Miles Malleson as well as in making a few new ones.

Of the celebration party at Festival Hall, under the kind aegis of its manager, T. E. Bean, that took place the next afternoon, I do not know what to say or how to say it. I had been told that there would be music and presentations to me, but I could not know beforehand how lovely the music would be, either the orchestral part under Colin Davis or the solo work by Lili Kraus. Nor could I know how touching and generous would be the presentation speeches: by Ralph Schoenman, the Master of Ceremonies; Victor Purcell; Mrs Sonning of Denmark; Ernst Willi, the Swiss sculptor; Morley Nkosi of Africa; Vanessa Redgrave, the actress; and my cousin Ian Bedford. Some of those who could not be there had sent gifts which were presented to me—a bust of Socrates from my cousin Flora Russell and an excellent portrait of me from its painter Hans Erni. And many people had sent messages which Schoenman read out or had printed in the 'Tribute Programme'. It had a photograph of me taken by T. E. Morris of Portmadoc on its cover. I have been told that it has been sent to people all over the world. The Musicians Union refused to have the music recorded and the BBC refused to record any of the proceedings. The gifts, the programme, the record that was privately made of the proceedings, and, especially, the warm friendliness that I felt in the audience as well as in the actors, I still, and always shall, treasure. At the time I was so deeply moved that I felt I could not utter a word, much less find words that might express my feeling of gratitude and of what the occasion meant to me. But, mercifully, words came. I do not think that I can say again so freshly or with such entire, unconsidered sincerity what I felt then, so I give my speech itself, taking it from the recording:
'Friends,

'This is an occasion that I hardly know how to find words for. I am more touched than I can say, and more deeply than I can ever hope to express. I have to give my very warmest possible thanks to those who have worked to produce this occasion: to the performers, whose exquisite music, exquisitely performed, was so full of delight; to those who worked in less conspicuous ways, like my friend Mr Schoenman; and to all those who have given me gifts—gifts which are valuable in themselves, and also as expressions of an undying hope for this dangerous world.

'I have a very simple creed: that life and joy and beauty are better than dusty death, and I think when we listen to such music as we heard today we must all of us feel that the capacity to produce such music, and the capacity to hear such music, is a thing worth preserving and should not be thrown away in foolish squabbles. You may say it's a simple creed, but I think everything important is very simple indeed. I've found that creed sufficient, and I should think that a great many of you would also find it sufficient, or else you would hardly be here.

'But now I just want to say how it's difficult, when one has embarked upon a course which invites a greater or less degree of persecution and obloquy and abuse, to find instead that one is welcomed as I have been today. It makes one feel rather humble, and I feel I must try to live up to the feelings that have produced this occasion. I hope I shall; and I thank you from the bottom of my heart.'

The last formal celebration of my birthday took place the following week when Fenner Brockway most kindly invited me to a luncheon in my honour at the House of Commons. I was somewhat nervous of this as it seemed unlikely to me that any Members of either House would turn up to do me honour. My tension mounted as we waited in an anteroom to be led to the Harcourt Room where the banquet was to take place and, again, stood at the door rather wistfully watching the Members fortify themselves with preprandial drinks. But, when the party began, it was pleasant and friendly, and I thought it generous of many of those present to be there. I had not for some time been pulling my punches in regard to the activities of politicians, nor, I fear, did I on this occasion, seeing a chance and, indeed, an obligation, to speak to them direct.

When all this pleasant fuss to do with my becoming a nonagenarian had passed, we retired to Wales, returning to London only for a few days in July for the purpose of talking with U Thant about international nuclear and disarmament policies. This was the first time that I had met him and I was greatly impressed not only by his energy and clear grasp of affairs, but by his balanced objectivity and thoughtfulness and his delightful good humour. At this time, too, I paid my first visit to Woburn Abbey. I found the grandeurs of the house very pleasing and the lovely serenity of the Park, with its great trees sheltering Father David's deer and its wide quiet stretches of green turf, very calming.

The last months of that year were taken up with the Cuban crisis and then with the Sino-Indian Border dispute. Early in December, Penguin accepted my offer to write my account of these two happenings which I did in January. It was published by Penguin and Allen & Unwin in April under the title *Unarmed Victory*. I have told in it all there is to tell of any interest about my thought and action at that time, and I do not propose to repeat it all here. Perhaps I should add, however, that I regret nothing that I did at that time in relation to these two crises. My point of view upon them, in spite of further study, remains the same. I will give my critics only this olive branch: I am sorry that I did not couch my telegram of October 23rd to President Kennedy more gently. Its directness made it unlikely to cut much ice, I agree. But I had as little hope then as I should have in similar circumstances now of wise and quick withdrawal on the part of the u s Government.

I had become so tried by the folly of some of the leading members of the Committee of 100 during the events of September and by the growing dissipation of the Committee's policies that, early in January, I resigned from the Main Committee in London. I did not wish, however, to go into these reasons in my public resignation. I based it upon the equally valid and conclusive reason that my increasing absences in Wales prevented me from participating usefully in the work of the Main Committee. I still have great sympathy with the early aims and actions of the Committee, and I should support any recrudescence of them if they seemed to me to stand any chance of success. Mass civil disobedience still seems to me one of the most effective ways of attacking present international policies which remain as bad as they were then, if not worse.

The British Government, meanwhile, had its own plans for what to do in the event of nuclear war. What these plans were we learned, in part, from an organization which called itself 'Spies for Peace'. This organization had succeeded in ascertaining the secret plans of Authority to be put into force on the outbreak of war. Britain was to be divided into a number of regions, each with its own government, each with autocratic power, each composed of a pre-arranged corps of officials who were to live in supposed safety in underground 'Regional Seats of Government' and decide (so far as the enemy allowed) what was to become of the rest of us, and, in particular, what was to be done about fall-out if and while we remained alive. It was feared that possibly the prospect of such measures might not please the populace, and must therefore be kept secret. 'Spies for Peace' had discovered some of the documents involved, and were anxious to publish them. They had no funds, and appealed to me. I gave them £50 with my blessing. As soon as possible the documents were published, and copies were distributed among the Aldermaston marchers.

Unfortunately (as I felt) the leaders of CND were shocked that secret methods should be employed by pacifists. They did what they could to impede the spread of knowledge which the 'Spies' had sought to secure. A fresh batch of documents which they had secured was taken to the editor of a leading pacifist journal under the impression that he would publicize their information. But he, horrified by the disclosures and the retribution their publication would undoubtedly call down, sent the documents to the mother of one of the 'Spies' and she, fearing a police raid, burnt them. So died our hope of learning Government plans for governmental salvation and the succour of such members of the public as might be allowed to live. This bitter blow to the clarification of our position and to a great impetus to work for peace was dealt by well-meaning and not unknowledgeable pacifists.

LETTERS

To and from Ernest Jones

Plas Penrhyn
2 February, 1957

Dear Dr Jones

I enclose a copy of a letter from an eminent Anglican divine. It seems to me a document worthy to go into your case-book. I should be very grateful if you felt inclined to send me any comments on it.

Yours sincerely
Russell

The following is the letter I sent to Dr Jones (without the Bishop's address or signature):

From the Bishop of Rochester

Personal
Bishopscourt
Rochester
Jan: 29. 1957

Dear Lord Russell

It has been laid upon my conscience to write to you, after your article in the *Sunday Times* on the 'Great Mystery' of survival after death; seeing that you at 84 stand yourself upon that threshold.

Your contemporaries, like myself, acclaim you the greatest brain of our generation. And many must believe, with me, that if only your moral stature had matched your intellectual power and other singular endowments, you could have saved us from a second World War. Instead, in your book on Companionate Marriage, *Marriage and Morals* (1929), the cloven hoof of the lecher cannot be disguised; and it is lechery that has been your Achilles heel, blinding your great mind from discerning that infinitely **greater Mind** behind all phenomena, such as has formed your enthralling study. Only the pure in heart can see God; and four wives, with three divorces, must be an awful and bitter humiliation, showing the man himself, entrusted with such a magnificent brain.

Moreover, I cannot but believe that you must at times be haunted by the remembrance of the murder, suicide, and untold misery, between the wars, caused by the experiments of young people with Companionate Marriage, of which you were the Apostle, with all the immense authority of your fame. I am an old man myself of 72, but with no outstanding gifts or learning; and yet I would, in humble sincerity, make my own, to you, what that Dr M. J. Routh, who died in his hundredth year as President of Magdalen, Oxford, (1854), wrote to a Quaker acquaintance in the condemned cell:

'Sir, this comes from one who, like yourself, has not long to live, being in his ninetieth year. He has had more opportunity than most for distinctly knowing that the scriptures of the New Testament were written by the Apostles of the Saviour of mankind. In these Scriptures it is expressly said that the blood of Jesus Christ cleanses from all sin, and that if we confess our sins, God, being merciful and just, will forgive us our sins on our repentance. Think, say, and do everything in your power to save your soul, before you go into another life.'

You may know that the great Bishop Joseph Butler of Durham, your peer as regards intellect, died with this verse from I John, I. 7, in his ears, and whispering: 'Oh! but this is comfortable.'

I pray God that you will recognise that, for some reason, I have been filled with a deep concern for you.

Yours sincerely
Christopher Roften

The Plat, Elsted
Nr. Midhurst, Sx.
Feb. 4, 1957

Dear Russell

I am a little surprised that you should find the Anglican's letter at all odd. I should have thought you received many such, and indeed I even wonder how many masses are already being said for your soul.

The interest of such letters is of course the calm identification of wickedness with sexual activity. Freud used to think that the main function of religion was to check man's innate aggressivity (the obvious source of all wickedness), but it is curious how often religious teachers bring it back again to sexuality. That makes one think there must be some deep connection between the two, and we believe nowadays that much aggressivity, possibly all, can ultimately be traced to the innumerable forms of sexual frustration. It remains noteworthy, however, that you, our leading apostle of true morality (love, charity, tolerance, etc) should be cast into perdition for not accepting the Catholic view of marriage.

If you want a psycho-analytic comment on the letter there is a clue in the omnipotence he attributes to you (ability to stop wars, etc). That can only point to a gigantic father figure (an earthly God), whose only sin, much resented by the son, was his sleeping with the mother. It is curious that such people are never shocked at God's adulterous behaviour with the Virgin Mary. It needs a lot of purification.

yours sincerely
Ernest Jones

Plas Penrhyn
14 March, 1957

Dear Jones

Thank you for your very pleasant letter of February 4. Ever since I got it, I have been luxuriating in the pleasure of seeing myself as a formidable father-figure inspiring terror in the Anglican hierarchy. What surprised me about the letter I sent you was that I had imagined eminent Anglican Divines to be usually fairly civilized people. I get hundreds of letters very similar to the one I sent you, but they are generally from people with very little education. I cannot make up my mind whether the writer of the letter is gnawed with remorse for the sins he has committed or filled with regret for those that he has not committed.

Yours sincerely
Russell

From and to Lord Russell of Liverpool

Old Warren Farm
Wimbledon Common
S.W.19
13/2[1959]

Dear Lor.. Russell

I am forwarding the enclosed as Monsieur Edmond Paris, and he is not alone, has got us mixed up. The first paragraph of his letter refers to you. The others are for me and I shall be replying to them. Would you please return the letter when you have read it.

Ys. truly
Russell of Liverpool

Plas Penrhyn
18 February, 1959

Dear Lord Russell

Thank you for your letter and for the enclosure which I return herewith. I have been wondering whether there is any means of preventing the confusion between you and me, and I half-thought that we might write a joint letter to *The Times* in the following terms: Sir, To prevent the continuation of confusions which frequently occur, we beg to state that neither of us is the other. Do you think this would be a good plan?

Yours sincerely
Russell

Old Warren Farm
Wimbledon Common
S.W.19
20/2[1959]

Dear Lord Russell

Many thanks for your letter of the 18th.

I am not sure whether you are in earnest or joking about a joint letter to *The Times* but, in either event, I think it is a good idea. Even were it not effective it would provide a little light amusement, and if you would care to write such a letter I would gladly add my signature below yours.

Incidentally, *à propos* this subject, you will find pages 61/2 of a book of my reminiscences to be published on March 19 by Cassell & Co. under the title of *That Reminds Me* of some interest. They contain details of two occasions on which I was mistaken for an Earl Russell. Your elder brother in India in 1927 and yourself in 1954.

Page 60 will also interest you.

Yours sincerely
Russell of Liverpool

Plas Penrhyn
23 February 1959

Dear Lord Russell of Liverpool

Thank you for your letter of February 20. I was both serious and joking in my suggestion of a joint letter. I enclose a draft which I have signed, but I am entirely willing to alter the wording if you think it too frivolous. I think, however, that the present wording is more likely to secure attention than a more solemn statement.

Yours sincerely
Russell

Plas Penrhyn
23 February, 1959

To The Editor of *The Times*

Sir

In order to discourage confusions which have been constantly occurring, we beg herewith to state that neither of us is the other.

Yours etc.
Russell of Liverpool
(*Lord Russell of Liverpool*)

Russell
(*Bertrand, Earl Russell*)

Old Warren Farm
Wimbledon Common
S.W.19
25/2/59

Dear Lord Russell

I have forwarded our letter to *The Times* but I have asked them, of course, to put your name before mine.

I like the wording immensely.

Russell of Liverpool

To and from A. J. Ayer

Plas Penrhyn
19 January, 1957

Dear Ayer

I have just finished reading your *Problem of Knowledge*. I have read the book with a great deal of pleasure and I agree with most of it. I like your way of dissecting problems; for example, what you say on such subjects as television and precognition seems to me to combine logic and sound sense in just proportion. The only point upon which I seriously disagree with you is as to perception. My view on this subject, although to scientific people it seems a mere collection of truisms, is rejected as a wild paradox by philosophers of all schools. You need not, therefore, be in any degree disquieted by not having my support. I will, however, make one point: on page 126 you say that from the fact that the perceived qualities of physical objects are causally dependent upon the state of the percipient, it does not follow that the object does not really have them. This, of course, is true. What does follow is that there is no reason to think that it has them. From the fact that when I wear blue spectacles, things look blue, it does not follow that they are not blue, but it does follow that I have no reason to suppose they are blue.

As I find that philosophers, as opposed to men of science, unanimously misunderstand my theory of perception, I am enclosing a note on the subject with no special reference to your book.

Yours very sincerely
Russell

New College
Oxford
26 May 1961

Dear Russell

I have just heard from Routledge that you have withdrawn permission for your preface to be included in the new translation of Wittgenstein's *Tractatus*. The reason why I come in to this is that I am editor of the series in which the book is to appear.

I assume that you are taking this step because of the difficulties which are being raised by Ogden's brother. I do not know what Ogden has told you; but I do hope that I can persuade you to reconsider your decision. The most important fact, as I see it, is that this new translation will supersede the old, so that if your preface is not included in it, it will practically cease to be available. I think this would be a great pity, as quite apart from the light it throws on Wittgenstein, it is a very interesting piece of work in itself.

The authors of the new translation, Messrs Pears and McGuinness, tell me that if there [are] any conditions which you now wish to make before allowing them to use your preface, they will do their very best to meet them.

I am very sorry to hear that you have been ill and hope that you are now recovered.

Yours sincerely
Freddie Ayer

Pears and McGuinness say that they have made every effort to satisfy Ogden but have found him quite intractable.

Plas Penrhyn
27 May, 1961

Dear *Ayer*

Thank you for your letter of May 26. I have never succeeded in understanding the points at issue between Ogden's brother and your party. I have no objection in principle to the reprinting of my introduction to the *Tractatus*. I was influenced by the fact that Wittgenstein and all his followers hated my introduction and that Wittgenstein only consented to its inclusion because the publishers made it a condition of their publishing the *Tractatus*. I did not know, until I received your letter this morning, that there was anyone who thought that my introduction had any value. Since you think that it has, I am quite willing again to grant permission for its republication. Would you kindly communicate the substance of this letter to Routledge.

Yours sincerely
Russell

New College
Oxford
31 May 1961

Dear *Russell*

Thank you very much for allowing us to reprint your Introduction to the *Tractatus*. Wittgenstein always complained at being misrepresented by anybody who wrote about him, and his followers simply echo what he said. But I am sure that your Introduction is an important addition to the work and the new translators entirely share my view. They were indeed very upset when they thought they were not going to be allowed to reprint it. With regard to Ogden's brother I am in the same position as yourself: I still do not understand what the substance of his grievance is.

Yours sincerely
Freddie Ayer

131

From and to Rudolf Carnap

Department of Philosophy
University of California
May 12, 1962

Dear Lord Russell

Throughout my life I have followed with the greatest interest not only your philosophical work but also, especially during the last years, your political activities, and I admire your courage and your intensity of energy and devotion. Now, on the occasion of your ninetieth birthday, I wish to send you a message of best wishes and of deep gratitude for all I owe to you. Your books had indeed a stronger influence on my philosophical thinking than those of any other philosopher. I say more about this in my intellectual autobiography (in a forthcoming Schilpp-volume on my philosophy), and especially also about the inspiring effect on me of your appeal for a new method in philosophy, on the last pages of your book *Our knowledge of the external world.*

I am in complete agreement with the aims for which you are fighting at present: serious negotiations instead of the cold war, no bomb-testing, no fallout shelters. But, not having your wonderful power of words, I limit myself to participation in public appeals and petitions initiated by others and to some private letters to President Kennedy on these matters. Even such letters are difficult for me. By nature I am inclined to turn away from the insane quarrels of parties and governments, and pursue my thinking in a purely theoretical field. But at present, when the survival of civilization is at stake, I realize that it is necessary at least to take a stand. I also admired your forceful and convincing argumentation in the debate with Edward Teller which I saw on television. I find it depressing to see a prominent scientist (in contrast to politicians from whom one has come to expect nothing better) strengthening the prejudices of the listeners.

I am going to be 71 on the same day you are having your birthday. May you have many more active years ahead, in good health, and with the satisfaction of seeing a more rational world order coming into being, to whose development you have contributed so much. I am going to retire in a few weeks from teaching and to devote myself to the further development of my theory of inductive probability, on which I have begun to publish in 1950 and which has occupied me ever since.

With deep affection and gratitude,

Yours
Rudolf Carnap

Plas Penrhyn
21st June 1962

Dear Professor Carnap

I am immensely grateful to you for your kind letter. It pleased me greatly. I had not realised that your birthday and mine fall on the same day. I am sorry not to have sent you my own good wishes, which are sincerely felt.

I believe that your efforts to bring clarity and precision to philosophy will have an everlasting effect on the thinking of men, and I am very happy to see that you will continue your work after your retirement. Nothing would be more fitting than that you should successfully realise your theory of inductive probability. I entirely understand your diffidence with respect to letters to public officials. It is difficult to employ a language which speaks of intense and sincere fears for our world to public men who receive our words with small awareness of that which promotes them. I must confess that I am deeply troubled. I fear that human beings are intent upon acting out a vast deathwish and that it lies with us now to make every effort to promote resistance to the insanity and brutality of policies which encompass the extermination of hundreds of millions of human beings.

In this country we are having a much greater success than seems evident in the United States, although it is obvious that protest in the United States requires far greater courage and dedication than its equivalent here. Nonetheless; I am hopeful that the effect of our minority resistance may grow and find a co-ordinated international expression. We are holding a great demonstration at the Air Ministry in Whitehall involving civil disobedience this coming September 9th, and I shall be taking part in the physical demonstration itself. I believe that men are starved for an answer to the terror and that they will respond if their sense of helplessness can be overcome.

I am sincerely grateful to you for your kindness in writing and I wish you earnestly success in your great work.

With my good wishes and respect
Bertrand Russell

From *The Observer*, May 13, 1962

PROS AND CONS OF REACHING NINETY

by

Bertrand Russell

There are both advantages and disadvantages in being very old. The disadvantages are obvious and uninteresting, and I shall say little about them. The advantages seem to me more interesting. A long retrospect gives weight and substance to experience. I have been able to follow many lives, both of friends and of public characters, from an early stage to their conclusion. Some, who were promising in youth, have achieved little of value; others have continued to develop from strength to strength through long lives of important achievement. Undoubtedly, experience makes it easier to guess to which of these two kinds a young person is likely to belong. It is not only the lives of individuals, but the lives of movements that come, with time, to form part of personal experience and to facilitate estimates of probable success or failure. Communism, in spite of a very difficult beginning, has hitherto continued to increase in power and influence. Nazism, on the contrary, by snatching too early and too ruthlessly at dominion, came to grief. To have watched such diverse processes helps to give an insight into the past of history and should help in guessing at the probable future.

To come to more personal matters; it is natural for those who are energetic and adventurous to feel in youth a very passionate and restless desire for some important achievement, without any clear prevision of what, with luck, it may be. In old age, one becomes more aware of what has, and what has not, been achieved. What one can further do becomes a smaller proportion of what has already been done, and this makes personal life less feverish.

It is a curious sensation to read the journalistic clichés which come to be fastened on past periods that one remembers, such as the 'naughty nineties' and the 'riotous twenties'. Those decades did not seem, at the time, at all 'naughty' or 'riotous'. The habit of affixing easy labels is convenient to those who wish to seem clever without having to think, but it has very little relation to reality. The world is always changing, but not in the simple ways that such convenient clichés suggest. Old age, as I am experiencing it, could be a time of very complete happiness if one could forget the state of the world. Privately, I enjoy everything that could make life delightful. I used to think that when I reached old age I would retire from the world and live a life of elegant culture, reading all the great books that I ought to have read at an earlier date. Perhaps it was, in any case, an idle dream. A long habit of work with some purpose that one believes important is difficult to break, and I might have found elegant leisure boring even if the world had been in a better state. However that might have been, I find it impossible to ignore what is happening.

Ever since 1914, at almost every crucial moment, the wrong thing has been done. We are told that the West is engaged in defending the 'Free World', but freedom such as existed before 1914 is now as dim a memory as crinolines. Supposedly wise men assured us in 1914 that we were fighting a war to end war, but it turned out to be a war to end peace. We were told that Prussian militarism was all that had to be put down; and, ever since, militarism has continually increased. Murderous humbug, such as would have shocked almost everyone when I was young, is now solemnly mouthed by eminent statesmen. My own country, led by men without imagination and without capacity for adaptation to the modern world, pursues a policy which, if not changed, will lead almost inevitably to the complete extermination of all the inhabitants of Britain. Like Cassandra, I am doomed to prophesy evil and not be believed. Her prophecies came true. I desperately hope that mine will not.

Sometimes one is tempted to take refuge in cheerful fantasies and to imagine that perhaps in Mars or Venus happier and saner forms of life exist, but our frantic skill is making this a vain dream. Before long, if we do not destroy ourselves, our destructive strife will have spread to those planets. Perhaps, for their sake, one ought to hope that war on earth will put an end to our species before its folly has become cosmic. But this is not a hope in which I can find any comfort.

The way in which the world has developed during the last fifty years has brought about in me changes opposite to those which are supposed to be typical of old age. One is frequently assured by men who have no doubt of their own wisdom that old age should bring serenity and a larger vision in which seeming evils are viewed as means to ultimate good. I cannot accept any such view. Serenity, in the present world, can only be achieved through blindness or brutality. Unlike what is conventionally expected, I become gradually more and more of a rebel. I was not born rebellious. Until 1914, I fitted more or less comfortably into the world as I found it. There were evils— great evils—but there was reason to think that they would grow less. Without having the temperament of a rebel, the course of events has made me gradually less and less able to acquiesce patiently in what is happening. A minority, though a growing one, feels as I do, and, so long as I live, it is with them that I must work.

From Mrs Roosevelt

55 East 74th Street
New York City
September 22, 1960

My Lord
I am most grateful to you for taking part with me in our television program on British defence policy in London. It was a lively and exciting discussion and I feel the result was satisfying.

Sincerely
Eleanor Roosevelt

From and to Max Born

Haus Filser
Freibergstrasse
Obersdorf (Allgäu)
Germany
12.7.51

Dear Professor Russell
Your book *A History of Western Philosophy* which I never had time to read at home has accompanied me on my holiday journey and given me so much pleasure that I take the liberty to write to you a few words of thanks.

I confess that before putting the book into my suitcase I asked a few of my philosophical friends in Scotland about it, and was warned not to read it as it would give me a distorted picture of the actual men and events. When I was, a few weeks ago, in Göttingen I discussed your book with one of the local philosophers and found a still stronger negative attitude, based mainly on your treatment of Plato and of the German idealistic school. This encouraged me greatly to read your book. For I have been tortured at school with Plato, and I have always thoroughly disliked German metaphysics, in particular Hegel. Thus I decided to read your last chapter first, and as I wholeheartedly agreed to your own philosophy, I started cheerfully with page 1 and continued reading with ever increasing fascination and pleasure until I reached your moderate, though decided refutations of some of the modern schools of 'subjectivistic madness'. I was myself once a pupil of Edmund Husserl but found his 'phenomenology' unsatisfactory and its modern version by Heidegger rather disgusting. I suppose you found it not worth while to mention it.

My son and his wife who are with us on this journey share my admiration for your work and have gone so far to call their new-born boy Max Russell combining thus my name with yours.

On my way out I stayed a week with Niels Bohr at Copenhagen and had some most interesting talks with him on the philosophical foundations of quantum theory.

Yours Sincerely
Max Born

Marcard str. 4
Bad Pyrmont
18 March, 1958

Dear Professor Russell

I have read Khrushchev's long declaration in the *New Statesman*. I find it just as depressing as the letter from Dulles published some weeks ago. The commentary by Kingsley Martin that these fellows are amazingly similar in their mental make-up is quite correct. One could just as well call them Khrushless and Dullchev, and, what they believe in, not an ideology, but an idiotology. I wonder whether you will write a summary containing your impressions of this exchange of opinions which you have originated.

Meanwhile we 'Eighteen' here are involved in the fight against rocket and nuclear armament of West-Germany. Von Weizsäecker is in Pugwash and will be back on April 17th when we meet again on the Rhine.

I have stirred up another ugly matter, concerning space travel, which is used by the military party to camouflage the expensive development of rocket missiles. All newspapers, the radio, the cinemas are full of this affair and I have a lively time. The great majority of the people are on our side but the Government (Adenauer, Strauss) are clever and use all means.

Yours sincerely
M. Born

Plas Penrhyn
22 March, 1958

Dear Dr Born

Thank you very warmly for your letter of March 18 which expressed feelings exactly similar to mine as regards Khrushless and Dullchev and what you so aptly call their idiotology. I am sending my reflections on this matter to the *New Statesman* where they will be published shortly.

I wish you all success in your campaign about space travel.

Yours sincerely
Bertrand Russell

Plas Penrhyn
25 November, 1961

Dear Max Born

Before it is too late for any of us to say anything, I wish to tell you that I feel for you a profound admiration, not only for your intellect which I have respected for forty years, but for your character of which my knowledge is more recent. I have found in you a kind of generosity and a kind of freedom from self-assertion which is very rare even among those whom, on the whole, I admire. You appear to me a man possessed of nobility—unfortunately a rare quality.

Forgive me for writing so openly, but what I have said is said in profound sincerity.

Yours very sincerely
Bertrand Russell

The following statement launched the Committee of 100 in the autumn of 1960

ACT OR PERISH

A call to non-violent action

by Earl Russell and Rev. Michael Scott

We are appealing for support for a movement of non-violent resistance to nuclear war and weapons of mass extermination. Our appeal is made from a common consciousness of the appalling peril to which Governments of East and West are exposing the human race.

DISASTER ALMOST CERTAIN

Every day, and at every moment of every day, a trivial accident, a failure to distinguish a meteor from a bomber, a fit of temporary insanity in one single man, may cause a nuclear world war, which, in all likelihood, will put an end to man and to all higher forms of animal life. The populations of the Eastern and Western blocs are, in the great majority, unaware of the magnitude of the peril. Almost all experts who have studied the situation without being in the employment of some Government have come to the conclusion that, if present policies continue, disaster is almost certain within a fairly short time.

PUBLIC MISLED

It is difficult to make the facts known to ordinary men and women, because Governments do not wish them known and powerful forces are opposed to dissemination of knowledge which might cause dissatisfaction with Government policies. Although it is possible to ascertain the probabilities by patient and careful study, statements entirely destitute of scientific validity are put out authoritatively with a view to misleading those who have not time for careful study. What is officially said about civil defence, both here and in America, is grossly misleading. The danger from fall-out is much greater than the Authorities wish the population to believe. Above all, the imminence of all-out nuclear war is ignorantly, or mendaciously, underestimated both in the statements of politicians and in the vast majority of newspapers. It is difficult to resist the conclusion that most of the makers of opinion consider it more important to secure defeat of the 'enemy' than to safeguard the continued existence of our species. The fact that the defeat of the 'enemy' must involve our own defeat, is carefully kept from the consciousness of those who give only a fleeting and occasional attention to political matters.

ACTION IMPERATIVE

Much has already been accomplished towards creating a public opinion opposed to nuclear weapons, but not enough, so far, to influence Governments. The threatening disaster is so enormous that we feel compelled to take every action that is possible with a view to awakening our compatriots, and ultimately all mankind, to the need of urgent and drastic changes of policy. We should wish every parent of young children, and every person capable of feelings of mercy, to feel it the most important part of their duty to secure for those who are still young a normal span of life, and to understand that Governments, at present, are making this very unlikely. To us, the vast scheme of mass murder which is being hatched—nominally for our protection, but in fact for universal extermination—is a horror and an abomination. What we can do to prevent this horror, we feel to be a profound and imperative duty which must remain paramount while the danger persists.

CONSTITUTIONAL ACTION NOT ENOUGH

We are told to wait for the beneficent activities of Congresses, Committees, and Summit meetings. Bitter experience has persuaded us that to follow such advice would be utterly futile while the Great Powers remain stubbornly determined to prevent agreement. Against the major forces that normally determine opinion, it is difficult to achieve more than a limited success by ordinary constitutional methods. We are told that in a democracy only lawful methods of persuasion should be used. Unfortunately, the opposition to sanity and mercy on the part of those who have power is such as to make persuasion by ordinary methods difficult and slow, with the result that, if such methods alone are employed, we shall probably all be dead before our purpose can be achieved. Respect for law is important and only a very profound conviction can justify actions which flout the law. It is generally admitted that, in the past, many such actions have been justified. Christian Martyrs broke the law, and there can be no doubt that majority opinion at the time condemned them for doing so. We, in our day, are asked to acquiesce, passively if not actively, in policies clearly leading to tyrannical brutalities compared with which all former horrors sink into insignificance. We cannot do this any more than Christian Martyrs could acquiesce in worship of the Emperor. Their steadfastness in the end achieved victory. It is for us to show equal steadfastness and willingness to suffer hardship and thereby to persuade the world that our cause is worthy of such devotion.

TOWARDS WORLD PEACE

We hope, and we believe, that those who feel as we do and those who may come to share our belief can form a body of such irresistible persuasive force that the present madness of East and West may give way to a new hope, a new realisation of the common destinies of the human family and a determination that men shall no longer seek elaborate and devilish ways of injuring each other but shall, instead, unite in permitting happiness and co-operation. Our immediate purpose, in so far as it is political, is only to persuade Britain to abandon reliance upon the illusory protection of nuclear weapons. But, if this can be achieved, a wider horizon will open before our eyes. We shall become aware of the immense possibilities of nature when harnessed by the creative intelligence of man to the purposes and arts of peace. We shall continue, while life permits, to pursue the goal of world peace and universal human fellowship. We appeal, as human beings to human beings: remember your humanity, and forget the rest. If you can do so, the way lies open to a new Paradise; if you cannot, nothing lies before you but universal death.

The following is the text of my leaflet 'On Civil Disobedience'

RUSSELL ON CIVIL DISOBEDIENCE

On April 15th, 1961, Earl Russell addressed the first Annual Conference of the Midlands Region Youth Campaign for Nuclear Disarmament, in Birmingham.

In putting the case for Civil Disobedience, Earl Russell makes a balanced appeal for nuclear disarmament in the interests of humanity, and his words will be of interest to all who support the Campaign and to those whose minds are open to rational persuasion.

Friends

My main purpose this afternoon is to set out the case for non-violent civil disobedience as one of the methods to be employed in combatting the nuclear peril. Many people believe that this method is not likely to achieve its purpose, and some have moral objections to it on principle. Most of them will admit that non-violent civil disobedience is justified when the law demands the individual concerned to do something which he considers wicked. This is the case of conscientious objectors. But our case is a somewhat different one. We advocate and practise non-violent civil disobedience as a method of causing people to know the perils to which the world is exposed and in persuading them to join us in opposing the insanity which affects, at present, many of the most powerful Governments in the world. I will concede that civil disobedience as a method of propaganda is difficult to justify except in extreme cases, but I cannot imagine any issue more extreme or more overwhelmingly important than that of the prevention of nuclear war. Consider one simple fact: if the present policies of many great powers are not radically changed, it is in the highest degree improbable that any of you here present will be alive ten years hence. And that is not because your peril is exceptional. It is a universal peril.

'But', objectors will say, 'why cannot you be content with the ordinary methods of political propaganda?' The main reason why we cannot be content with these methods alone is that, so long as only constitutional methods were employed, it was very difficult—and often impossible—to cause the most important facts to be known. All the great newspapers are against us. Television and radio gave us only grudging and brief opportunities for stating our case. Politicians who opposed us were reported in full, while those who supported us were dubbed 'hysterical' or were said to be actuated by personal hostility to this or that politician. It was very largely the difficulty of making our case known that drove some of us to the adoption of illegal methods. Our illegal actions, because they had sensational news value, were reported, and here and there, a newspaper would allow us to say why we did what we did.

It was a most noteworthy fact that not only was our demonstration of February 18th very widely reported in every part of the world but, as an immediate consequence, all sorts of newspapers—both here and abroad—demanded and printed statements of our case which, until then, they would have rejected. I think also that the spectacle, even in photographs, of so very many serious people, not looking like freaks as newspapers had said we did, caused a widespread belief that our movement could not be dismissed as an outbreak of hysterical emotionalism.

Both popular and official ignorance of the main facts concerned has begun to grow less, and we hope that, in time some members of the Government, and perhaps one or two great newspapers may acquire some knowledge as to the terrible problems about which they light-heartedly dogmatize.

Some of our critics who oppose non-violent civil disobedience on principle say that we rely upon bullying and not upon persuasion. Alas, we are very far removed from being strong enough to bully anybody; and, if we ever were strong enough, present methods would have become unnecessary. I will take as typical of the arguments of our opponents a letter in *The Guardian* of March 29th from the Bishop of Willesden. You may think it rash to oppose a Bishop on a moral issue, but—greatly daring—I will attempt the task. The Bishop says that our demonstrations are intended to force our views upon the community, rather than merely to assert them. He has not, himself, experienced, as we have, the difficulty of asserting anything loud enough to be heard when all the major organs of publicity are combined in an attempt to prevent our case from being known. Non-violent civil disobedience, according to the Bishop, is a use of force by a minority to compel the majority to submit. This seems to me one of the most far-fetched and absurd arguments that I have ever heard. How can a minority of unarmed people, pledged to non-violence, impose their will against all the forces of the Establishment backed by public apathy? The Bishop goes on to say that such methods can lead to anarchy or dictatorship. There have, it is true, been many instances of minorities acquiring dictatorship. The Communists in Russia and the Nazis in Germany are outstanding examples. But their methods were not non-violent. Our methods, which are non-violent, can only succeed by persuasion.

There are two arguments which are often employed against non-violent civil disobedience. One is that it alienates people who might otherwise be supporters, and the other is that it causes dissension within the anti-nuclear movement. I will say a few words about each of these. I have no wish whatever to see non-violent civil disobedience adopted by *all* opponents of nuclear weapons. I think it is well that organisations both practising and abstaining from non-violent civil disobedience should exist to suit different temperaments. I do not believe that the existence of an organisation practising non-violent civil disobedience prevents anybody from joining an organisation which does not. Some may say that they are deterred by distaste for fanatical extremists, but I think these are all people who would in any case find something to deter them. I think, on the contrary, that our movement has a vigour and magnetism which attracts large numbers who might otherwise remain indifferent.

As for dissensions, they, I agree, are regrettable, but they are totally unnecessary. There is no reason why societies practising different techniques should not exist side by side without finding fault with each other. I think this has come to be recognized. I have, for my part, a very great admiration for what the c n d has done and I hope its work will continue to prosper. But I think the work of those who believe in non-violent civil disobedience is at least equally valuable, especially while to the newspapers it has the attraction of novelty.

Many people say that, while civil disobedience may be justified where there is not democracy, it cannot possibly be right where everybody has a share of political power. This sort of argument is one which is wilfully blind to very obvious facts. In practically every so-called democratic country there are movements similar to ours. There are vigorous movements in the United States. In Canada they are not far from acquiring power. Naturally the movement in Japan is very powerful and very convinced. Moreover, take the problem of people under 21. If the Governments have their way, these people will all be slaughtered without having any legal means of giving weight to their wish to survive. Consider, again, the way in which opinion is manufactured in a nominally democratic country. Great newspapers belong to rich and powerful people. Television and radio have strong reasons for not offending the Government. Most experts would lose their position and their income if they spoke the truth.

For these reasons the forces that control opinion are heavily weighted upon the side of the rich and powerful. Those who are neither rich nor powerful can find no ways of counter-balancing this over-weight except such as the Establishment can decry with the support of all who profit by the *status quo*. There is in every great modern State, a vast mechanism intended to prevent the truth from being known, not only to the public, but also to the Governments. Every Government is advised by experts and inevitably prefers the experts who flatter its prejudices. The ignorance of important public men on the subject of nuclear warfare is utterly astounding to those who have made an impartial study of the subject. And from public men this ignorance trickles down to become the voice of the people. It is against this massive artificial ignorance that our protests are directed. I will give a few instances of this astonishing ignorance:

The *Daily Mail* in a report on civil defence stated that fall-out decays rapidly once it is down on the ground and that, therefore, people who had taken refuge in shelters would not have to stay there very long. As a matter of fact, to take only two of the most dangerous ingredients of fallout—Strontium 90 has a half life of 28 years and Carbon 14 has a half life of 5,600 years. These facts make it seem as if people would have to stay in the shelters as long as from the building of the Pyramids to the present day.

To take a more important example, the Prime Minister recently stated without any qualification that 'there will be no war by accident'. I have not come across one non-Government expert who has studied this subject who does not say the opposite. C. P. Snow, who has an exceptional right to speak with authority, said in a recent article 'Within at the most ten years, some of these bombs are going off. I am saying this as responsibly as I can. *That* is a certainty.' John B. Witchell, an engineer, who resigned his position as a member of Canada's Atomic Research Board in protest against the Government's nuclear armament policies, stated in a recent speech: 'The demand for instantaneous retaliation leads to a hair-trigger situation which renders nuclear war a statistical certainty.' He went on to say that those whom he calls 'the official liars' will say that mistakes will be impossible. He replied to them: 'Let me say emphatically, positively, there can be no safeguard which can be considered adequate.'

I could give many other quotations expressing the same view, and none expressing the opposite view except from Government employees. Mr Macmillan should know these facts, but evidently does not.

I will give another example of the Prime Minister's cheerful ignorance: Speaking in Ottawa quite recently he alluded to the signs of neutralism in Britain and told the Canadians not to be worried by them. He said, 'If ever the call comes to them, the young will go straight from the ranks of the neutralists into the ranks of Her Majesty's Forces, as they have so often done in the past'. They will have to be rather quick about it, as his own Government has told us that they will only have four minutes' notice. At the end of the four minutes they will be dead, whether in Her Majesty's Forces or still among the neutralists. The ancient rhetorical language associated with war is so ingrained that Mr Macmillan is quite unable to realise its complete remoteness from modern military facts.

It is not only that the organs of publicity are slow to publish facts which militate against official policy. It is also that such facts are unpleasant and, therefore, most people soon forget them. What proportion of the inhabitants of Britain know the official report by the u s Defence Minister of probable casualties in a nuclear war with present armament? His official guess was 160 million in the u s, 200 million in the u s s r and everybody in Britain and Western Europe. He did not regard this as a reason for changing American policy. When one combines this estimate with the near certainty of a nuclear war if present policies continue, it is obviously not unjust to say that the Government of Britain is favouring a course which if persisted in, will lead to the death of every one of us. It may seem odd that a majority of the British public supports the policy leading to this dreadful disaster. I do not think that British voters would continue to do so if the facts were brought to their notice so emphatically that they could no longer forget them. This is part of our purpose and part of what makes spectacular action necessary.

Most people in Britain are not aware of the attitude taken by armament experts in America to the British alliance and to the British desire to be a nuclear Power. The most learned and detailed account of American policy in these matters is Herman Kahn's big book *On Thermonuclear War*.

He is remarkably cold blooded and makes careful arithmetical estimates of probable casualties. He believes that both America and Russia could more or less survive a nuclear war and achieve economic recovery in no very long time. Apparently—though on this he is vague—they are both to set to work at once on preparations for another nuclear war, and this sort of thing is to go on until not enough people are left alive for it to be possible to make a bomb.

All this has shocked liberal-minded Americans who have criticised Mr Kahn with great severity, not realizing, apparently, that he is only expounding official American policy.

There is, however, another aspect of his discussions which is of special interest to Britain. He holds that Britain as an ally adds nothing to the strength of America. He argues at length that, if Russia were to attack Britain without attacking the United States, the United States would not intervene in spite of obligations under N A T O. He shows no objection to British neutrality, and explicitly regrets the lack of success for the suggestion that Britain should form a non-nuclear club of which it should be a member. Britons who are orthodox in armament policy do not seem to be aware of this American opinion. It hurts their national pride since it considers British military power negligible and the protection of Britain during war totally impossible. British opponents of British neutralism all argue vehemently that the West would be weakened if Britain became neutral. But, apparently, this is not the opinion of orthodox American armament experts.

It is not only unpleasant facts that the public ignores: it is also some facts which ought to be found pleasant. Khrushchev has repeatedly offered complete disarmament by agreement combined with any degree of inspection that the West may desire. The West shrugs its shoulders and says 'of course, he is not sincere'. This, however, is not the argument that really weighs with Western Governments. Khrushchev proclaims his hope that Communists will conquer the world by peaceful propaganda. Western Governments fear that they cannot produce equally effective counter-propaganda. As Dulles said, in an unguarded moment, 'We are losing this cold war, but we might win a hot one'. He did not explain what he meant by 'winning', but I suppose he meant that, at the end, there might be 6 Americans and only 4 Russians.

Doubts as to sincerity have at least as much justification if entertained by the Russians towards us as they have if entertained by us towards the Russians. The British Commonwealth has lately voted unanimously for universal and complete disarmament. Since in this matter there is complete agreement with Khrushchev, while America is adverse, it might have been thought that the vote of the British Commonwealth, including Britain, would lead to a rapprochement with the Soviet Government. Instead of this, however, Kennedy and Macmillan have recently been tightening up the alliance and proposing agreements which would make British disarmament totally impossible. We cannot therefore take the British vote in the Commonwealth as indicating the sincere wishes of the British Government.

I think that while we are engaged in campaigning for British unilateralism, it is important to bear in mind the more distant objectives which give international meaning to our efforts. Let us consider for a moment what international aims must form part of any attempt to put an end to nuclear war.

The first thing to realize is that, if there are not to be nuclear wars, there must not be wars, because any war is sure to become nuclear no matter what treaties to the contrary may have been concluded. And if there is not to be war, there must be machinery for settling disputes by negotiation. This will require an international authority which shall arbitrate disputes and be sufficiently powerful to compel obedience to its awards. None of this can possibly come about while relations between East and West are as strained as they are now, and while weapons of mass extermination keep the whole world in a state of nuclear terror. Before anything that seriously diminishes the risk of nuclear war can be achieved, there will have to be a treaty between America and Russia and China, and an agreement to ban—not only nuclear weapons—but also chemical and biological weapons. All this may seem beyond the power of Britain to help or hinder. I do not think that it is. Negotiations between East and West ever since 1945 have been abortive because only the two contesting blocs were represented in the negotiations, and each of them, from motives of prestige, felt unable to make the slightest concession to the other. If there is ever to be a detente between Russia and America, it will have to be brought about by the friendly mediation of neutrals. Britain, if neutral, could play an important part in this beneficent work, whereas Britain can do nothing in this direction while remaining a member of N A T O.

These, as yet somewhat distant, vistas should, I think, be in our minds while we are engaged in what might seem an exclusively national campaign. We have to remember that weapons of mass extermination, once invented, remain a potential threat even if none are actually in being. For this reason, we have to remember, further, that, unless war is completely eliminated, the human race is doomed. To put an end to war, which has dominated human life for 6,000 years, is no easy task. It is a heroic task, a task worthy of all the energies and all the thought of every sane man throughout the world. I think this larger vista may help in difficult times to prevent discouragement and disillusion. I think that our campaign is the best thing that Britons not in Government posts can do, though it is only a small part of what the world needs.

Extempore comment added by Lord Russell to the foregoing speech

And I would like to say in conclusion that what I suppose most of us feel most strongly and what makes us willing to make sacrifices for the cause is the extraordinary wickedness of these weapons of mass destruction. We used to think that Hitler was wicked when he wanted to kill all the Jews, but Kennedy and Macmillan and others both in the East and in the West pursue policies which will probably lead to killing not only all the Jews but all the rest of us too. They are much more wicked than Hitler and this idea of weapons of mass extermination is utterly and absolutely horrible and it is a thing which no man with one spark of humanity can tolerate and I will not pretend to obey a government which is organising the massacre of the whole of mankind. I will do anything I can to oppose such Governments in any non-violent way that seems likely to be fruitful, and I should exhort all of you to feel the same way. We cannot obey these murderers. They are wicked and abominable. They are the wickedest people that ever lived in the history of man and it is our duty to do what we can.

[The last phrase of these extempore observations—'They are the wickedest

9. Bertrand Russell addressing a nuclear disarmament meeting at Trafalgar Square during a snowstorm, February 1962

10. Bertrand Russell at his home in Penrhyndeudraeth, 1964

[*Keystone Press Agency Ltd.*]

people that ever lived'—was taken up by the Press and published throughout Britain and the world, usually without the preceding extempore remarks and with no indication that they had been preceded by a carefully built up speech giving the documentation necessary to support such a conclusion.]

My Statement at Bow Street, September 12, 1961

If the Court permits, I should like to make a short statement as to the reasons for my present course. This is my personal statement, but I hope that those who are accused of the same so-called crime will be in sympathy with what I have to say.

It was only step by step and with great reluctance that we were driven to non-violent civil disobedience.

Ever since the bomb was dropped on Hiroshima on August 6th, 1945, I have been profoundly troubled by the danger of nuclear warfare. I began my attempt to warn people by entirely orthodox methods. I expressed my fears in a speech in the House of Lords three months after the bombs were dropped in Japan. I called together scientists of the highest eminence from all parts of the world and am now Chairman of their periodic meetings. They issue wise and reasoned reports concerning nuclear warfare, its probable disastrous results, and ways of preventing its occurrence. No newspaper notices these reports and they have no effect either on Governments or on public opinion. The popular Press minimises and ridicules the effort of those working against nuclear warfare, and television, with rare exceptions, is closed to us. In recent months one television company, and only one, offered me two minutes for general platitudes, but when I said I should wish to speak on Berlin the offer was withdrawn.

It has seemed to some of us that, in a country supposed to be a democracy, the public should know the probable consequences of present Great-Power policies in East and West. Patriotism and humanity alike urged us to seek some way of saving our country and the world. No one can desire the slaughter of our families, friends, our compatriots and a majority of the human race in a contest in which there will be only vanquished and no victors. We feel it a profound and inescapable duty to make the facts known and thereby save at least a thousand million human lives. We cannot escape this duty by submitting to orders which, we are convinced, would not be issued if the likelihood and the horror of nuclear war were more generally understood.

Non-violent civil disobedience was forced upon us by the fact that it was more fully reported than other methods of making the facts known, and that caused people to ask what had induced us to adopt such a course of action. We who are here accused are prepared to suffer imprisonment because we believe that this is the most effective way of working for the salvation of our country and the world. If you condemn us you will be helping our cause, and therefore humanity.

While life remains to us we will not cease to do what lies in our power to avert the greatest calamity that has ever threatened mankind.

The text of a leaflet issued while I was in Brixton Prison

A MESSAGE FROM BERTRAND RUSSELL

To all, in whatever country who are still capable of sane thinking or human feeling:

Friends

Along with valued colleagues I am to be silenced for a time—perhaps for ever, for who can tell how soon the great massacre will take place?

The populations of East and West, misled by stubborn governments in search of prestige and by corrupt official experts bent on retaining their posts, tamely acquiesce in policies which are almost certain to end in nuclear war.

There are supposed to be two sides, each professing to stand for a great cause. This is a delusion—Kennedy and Khrushchev, Adenauer and de Gaulle, Macmillan and Gaitskell, are pursuing a common aim: the ending of human life.

You, your families, your friends and your countries are to be exterminated by the common decision of a few brutal but powerful men. To please these men, all the private affections, all the public hopes, all that has been achieved in art, and knowledge and thought and all that might be achieved hereafter is to be wiped out forever.

Our ruined lifeless planet will continue for countless ages to circle aimlessly round the sun unredeemed by the joys and loves, the occasional wisdom and the power to create beauty which have given value to human life.

It is for seeking to prevent this that we are in prison.

Bertrand Russell

From Augustus John

Fryern Court,
Fordingbridge, Hants.
[postmarked 15 Feb 1961]

Dear Lord Russell

Your message was brought to me while I was working in the studio (not the one you knew but one further off) by the gardener. I told him how to reply, which he said he understood but I don't know if he did so correctly. All I wanted to say was that I believed in the object of the demonstration and would like to go to prison if necessary. I didn't want to parade my physical disabilities though I *still* have to follow the instructions of my doctor, who I think saved my life when I was in danger of coronary thrombosis. A very distinguished medical authority who was consulted, took a *very* pessimistic view of my case, but my local doctor, undeterred, continued his treatment and I feel sure, saved my life.

All this I meant *privately* & am sure you understood, even if the gardener garbled it when telephoning. I wish the greatest success for the demonstration on the 18th although I can only be with you in spirit.

Yours sincerely
Augustus John

P.S. This requires no answer.

My speech in Trafalgar Square, October 29, 1961

Friends

During the last decades there have been many people who have been loud
in condemnation of the Germans for having permitted the growth of Nazi evil
and atrocities in their country. 'How', these people ask, 'could the Germans
allow themselves to remain unaware of the evil? Why did they not risk their
comfort, their livelihood, even their lives to combat it?'

Now a more all-embracing danger threatens us all—the danger of nuclear
war. I am very proud that there is in this country a rapidly growing company
of people who refuse to remain unaware of the danger, or ignorant of the facts
concerning the policies that enable, and force, us to live in such danger. I am
even prouder to be associated with those many among them who, at whatever
risk of discomfort and often of very real hardship, are willing to take drastic
action to uphold their belief. They have laid themselves open to the charges
of being silly, being exhibitionist, being law-breakers, being traitors. They
have suffered ostracism and imprisonment, sometimes repeatedly, in order to
call attention to the facts that they have made the effort to learn. It is a great
happiness to me to welcome so many of them here—I wish that I could say
all of them, but some are still in prison. We none of us, however, can be
entirely happy until our immediate aim has been achieved and the threat of
nuclear war has become a thing of the past. Then such actions as we have taken
and shall take will no longer be necessary.

We all wish that there shall be no nuclear war, but I do not think that the
country realizes, or even that many of us here present realize, the very considerable likelihood of a nuclear war within the next few months. We are all
aware of Khrushchev's resumption of tests and of his threat to explode a 50
megaton bomb.

We all deplore these provocative acts. But I think we are less aware of the
rapidly growing feeling in America in favour of a nuclear war in the very near
future. In America, the actions of Congress are very largely determined by
lobbies representing this or that interest. The armament lobby, which represents both the economic interests of armament firms and the warlike ardour
of generals and admirals, is exceedingly powerful, and it is very doubtful
whether the President will be able to stand out against the pressure which it
is exerting. Its aims are set forth in a quite recent policy statement by the Air
Force Association, which is the most terrifying document that I have ever read.
It begins by stating that preservation of the *status quo* is not adequate as a
national goal. I quote: 'Freedom must bury Communism or be buried by
Communism. Complete eradication of the Soviet system must be our national
goal, our obligation to all free people, our promise of hope to all who are not
free.' It is a curious hope that is being promised, since it can only be realised
in heaven, for the only 'promise' that the West can hope to fulfil is the promise
to turn Eastern populations into corpses. The noble patriots who make this
pronouncement omit to mention that Western populations also will be
exterminated.

'We are determined', they say, 'to back our words with action even at the risk of war. We seek not merely to preserve our freedoms, but to extend them.' The word 'freedom', which is a favourite word of Western warmongers, has to be understood in a somewhat peculiar sense. It means freedom for war-mongers and prison for those who oppose them. A freedom scarcely dis-tinguishable from this exists in Soviet Russia. The document that I am discussing says that we should employ bombs against Soviet aggression, even if the aggression is non-nuclear and even if it consists only of infiltration. We must have, it says, 'ability to fight, win, and purposefully survive a general nuclear war'. This aim is, of course, impossible to realize, but, by using their peculiar brand of 'freedom' to cause belief in lies, they hope to persuade a deliberately uninformed public opinion to join in their race towards death. They are careful to promise us that H-bombs will not be the worst things they have to offer. 'Nuclear weapons', they say, 'are not the end of military develop-ment. There is no reason to believe that nuclear weapons, no matter how much they may increase in number and ferocity, mark the end of the line in military systems' development.' They explain their meaning by saying, 'We must utilise us space technology as a prime factor in the international power equation'. They lead up to a noble peroration: 'Soviet aims are both evil and implacable. The people (i.e. the American people) are willing to work toward, and fight for if necessary, the elimination of Communism from the world scene. Let the issue be joined.'

This ferocious document, which amounts to a sentence of death on the human race, does not consist of the idle vapourings of acknowledged cranks. On the contrary, it represents the enormous economic power of the armament industry, which is re-enforced in the public mind by the cleverly instilled fear that dis-armament would bring a new depression. This fear has been instilled in spite of the fact that Americans have been assured in the *Wall Street Journal* that a new depression would not be brought about, that the conversion from armaments to manufactures for peace could be made with little dislocation. Reputable economists in other countries support this Wall Street view. But the armament firms exploit patriotism and anti-communism as means of transferring the taxpayers' money into their own pockets. Ruthlessly, and probably consciously, they are leading the world towards disaster.

Two days ago *The Times* published an article by its correspondent in Washington which began: 'The United States has decided that any attempt by East Germany to close the Friedrichstrasse crossing between West and East Berlin will be met by force.'

These facts about both America and Russia strengthen my belief that the aims that I have been advocating for some years, and upon which some of us are agreed, are right. I believe that Britain should become neutral, leaving NATO—to which, in any case, she adds only negligible strength. I believe this partly because I believe that Britain would be safer as a neutral, and with-out a bomb of her own or the illusory 'protection' of the American bomb, and without bases for foreign troops; and, perhaps more important, I believe it because, if Britain were neutral, she could do more to help to achieve peace in the world than she can do now. I do not believe that either America or Russia should disarm unilaterally, because whichever did not do so first would automatically become ruler of the world. I believe that they should disarm as a result of negotiations and agreement to do so. In order to achieve this agreement, I think that Britain might have a very important role to play, for I believe that it can only be brought about if the neutrals form a sort of balancing committee to put forward and argue possible compromises. Then Britain could profitably add her political experience to this committee. In the present state of affairs she can do nothing to forward governmental movement towards peace. I should like to think that the example of Britain unilaterally disarming and, untramelled, taking up the cudgels for peace would persuade some other countries to disarm unilaterally. Then we should be able to throw a heavy weight towards persuading America and Russia to disarm multi-laterally.

I have heard the criticism that we uphold only negative aims. I should like to point out that the policy just outlined is quite positive. All our aims, the most immediate and the most distant, are positive—whether they happen to be stated in negative terms or not.

But to return—

The British Government is less ruthless than the American, but shrinks from open opposition to American Jingoism. It is our hope that, before it is too late, we may overcome this shrinking timidity. Our methods must be dominated by the knowledge that the time is short. We are censured as disobeying orders by the very men who, in the Nuremberg Trials, punished the Germans for *not* disobeying orders. There are Committees of 100 starting up in various parts of this country. But not only here. Since September 17th, the support given us from all parts of the world from individuals, by already established movements having similar aims, even by newly established Committees of 100 in other countries, has been astounding. All these people throughout the world must be encouraged. We must build up—and we must do it quickly—a great world-wide mass movement of people demanding the abandonment of nuclear weapons, the abandonment of war as a means of settling disputes. Although the time may be short, our movement is gaining strength day by day. I repeat, and shall go on repeating:

We *can* win, and we *must*.

Note to above speech:

[After Khrushchev's abandonment of violence in the Cuba crisis, the danger of war became less immediate, and Russian policy became somewhat milder.]

SUGGESTIONS FOR U THANT   RE: BALANCING COMMITTEE

The Assembly should empower the Secretary General to appoint a small committee consisting entirely of members of uncommitted nations which should be charged with the task of investigating matters in debate between East and West as they arise, with a view to suggesting compromise solutions which both sides could accept without loss of face. These solutions should be such as to give no net advantage to either side since if they favoured one side, the other would not accept them. They should also be such as to diminish friction at danger points such as Berlin.

This 'Balancing Committee' should publish the suggestions on whatever problems it investigated and seek to rally to the support of these suggestions first neutral opinion and then, if possible, the opinion of Eastern and Western negotiators. The members of the 'Balancing Committee' should command public respect in their several countries but should not be responsible to the national governments of the states from which they come.

The Committee should be small, since, otherwise, it will not reach decisions until they are out of date. It may be hoped that in time the suggestions of the 'Balancing Committee' would acquire moral authority and be difficult for either side to resist.

Statement re: CUBA CRISIS

YOU ARE TO DIE	Not in the course of nature, but within a few weeks, and not you alone, but your family, your friends, and all the inhabitants of Britain, together with many hundreds of millions of innocent people elsewhere.
WHY?	Because rich Americans dislike the Government that Cubans prefer, and have used part of their wealth to spread lies about it.
WHAT CAN YOU DO?	You can go out into the streets and into the market place, proclaiming: 'Do not yield to ferocious and insane murderers. Do not imagine that it is your duty to die when your Prime Minister and the President of the United States tell you to do so. Remember rather your duty to your family, your friends, your country, the world you live in, and that future world which, if you so choose, may be glorious, happy, and free.'
AND REMEMBER:	CONFORMITY MEANS DEATH ONLY PROTEST GIVES A HOPE OF LIFE

BERTRAND RUSSELL
23rd October, 1962

The two following letters concerned with the Sino-Indian Border dispute were not published in Unarmed Victory. *I therefore publish them here.*

Peking, November 24, 1962

The Earl Russell
London

My dear Lord
I have received with honour your letters dated November 16 and 19, 1962 and read with great pleasure your statement welcoming and supporting the

Chinese Government's statement of November 21. I am deeply moved by your good wishes and efforts for a peaceful settlement of the Sino-Indian boundary question and your deep interest in world peace. I am sincerely grateful to you for the profound friendship for the Chinese people and the condemnation of u s occupation of China's territory Taiwan, which you have expressed in your letters.

The Chinese Government issued a statement on October 24, 1962, putting forward three proposals. Unfortunately, they were repeatedly rejected by the Indian Government. In order to reverse the daily aggravating Sino-Indian border situation due to the Indian Government's refusal to enter into negotiations and its continued expansion of the armed border conflict, and in order to demonstrate its great sincerity for stopping the border conflict and settling the Sino-Indian Boundary question peacefully, the Chinese Government issued a statement on November 21, 1962, declaring three measures including the unilateral observation of cease-fire and withdrawal along the entire border by China on its own initiative. Now, I wish to tell you that as from 00:00 hours on November 22 the Chinese frontier guards have ceased fire along the entire Sino-Indian border. I believe that this accords with the desires you expressed in your messages.

You suggested in your letter of November 19: 'All troops to vacate this particular area—that which India has occupied since 1959 and until September 8, 1962, and felt by China to be her own.' I believe you have noted that the Chinese Government has declared in its statement of November 21 that, beginning from December 1, the Chinese frontier guards would withdraw to positions 20 kilometres behind the line of actual control which existed between China and India on November 7, 1959 and would then be far behind their positions prior to September 8, 1962. The Chinese Government hopes that the Indian Government will respond positively to the Chinese Government's November 21 statement and adopt corresponding measures. Once the Indian Government has done so, the Sino-Indian Border will become tranquil and a demilitarized zone 40 kilometres wide can be established between China and India. It goes without saying that administration will continue to be exercised by the administrative authorities of each side existing in the zone on their own side of the line of actual control between China and India.

The Chinese Government hopes that the Indian Government will be willing to change its past attitude and sincerely settle the Sino-Indian Boundary question through friendly negotiations. I hope that you will continue to use your distinguished influence to urge the Indian Government to respond positively to the Chinese Government's November 21 statement and adopt corresponding measures. At the same time, the Chinese Government also hopes that all friendly countries and peace-loving public figures will exert their influence to urge the Indian Government to return to the conference table. These efforts will be great contributions to peace.

Please accept my high regards.

Chou En-Lai

Prime Minister's House
New Delhi
December 4, 1962

CONFIDENTIAL
No. 2155-PMH/62
The Earl Russell
Plas Penrhyn, Penrhyndeudraeth
Merioneth, England

Dear Lord Russell

I must ask for your forgiveness for the delay in answering your letter of the 23rd November and your telegram which came subsequently. You can certainly write to me whenever you so wish, and I shall always welcome your views and advice.

I have given much thought to what you have written. I need not tell you that I am much moved by your passion for peace and it finds an echo in my own heart. Certainly we do not want this frontier war with China to continue, and even more certainly we do not want it to spread and involve the nuclear powers. Also there is the danger of the military mentality spreading in India and the power of the Army increasing.

But there are limits in a democratic society to what a Government can do. There is such strong feeling in India over the invasion by China that no Government can stand if it does not pay some heed to it. The Communist Party of India has been compelled by circumstances to issue a strong condemnation of China. Even so, the Communists here are in a bad way, and their organisation is gradually disappearing because of popular resentment.

Apart from this, there are various other important considerations which have to be borne in mind in coming to a decision. If there is a sense of national surrender and humiliation, this will have a very bad effect on the people of India and all our efforts to build up the nation will suffer a very serious setback. At present the popular upsurge all over India can be utilised for strengthening the unity and capacity for work of the nation, apart from the military aspect. There are obvious dangers about militarism and extreme forms of nationalism developing, but there are also possibilities of the people of our country thinking in a more constructive way and profiting by the dangers that threaten us.

If we go wholly against the popular sentiment, which to a large extent I share, then the result will be just what you fear. Others will take charge and drive the country towards disaster.

The Chinese proposals, as they are, mean their gaining a dominating position, specially in Ladakh, which they can utilise in future for a further attack on India. The present day China, as you know, is probably the only country which is not afraid even of a nuclear war. Mao Tse-tung has said repeatedly that he does not mind losing a few million people as still several hundred millions will survive in China. If they are to profit by this invasion, this will lead them to further attempts of the same kind. That will put an end to all talks of peace and will surely bring about a world nuclear war. I feel, therefore, that in order to avoid this catastrophe and, at the same time, strengthen our own people, quite apart from arms, etc., we must not surrender or submit to what we consider evil. That is a lesson I learned from Gandhiji.

We have, however, not rejected the Chinese proposal, but have ourselves suggested an alternative which is honourable for both parties. I still have hopes that China will agree to this. In any event we are not going to break the cease-fire and indulge in a military offensive.

If these preliminaries are satisfactorily settled, we are prepared to adopt any peaceful methods for the settlement of the frontier problem. These might even include a reference to arbitration.

So far as we are concerned, we hope to adhere to the policy of non-alignment although I confess that taking military help from other countries does somewhat affect it. But in the circumstances we have no choice.

I can assure you that the wider issues that you have mentioned are before us all the time. We do not want to do something which will endanger our planet. I do think, however, that there will be a greater danger of that kind if we surrender to the Chinese and they feel that the policy they have pursued brings them rich dividends.

Yours sincerely
Jawaharlal Nehru

CHAPTER IV

THE FOUNDATION

THE nuclear peril represented a danger which was likely to last as long as governments possessed nuclear weapons, and perhaps even longer if such destructive objects get into private hands. At first I imagined that the task of awakening people to the dangers should not be very difficult. I shared the general belief that the motive of self-preservation is a very powerful one which, when it comes into operation, generally overrides all others. I thought that people would not like the prospect of being fried with their families and their neighbours and every living person that they had heard of. I thought it would only be necessary to make the danger known and that, when this had been done, men of all parties would unite to restore previous safety. I found that this was a mistake. There is a motive which is stronger than self-preservation: it is the desire to get the better of the other fellow. I had discovered an important political fact that is often overlooked, as it had been by me: people do not care so much for their own survival—or, indeed, that of the human race—as for the extermination of their enemies. The world in which we live is one in which there is constant risk of universal death. The methods of putting an end to this risk are obvious to all, but they involve a very tiny chance that someone may play the traitor, and this is so galling that almost everybody prefers running the risk of nuclear war to securing safety. I thought, and I still think, that, if the risk of total destruction were made sufficiently vivid, it would have the desired effect. But how was an individual, or a collection of individuals, to bring about this vividness? In company with those who thought like me, I tried various methods with varying degrees of success. I tried first the method of reason: I compared the danger of nuclear weapons with the danger of the Black Death. Everybody said, 'How true', and did nothing. I tried alerting a particular group, but though this had a limited success, it had little effect on the general public or Governments. I next tried the popular appeal of marches of large numbers. Everybody said, 'These marchers are a nuisance'. Then I tried methods of civil disobedience, but they, too, failed to succeed. All these methods continue to be used, and I support them all when possible, but none has proved more than partially efficacious. I am now engaged in a new attempt which consists of a mixed appeal to Governments and public. So long as I live, I shall continue the search and in all probability I shall leave the work to be continued by others. But whether mankind will think itself worth preserving remains a doubtful question.

For many years I had been interested in the persecuted minorities and those people in many countries who, I thought, had been unjustly imprisoned. I tried to help, for instance, the Naga and Sobell about whom I have already told. A little later, I became concerned with the plight of the Gypsies, being especially interested in the efforts of Guy Puxton to give them a fit abiding place with at least the necessary amenities, such as decent sanitation and opportunity to obtain at least a minimum of proper education.

My scutcheon on the score of liberating prisoners, I confess, is not entirely unsmirched. Many years ago a young German Jewish refugee came to me asking for help. The Home Office had decreed that he was to be returned to Germany and, if he were returned, he would be executed. He seemed a silly young man but harmless enough. I went with him to the Home Office and said, 'Look, do you think that he is dangerous?' 'Well,' they said, 'no.' They agreed not to dispatch him to his homeland but said that he must have a fresh passport. They started at once putting him through the questions to be answered for this purpose. 'Who was your father?' 'I do not know.' 'Who was your mother?' 'I do not know.' 'Where and when were you born?' 'I do not know.' The Officials quailed. The only thing he was sure of was that he was a Jew. Seeing my stubborn and grim, if by this time slightly pink, visage, the officials persisted and gave him his passport. The last thing I heard of him was a message to the effect that to remain in England he knew that he had to pay his way and he had learnt that the surest means of obtaining money was to get an English girl pregnant. He could then apply for and receive a governmental hand-out. I was only slightly reassured by the comment that, up to date, he had failed in this scheme.

Many years ago, too, a young Pole appealed to me for help against imprisonment on the charge of writing obscene verse. I thought, 'A poet gaoled! Never! This cannot be!' And again I appealed to the Home Office. I then read some of his verse and found it so thoroughly disgusting that my sympathies were with the earlier verdict. But he was allowed to stay in England.

Though both these cases are somewhat embarrassing to remember, I cannot regret them. It seems to me nonsense to imprison people for silliness that is unlikely to harm the general public. If it were carried

155

to its logical conclusion, there are few men who would be free. Moreover, to deal with obscenity by means of the law and the threat of imprisonment does more harm than good. It merely adds an aura of delightful and enticing wickedness to what may be only foolish or may be evil. It does nothing to curtail it. I feel even more strongly in the matter of political prisoners and for similar reasons. To gaol a man merely for his political views, however tempting it may be, is more likely to spread than to stop the dissemination of those views. It adds to the sum of human misery and encourages violence, and that is all. In recent years I have become, as I have said, more and more involved in work against the incarceration and the persecution of individuals and groups because of their political and religious opinions. I have received a continually increasing number of written appeals for help from individuals and organizations all over the world and almost daily visits from representatives of the latter. I have been unable to travel to distant countries myself, so, in order to have as nearly as possible first-hand objective information, I have been obliged to send representatives to the various countries.

In 1963, my interests in the resistance fighters in Greece came to a head. They had opposed the Nazis there but were still languishing in prison because most of them had been 'Communists'. A number of their representatives came to see me, among them the Greek M PS who visited England in April and May. A 'Bertrand Russell Committee of 100' had been formed in Greece and they held a march, or tried to hold one, towards the end of April to which I sent a representative. Then came the murder of the M P Lambrakis at Salonika, with, it was fairly clear, the connivance of the Authorities. This deeply shocked me, in common with other liberal-minded people. Again, at request, I sent my representative to the funeral of Lambrakis in Athens. He returned with a very moving story. By the time that the Greek Royal visit to Buckingham Palace took place in July, feeling here had mounted to boiling point. I shared it. I spoke in Trafalgar Square against the visit and took part in a demonstration. The press were shocked at such unseemly doings on the part of Her Majesty's subjects, Cabinet Ministers gobbled, and the police planted bricks in the pockets of arrested demonstrators and charged them with carrying offensive weapons. One of the most persistent and bravest of British demonstrators was Betty Ambatielos whose Greek husband had been held a prisoner for many years. Two years later, he was freed and visited us in London, but others of the prisoners remained in gaol. Later he and, for a time, his wife were re-imprisoned and many more prisoners were thrown into concentration camps by the Greek Authorities. The contemplation of what their lives must be in these camps, herded together in the blazing sunlight, without water, without sanitation, with no care of any sort, is sickening.

That same April, 1963, I sent a representative to Israel to look into the situation of the Palestine Arab refugees. We wished to form some assessment of what, if anything, might most effectively be urged to help to settle matters between Jews and Arabs concerning the question of the Palestine refugees. Since then I have, often at request, sent other representatives to both Israel and Egypt to discuss the separate and the joint problems of those countries. In turn, they have sent their emissaries to me. I was also much concerned, and still am, with the plight of the Jews in the Soviet Union, and I have carried on a considerable and continuing correspondence with the Soviet Government in regard to it. In addition, a very large number of Jewish families in Eastern Europe have been separated by the Second World War and wish to rejoin their relations abroad, usually in Israel. At first I appealed for permission for them to emigrate individually, but later, under the pressure of hundreds of requests, I began to make appeals on behalf of whole groups. As such work developed, I found myself working for the release of political prisoners in over forty countries where they are held, half forgotten, for deeds which were often praiseworthy. Many prisoners in many lands have been freed, we are told, as a result of my colleagues' and my work, but many remain in gaol and the work goes on. Sometimes I have got into difficulty about this work and had to bear considerable obloquy, as in the case of Sobell and, later, in regard to the freeing of Heintz Brandt. The abduction and imprisonment by the East Germans of Brandt, who had survived Hitler's concentration camps, seemed to me so inhuman that I was obliged to return to the East German Government the Carl von Ossietsky medal which it had awarded me. I was impressed by the speed with which Brandt was soon released. And perhaps it was my work for prisoners, in part at any rate, that won me the Tom Paine award bestowed upon me by the American Emergency Civil Liberties Committee in January, 1963.[1]

Through the last years, and especially recently, since I have been able to act in this work as part of an organization, I have sent fact-finding representatives to many parts of the world. They have gone to most European countries, 'East' and 'West', and to many eastern countries—Cambodia, China, Ceylon, India, Indonesia, Japan, Vietnam. They have gone to Africa—Ethiopia and Egypt and the newer countries of both East and West Africa. And, of course, they have gone to countries of the Western Hemisphere, both north and south. These in-

[1] In seeking to liberate prisoners, my colleagues and I made no distinction of party or creed, but only of the justice or injustice of the punishment inflicted and the unnecessary cruelty caused by the imprisonment.

vestigators have been generously welcomed by the Heads of the countries to which they journeyed and by many of the Government officials and heads of organizations dealing with problems in which they are interested. And, naturally, they have talked with members of the general public. I have myself carried on prolonged correspondence with the various Heads of State and officials, and have discussed in London a variety of international problems with them, particularly with those from Eastern Europe and Asia and Africa. The gatherings for the Commonwealth Conference, especially, made possible many of these meetings. Some of them were entertaining and adorned with the proper trappings—flashing eyes, robes, scimitars, jewels and tall, fierce attendants—as was my meeting with the Sheikh of Bahrein in 1965, the memory of which I rejoice in. On special subjects, of course, I am in frequent touch with the Embassies in London.

All this work steadily mounted in demand. By 1963, it was rapidly becoming more than one individual could carry on alone even with the extraordinarily able and willing help that I had. Moreover, the expenses of journeys and correspondence—written, telegraphed and telephoned— and of secretaries and co-workers was becoming more than my private funds could cover. And the weight of responsibility of being an entirely one-man show was heavy. Gradually the scheme took shape, hatched, again, I think, by the fertile mind of Ralph Schoenman, of forming some sort of organization. This should be not just for this or that purpose. It should be for any purpose that would forward the struggle against war and the armaments race, and against the unrest and the injustices suffered by oppressed individuals and peoples that in very large part caused these. Such an organization could grow to meet the widely differing demands. It could, also, reorientate itself as circumstances changed. A good part of my time, therefore, in 1963, was taken up with discussing plans for the formation of such an organization. Many of my colleagues in these discussions had been working with me since the early days of the Committee of 100.

My colleagues were inexperienced in organization and I myself am not at all good at it, but at least we brought our aims into some sort of cohesive progression, and, where we erred, it was on the side of flexibility which would permit of change and growth. We faced the fact that in the early days of the organization our work must be carried on much as it had been, with me bearing most of the public responsibility and holding the position of final arbitrator of it. We hoped to strengthen the organization gradually. We felt that not only the day-to-day work for it, but the responsibility and the planning should, in time, be borne by it as an entity. As I look back upon our progress, it seems to me that we achieved far more than we had dared to hope to do in its first three years.

Many people have worked to build up the Foundation, but I wish to stress not only my own but the Foundation's debt to Ralph Schoenman. He has carried on its work sometimes almost single-handed and many of its most fertile ideas are owing to him. His ingenuity, moreover, and his almost super-human energy and courageous determination have been largely responsible for carrying them out. I should like to record, also, something of both the Foundation's and my debt to another recent friend, Christopher Farley. Without his judgment and thoughtfulness we should be hard put to it to keep on as even a keel as we manage to keep. But he is reticent and unassuming and too often remains in the background. He takes a point quickly, and I thought at first that his occasional hesitation in pronouncing upon it was owing to timidity. I now know that it is owing to his extreme scrupulousness. It was some time before I realized the depth of feeling with which he pursues justice or the compassion and patience with which this pursuit is tempered. I learned only gradually that his obvious knowledge of present-day men and affairs is enriched by wide reading and a very considerable study of the past. The tendency to dogmatism and clap-trap and humbug which this combination might induce in a more superficial mind is burnt away by his intense perception of ironies and absurdity and the liveliness of his many interests. His observations are both sensitive and his own. All this makes him a helpful, interesting and delightful companion.

During the spring and early summer of 1963 we sent out letters over my name to a number of people who we thought might be willing to be sponsors of the new Foundation. By the end of the summer nine of these had agreed. With such backing, we felt ready to make our plans public, especially as there was reason to expect others to join us soon. And, in fact, soon after the establishment of the Foundation was announced, seven others did join.

We knew our aims—chief of which was to form a really international organization—and the long term means towards them that we must strive to achieve, and the outlines of work that we must carry on, work such as we had been carrying on for some time. We also recognized the fact that the attainment of our purposes necessitated vast sums of money. Rather against my will my colleagues urged that the Foundation should bear my name. I knew that this would prejudice against the Foundation many people who might uphold our work itself. It would certainly prejudice well-established and respectable organizations and, certainly, a great number of individuals in Britain, particularly those who were in a position to support us financially. But my colleagues contended that, as I had been carrying on the work for years, helped by them during the last few years, and my name was identified with it in many parts of the world, to omit my name would mean a set-back for the work. I was pleased by their determination, though still somewhat dubious of its wisdom. But in the end I agreed. When, however, we decided to seek charitable status for our organization, it became evident to my friends as well as to myself that it would be impossible to obtain it in Great Britain for any organization bearing my name.

Finally, our solicitors suggested that we compromise by forming two Foundations: The Bertrand Russell Peace Foundation and the Atlantic Peace Foundation, for the second of which we obtained charitable status. These two Foundations were to work, and do work, in co-operation, but the latter's objects are purely educational. Its purpose is to establish research in the various areas concerned in the study of war and peace and the creation of opportunities for research and the publication of its results. As the Charity Commission registered this Foundation as a charity, income tax at the standard rate is recoverable on any subscription given under a seven-year covenant, which, in turn, means that such subscriptions are increased by about sixty per cent.

The Bertrand Russell Peace Foundation was to deal with the more immediately political and controversial side of the work, and contributions to it, whether large or small, are given as ordinary gifts. During its first three years of existence many thousands of pounds have been contributed to it, some from individuals, some from organizations, some from Governments. No contribution with strings tied to it is accepted. Particularly in the case of Government contributions, it is made clear to the donors that the source of the money will not in any way prejudice the methods or results of its expenditure.

Unfortunately, I fell very ill at the beginning of September when we had decided to make our plans public, but by the end of the month, on September 29, 1963, we were able to release them. After I had made a vehement statement, we gave the press men the leaflet that my colleagues had prepared about each Foundation. That concerning the Bertrand Russell Peace Foundation gave a list of the then sponsors, and a letter that U Thant had written for the purpose on the outside. I had talked with him about our plans among other things and written to him about them. He had been warmly sympathetic, but explained that he could not be a sponsor because of his position as Secretary-General of the United Nations. He offered, however, to write the carefully worded but encouraging letter which we printed.

Reading a list of our ambitious projects, the journalists asked whence we proposed to obtain the funds. It was a pertinent question and not unexpected. Since we had not wished to divulge our plans till September 29th, we had been unable to campaign for funds. Our answer could only be that we were determined to raise the necessary funds and were sure that we could, in time, do so—a reply naturally received with acid scepticism.

Looking back upon the occasion, I cannot say that I blame the assembled pressmen for their attitude, nor the press in general for the anything but encouraging start that was given us. Anyone who is willing to back his vision of the future by action should be prepared to be thought a 'crack-pot', and we were prepared. Moreover, we were elated. It was a kind of freedom to be able to work again publicly towards the ends that we had in view. And, of course, our first efforts were towards obtaining funds to carry on with.

We approached an endless number of individuals; with singularly little success among the rich: 'Oh yes', they said more often than not, 'we think that you are doing a wonderful work. We entirely believe in it and wish it success. But, of course, we already have so many commitments . . . .' Though all such financial begging is always awkward and distasteful, we only occasionally met with unpleasantness and only once with virulent discourtesy. This was at a party of rich Jews given in order that I might speak of our work for the Jews in Soviet countries in whom they professed themselves mightily interested. The unpleasant occasions were unexpected since they occurred when, upon apparently knowledgeable advice, we approached people who had expressed themselves passionately interested in the special project about which we approached them and to be friendly towards us, to 'greatly admire' me and my work as it was always put. We received many surprises, both pleasant and exasperating: one morning a message came that two people were leaving in their wills their very considerable estate on the continent to the Foundation; another morning came a letter from Lord Gladwyn, a former British Ambassador in Paris, that I append to this chapter along with my reply, as it gives the tone and reasoning of part of the huge correspondence that building up the Foundation had entailed. I believe that this exchange of letters, in spite of Lord Gladwyn's suggestion, has not before been published. In his letter, it will be noted, he advocated my advancing my proposals in the House of Lords 'where they could be subjected to intelligent scrutiny'. I refrained, in my reply, from remarking that on the occasions when I had advanced proposals in the House of Lords, I had never perceived that my audience, with a few exceptions, showed any peculiar degree of intelligence—but perhaps the general level has risen since the advent of Lord Gladwyn.

However, many people in many parts of the world helped us. Artists —painters and sculptors and musicians—of different countries have been especially generous. Indeed, one of our first money-raising ventures was an art sale of their paintings and sculpture given by the artists, which took place, through the kindness of the Duke of Bedford, at Woburn Abbey. I could not attend the opening of the sale, but I went some time later, arriving, to my amusement, on the same day that the Miss World beauties were being entertained at Woburn and I was privileged to meet them. The sale was fairly successful and we have since then been given other works of art and sold them to the great profit of our work. Though musicians were generous to us, their generosity was more often then not, thwarted by their agents or impresarios and the managers of concert halls. Actors and playwrights made us many promises of benefit performances or special plays of one sort or another, but nothing came of them. We had better fortune with the Heads of Governments, perhaps because they were better able to understand what we were doing. One of the difficulties in our begging was that much of our work—that concerning special prisoners or broken families and minority groups, for instance—could not be talked of until it was accomplished, if then, or it would be automatically rendered ineffective. The same was even more true of discussions and schemes concerning international adjustments. When asked, therefore, precisely what we had to show for our work, we had to speak chiefly in vague and general terms, which carried conviction only to the astute and the already converted.

The drawback to this more or less haphazard gathering of money was that it was impossible to be sure what monies we should have when. No huge sum came in at one time which could be used as a back-log, and promises were not always kept promptly. The result was that we sometimes had enough to go ahead with fairly ambitious schemes, but sometimes we had next door to nothing. The latter periods would have been impossible to weather had it not been for the dedication to the idea and ideas of the Foundation and the dogged determination of the people working with me, especially of Ralph Schoenman and Christopher Farley and Pamela Wood. These three in their different ways held the work together and pulled it through bad as well as good times. Many others from many different countries aided our work, some as volunteers and some on the payroll, but, for one good reason or another, until the present time, they have proved to be transient workers and sometimes too dearly paid for. Now, however, a staff of colleagues has been built up that appears stable and quite capable of dealing, each with one or more of the various aspects of the work.

For the most part the British press has done very little to help us. They have treated us with silence or, if they can find something to make us look ridiculous or wicked, with covert jeers. Perhaps this is not astonishing, since we have been working, though quite legally, against our country's established policies—not those which Mr Harold Wilson's

Government promised before it came to office both for the first and second time, but against the policies which it has adopted in office, For the same reason at different times the press of other countries have railed at us or refused to mention us. And, of course, journalists and commentators are apt to deal with me personally by saying that I am senile. The journalists in the United States, especially do this since for years I have been worrying over the increase of violence in that country and most of my recent writing has been very vehemently against their Government's warlike policies. This method of diminishing my effectiveness alarms and angers my friends and affronts me, but, from the point of those who differ with me, I dare say it is about their only retort. In any case, if the charge is true, I fail to see why anyone troubles to remark on my babblings.

Those who wish to make up their own minds as to whether or not I am senile or, even, sillier than they had formerly believed me to be, have been given ample opportunity to do so as I have given countless newspaper and TV interviews and made several films. The general rule to which I adhere in determining to which requests for interviews to accede to is to refuse all those that show signs of being concerned with details of what is known as my 'private life' rather than my work and ideas. The latter, I am glad to have publicized, and I welcome honest reports and criticisms of them. The best of these TV interviews that I have seen during the last years seemed to me to be one in early October, 1963, with John Freeman; one made in early April, 1964, in which Robert Bolt was the interlocutor (there is also a later one, made in 1967, with him, but I have not seen it); and one made in September, 1965, with Ralph Milliband. But many, of course, I have never seen. The two most important public speeches that I have made have been those concerned with the perfidy of the Labour Government under the premiership of Harold Wilson, one in mid-February 1965, and one eight months later. The first deals with the general international policies of the Government, the second dwells upon its policies in regard, especially, to Vietnam and is, therefore, reprinted in my book *War Crimes in Vietnam*. At the end of the second, I announced my resignation from the Party and tore up my Labour card. To my surprise, this intensely annoyed two of the other speakers on the platform, a Member of Parliament and the Chairman of the CND. The latter remarked to the press that I had stage-managed the affair. If I had been able to do so, I do not know why I should not have done so, but, in actual fact, all the management was in the hands of the Youth CND under whose auspices the meeting was held. The MP, who had often expressed views similar to mine on Vietnam, arrived late at the meeting and stalked out because of my action. I was rather taken aback by this singular behaviour as both these people had been saying much what I said. The only difference seemed to be that they continued in membership of the Party they denounced.

There are four other charges brought against me which I might mention here since I suppose they are connected, also, with 'The folly of age'. The most serious is that I make extreme statements in my writings and speeches for which I do not give my sources. This is levelled, I believe, against my book *War Crimes in Vietnam*. If anyone cares to study this book, however, I think that they will find it well documented. If I occasionally make a statement without giving the basis of it, I usually do so because I regard it as self-evident or based upon facts noted elsewhere in the book or so well known that there is no need to name the source.

Another charge, allied to this one, is that I myself compose neither speeches nor articles nor statements put out over my name. It is a curious thing that the public utterances of almost all Government officials and important business executives are known to be composed by secretaries or colleagues, and yet this is held unobjectionable. Why should it be considered heinous in an ordinary layman? In point of fact, what goes out over my name is usually composed by me. When it is not, it still presents my opinion and thought. I sign nothing—letters or more formal documents—that I have not discussed, read and approved.

Two other rumours which I have learned recently are being put about, I also find vexatious. They are that letters and documents sent to me are withheld by my secretaries lest they trouble me, and that my secretaries and colleagues prevent people who wish to see me from doing so. But I myself open and read all that is addressed to me at home. My mail, however, is so large that I cannot reply to everything, though I indicate to my secretary what I wish said and read the replies drafted by my secretary before they are sent. Again, it is the number of people who wish to see me about this or that which makes it impossible to see them all. During a week, for instance, that I spent in London towards the end of 1966 in order to open the preparatory meetings of the War Crimes Tribunal, I received visits each day, morning, afternoon and evening, from people wishing to talk with me. But, as well over one hundred people asked to talk with me during this week, many, over a hundred, had to be refused.

I have remarked upon these charges at such length not only because I dislike being thought to be silly, but because it exasperates me to have my arguments and statements flouted, unread or unlistened to, on such grounds. I also dislike my colleagues coming under fire for doing, most generously, what I have asked them to do.

Less than two months after the Foundation was established I, in common with the rest of the world, was shocked by the news of the murder of President Kennedy. Perhaps I was less surprised by this vicious attack than many people were because for a number of years I had been writing about the growing acceptance of unbridled violence in the world and particularly in the United States. Some of my articles on this subject were published, but some were too outspoken for the editors of the publications that had commissioned them.

As I read the press reports in regard to the President's assassination and, later, the purported evidence against Oswald and his shooting by Ruby, it seemed to me that there had been an appalling miscarriage of justice and that probably something very nasty was being covered up. When in June, 1963, I met Mark Lane, the New York lawyer who, originally, had been looking into the affair on behalf of Oswald's mother, my suspicions were confirmed by the facts which he had already gathered. Everyone connected with the Foundation agreed with my point of view, and we did everything that we could, individually and together, to help Mark Lane and to spread the knowledge of his findings. It was quite clear from the hushing-up methods employed and the facts that were denied or passed over that very important issues were at stake. I was greatly impressed, not only by the energy and astuteness with which Mark Lane pursued the relevant facts, but by the scrupulous objectivity with which he presented them, never inferring or implying meanings not inherent in the facts themselves.

We thought it better if the Foundation itself were not involved in supporting those who were ferreting out the facts of the matter and propagating knowledge of them. We therefore started an autonomous committee with the unsatisfactory name of 'The British Who Killed Kennedy? Committee'. We got together a fair number of sponsors and even a secretary, but not without difficulty, since many people thought the affair none of our British business. A few understood what skul-duggery on the part of American Authorities might portend, not only for the inhabitants of the United States, but for the rest of the world as well. Those few had a hard time. We were well and truly vilified. A threatening telephone call from the United States Embassy was received by one of our number. Committees similar to ours were set up in some other countries and some of their officers received similar warnings. Finally, the Foundation had to take our Committee under its wing, and its members toiled both night and day in consequence of this extra work. By August, when I wrote an article called '16 Questions on the Assassination', meetings were being held, and other statements and articles were being issued. Feeling ran high. Mark Lane himself travelled about this country as well as about others, including his own, recounting the facts that he was unearthing which refuted the official and generally accepted pronouncements concerning the matter. I was sent the Warren Commission's Report before it was published in September, 1965, and at once said, to the apparent annoyance of many people, what I thought of it. Word went about that I was talking through my hat and had not even read the report, and could not have done so. In point of fact, Lane had sent me an early copy which I had read and had time to consider. Now that the Warren Commission Report has been examined minutely and it is 'respectable' to criticize it, many people agree with me and have blandly forgotten both their and my earlier attitudes. At the time, they were too timid to listen to or to follow the facts as they appeared, accepting blindly the official view of them. They did all that they could to frustrate our efforts to make them known.

Since shortly before April, 1963, more and more of my time and thought has been absorbed by the war being waged in Vietnam. My other interests have had to go by the board for the most part. Some of my time, of course, is spent on family and private affairs. And once in a blue moon I have a chance to give my mind to the sort of thing I used to be interested in, philosophical or, especially, logical problems. But I am rusty in such work and rather shy of it. In 1965, a young mathematician, G. Spencer Brown, pressed me to go over his work since, he said, he could find no one else who he thought could understand it. As I thought well of what little of his work I had previously seen, and since I feel great sympathy for those who are trying to gain attention for their fresh and unknown work against the odds of established indifference, I agreed to discuss it with him. But as the time drew near for his arrival, I became convinced that I should be quite unable to cope with it and with his new system of notation. I was filled with dread. But when he came and I heard his explanations, I found that I could get into step again and follow his work. I greatly enjoyed those few days, especially as his work was both original and, it seemed to me, excellent.

One of the keenest pleasures of these years has been my friendship, a friendship in which my wife shared, with Victor Purcell, and one of the losses over which I most grieve is his death in January, 1965. He was a man of humour and balanced judgment. He had both literary appreciation and attainment, and very considerable learning as well as great knowledge of the present day scene. He had achieved much both as a Government administrator in South East Asia and as a Don at Cambridge. His talk was a delight to me. For many years I had known him through his political writings which he used to send to me from time to time and about which I would write to him. A little later I rejoiced in his witty verses written under the pseudonym of Myra Buttle (a pun for My Rebuttal). I had never met him till he spoke at the birthday party given for me at the Festival Hall in 1962. I did not even begin to know him till he was drawn into discussions with us about the Foundation's doings in relation to South East Asia. He spoke at a meeting at Manchester in April, 1964, under the auspices of the Foundation at which I spoke also, and, soon afterwards, he did an admirable pamphlet for us surveying 'The Possibility of Peace in South East Asia'. During this time we saw something of him in London, but it was not until May, 1964, that we really came to know each other when he paid us a short visit in North Wales. We talked endlessly. We capped each other's stories and quotations, and recited our favourite poems and prose to each other. We probed each other's knowledge especially of history, and discussed serious problems. Moreover, it was a comfort to find someone who understood at once what one was driving at and, even when not entirely in agreement, was willing to discuss whatever the subject might be with tolerance and sympathy. He came again to visit us in December, little more than a fortnight before his death, and suddenly we felt, as he said, that we were old friends, though we had seen each other so little. I remember, especially, about this last visit, his suddenly bursting into a recitation of *Lycidas*, most beautifully given, and again, reading his latest work by Myra Buttle, singing those lines parodied from song. He was a brave and thoughtful, a compassionate and boisterous man. It startles me sometimes when I realize how much I miss him, not only for the enjoyment but for the help that he could and, I feel sure, would have given me. It is seldom, I think, that one of my age makes a new friend so satisfying and so treasured, and astonishing that all this affection and trust and under-standing should have grown up in so short a time.

My book on the situation in Vietnam and its implications, called *War Crimes in Vietnam*, appeared early in January 1967, in both cloth and paper editions. It was published in Britain by Allen and Unwin, to whose generosity and liberal attitude, in the person of Sir Stanley Unwin especially, I have owed much ever since the First World War. The book is comprised of a few of the innumerable letters, statements, speeches and articles delivered by me since 1963. To these are added an Introduction giving the general background of the situation at the beginning of 1967 and of my own attitude to it; a Postscript describing briefly the War Crimes Tribunal for which I had called; and an appendix containing some of the findings of Ralph Schoenman during one of his visits of many weeks to Vietnam. *War Crimes in Vietnam* is so thorough an account of my attitude towards the war and the facts upon which I base it, and, in any case, I have published and broadcast so much on them during the past few years, that I shall not go into them here. The book was reviewed with considerable hostility in some journals, so it was a pleasure to learn that the paperback edition was sold out within a fortnight of its publication and that the book has been published in the United States and translated and published in many languages throughout the world.

Schoenman's reports were of extreme importance since they contain not only first-hand observation but verbatim accounts given by victims of the war attested to both by the victims themselves and by the reliable witnesses present at the time the accounts were given. The reports also paved the way for the more formal investigations conducted in Indo-China by teams sent by the International War Crimes Tribunal. It was in part upon such reports as Schoenman's and of those of Christopher Farley who, in November, 1964, was the first member of the Foundation to go to Vietnam to obtain first-hand impressions, that I base my attitude and statements in regard to the Vietnam war, as well as upon reports of other special investigators. Chiefly, however, I base my opinions upon the facts reported in the daily newspapers, especially those of the United States. These reports seem to have been published almost by chance since they appear not to have affected editorial policy.

Occasionally I have been invited by the North Vietnamese to give my opinion about various developments in the war. They asked my advice as to the desirability of permitting Mr Harrison Salisbury, Assistant Managing Editor of the *New York Times*, to visit Hanoi as a journalist. Mr Salisbury had previously attacked me in his introduction to the Warren Commission's Report, in which he wrote of the Commission's 'exhaustive examination of every particle of evidence it could discover'. These comments were soon seen to be ridiculous, but I suspected that he would have great difficulty in ignoring the evidence of widespread bombardment of civilians in North Vietnam. I recommended that his visit was a risk worth taking, and was pleased to read, some weeks later, his reports from Hanoi, which caused consternation in Washington and probably lost him a Pulitzer Prize.

I have been, of course, in close touch with the two representatives of North Vietnam who are in London and with the North Vietnamese Chargé d'Affaires in Paris. I have corresponded with various members of the South Vietnam National Liberation Front and with members of the United States armed forces as well as with American civilians, both those who support and those who oppose the war. There is no lack of information if one wishes to have it. But there is great difficulty in making it known to the general public and in persuading people to pay attention to it. It is not pleasant reading or hearing.

The more I and my colleagues studied the situation, the more persuaded we became that the United States' attitude on Vietnam was wholly indefensible and that the war was being conducted with unprecedented cruelty by means of new methods of torture. We concluded, after careful examination of the great body of facts that we had amassed, that the war must be ended quickly and that the only way to end it was to support the North Vietnamese and the Liberation Front unequivocally. Moreover, we feared that so long as the war continued it would be used by America as an excuse for escalation which was likely to end in a general conflagration. We set up the Vietnam Solidarity Campaign, which brought together those groups which saw the Vietnam war as flagrant aggression by the world's mightiest nation against a small peasant people. Supporters of the Campaign held that justice demanded that they support the Vietnamese entirely. I delivered the opening address to the founding of the Solidarity Campaign in June 1966, and this was later published in my book on Vietnam. The Campaign sent speakers all over the country, together with the Foundation's photographic exhibition on the war, and formed a nucleus of support in Britain for the International War Crimes Tribunal.

The Tribunal, of which my Vietnam book told, caught the imagination of a wide public the world over. For four years I had been searching for some effective means to help make known to the world the unbelievable cruelty of the United States in its unjust attempt to subjugate South Vietnam. At the time of the Korean War I had been unable to believe in the allegations brought by Professor Joseph Needham and others charging the Americans with having used that war as a proving-ground for new biological and chemical weapons of mass destruction. I owe Professor Needham and the others my sincere apologies for thinking these charges too extreme. By 1963, I had become convinced of the justice of these allegations since it was clear that similar ones must be brought against the United States in Vietnam. Early in that year, I wrote to the *New York Times* describing American conduct in Vietnam as barbarism 'reminiscent of warfare as practised by the Germans in Eastern Europe and the Japanese in South-East Asia.' At the time this seemed too strong for the *New York Times*, which first attacked me editorially, then cut my reply and finally denied me any access to its letters columns. I tried other publications and determined to find out more about what was at that time a 'secret war'. The more I discovered, the more appalling American intentions and practice appeared. I learned not only of barbaric practices, but also of the most cynical and ruthless suppression of a small nation's desire for independence. The destruction of the Geneva Agreements, the support of a dictatorship, the establishment of a police state, and the destruction of all its opponents were intolerable crimes. The following year I

169

started sending observers regularly to Indo-China, but their reports were continually overtaken by the enlargement of the war. The pretexts for the 'escalation', particularly the attack upon North Vietnam, reminded me of nothing less than those offered a quarter of a century earlier for Hitler's adventures in Europe. It became clear to me that the combination of aggression, experimental weapons, indiscriminate warfare and concentration camp programmes required a more thorough and formal investigation than I was able to manage.

In the summer of 1966, after extensive study and planning, I wrote to a number of people around the world, inviting them to join an International War Crimes Tribunal. The response heartened me, and soon I had received about eighteen acceptances. I was especially pleased to be joined by Jean-Paul Sartre, for despite our differences on philosophical questions I much admired his courage. Vladimir Dedijer, the Yugoslav writer, had visited me earlier in Wales, and through his wide knowledge of both the Western and Communist worlds proved a valuable ally. I also came to rely heavily on Isaac Deutscher, the essayist and political writer, whom I had not seen for ten years. Whenever there were too many requests for television and other interviews about the Tribunal, I could rely on Deutscher in London to meet the press and give an informed and convincing assessment of world affairs and of our own work. I invited all the members to London for preliminary discussions in November, 1966, and opened the proceedings with a speech to be found at the end of this chapter. It seemed to me essential that what was happening in Vietnam should be examined with scrupulous care, and I had invited only people whose integrity was beyond question. The meeting was highly successful, and we arranged to hold the public sessions of the Tribunal over many weeks in the following year, after first sending a series of international teams to Indo-China on behalf of the Tribunal itself.

When the Tribunal first proposed to send a selection of its members to investigate atrocities, the proposal was ridiculed on the ground that there were no atrocities on the American side. When this contention was shown up, it was said that American military authorities would deal with this. When this was shown up, it was said that eminent legal authorities made themselves a laughing-stock by undertaking such work. Far better, it was argued, to let the atrocities go unpunished. The Press, the military authorities, and many of the American and British legal luminaries, consider that their honour and humanity will be better served by allowing their officers to burn women and children to death than by adopting the standards applied in the Nuremberg Trials. This comes of accepting Hitler's legacy.

When our opponents saw the seriousness of what we were preparing, there was the sort of outcry to which, over the years, I have become accustomed. Three African Heads of State who had sponsored the Foundation resigned, and it was not difficult to discover the hand behind their defection. One of them even sent me a photostat of a letter which I had sent about the Tribunal to President Johnson at the White House, a piece of clumsiness which even the Central Intelligence Agency must have deplored. The next move was for various journalists to question the impartiality of our Tribunal. It amused me considerably that many of these same critics had shortly before this been among the staunchest supporters of the Warren Commission on the Assassination of President Kennedy.[1] Their new-found interest in impartiality did, however, give us the opportunity to explain our own position. Clearly, we had all given considerable thought to some of the evidence we were about to assess. Our minds were not empty, but neither were they closed. I believed that the integrity of the members of the Tribunal, the fact that they represented no state power and the complete openness of the hearings would ensure the objectivity of the proceedings. We also decided to accept possible evidence from any source, so I wrote to President Johnson inviting him to attend the Tribunal. Unfortunately, he was too busy planning the bombardment of the Vietnamese to reply.

All this stir concerning the Tribunal naturally caused fresh interest in the Foundation itself. The Atlantic Peace Foundation remained a registered charity; the Bertrand Russell Peace Foundation became a company limited by guarantee, and has branches in several countries: Argentina, Australia and New Zealand, France, India, Italy, Japan, the Philippines, and the United States. In London it not only retained the small central offices off the Haymarket, which it had from its inception, but it provided a larger office for the War Crimes Tribunal. It also bought a larger freehold property into which much of the work has been transferred. All this placed the work on a firmer footing and prepared the way for further developments. For perhaps the first time, I was conscious of activity, centred on the Tribunal, involving world-wide support.

In the late 'forties and early 'fifties, I had been profoundly impressed by the horror of Stalin's dictatorship, which had led me to believe that there would be no easy resolution of the cold war. I later came to see that for all his ruthlessness, Stalin had been very conservative. I had assumed, like most people in the West, that his tyranny was expansionist, but later evidence made it clear that it was the West that had given him Eastern Europe as part of the spoils of the Second World War, and that, for the most part, he had kept his agreements with the

---

[1] Prominent members of that Commission had been the former director of the C.I.A. and an associate of the F.B.I.

West. After his death, I earnestly hoped that the world would come to see the folly and danger of living permanently in the shadow of nuclear weapons. If the contenders for world supremacy could be kept apart, perhaps the neutral nations could introduce the voice of reason into international affairs. It was a small hope, for I overestimated the power of the neutrals. Only rarely, as with Nehru in Korea, did they manage to add significant weight to pressures against the cold war.

The neutrals continued to embody my outlook, in that I consider human survival more important than ideology. But a new danger came to the fore. It became obvious that Russia no longer entertained hope of world-empire, but that this hope had now passed over to the United States. As my researches into the origins and circumstances of the war in Vietnam showed, the United States was embarking upon military adventures which increasingly replaced war with Russia as the chief threat to the world. The fanaticism of America's anti-communism, combined with its constant search for markets and raw materials, made it impossible for any serious neutral to regard America and Russia as equally dangerous to the world. The essential unity of American military, economic and cold war policies was increasingly revealed by the sordidness and cruelty of the Vietnam war. For people in the West, this was most difficult to admit, and again I experienced the silence or opposition of those who had come to accept my views of the previous decade. In the third world, however, our support was very considerable. Cruelty has not gone wholly unchallenged.

My views on the future are best expressed by Shelley in the following poem:

> Oh, cease! must hate and death return?
>   Cease! must men kill and die?
> Cease! drain not to its dregs the urn
>   Of bitter prophecy.
> The world is weary of the past,
> Oh, might it die or rest at last!

(478. 1096–1101)

LETTERS

On 'The Free Man's Worship'

27 July 1962

Dear Professor Hiltz

Thank you for your letter of June 27. As regards your 3 questions: (1) I have continued to think 'The Free Man's Worship' 'florid and rhetorical' since somewhere about 1920; (2) This observation concerns only the style; (3) I do not now regard ethical values as objective, as I did when I wrote the essays. However, my outlook on the cosmos and on human life is substantially unchanged.

Yours sincerely
Bertrand Russell

Thanks to Julian Huxley for his pamphlets: 'Psychometabolism'; 'Eugenics in Evolutionary Perspective'; 'Education and the Humanist Revolution'.

Plas Penrhyn
10 March, 1963

My Dear Julian

Thank you very much for sending me your three papers which I have read with very great interest. I loved your paper about psycho-metabolism, explaining why peacocks dance and women use lipstick, both of which had hitherto been mysterious to me. I do not know enough about the matters of which this paper treats to be able to offer any criticism. You touch occasionally on the mind-body problem as to which I have very definite views which are acceptable to some physiologists but are rejected with scorn and contempt by practically all philosophers, none of whom know either physics or physiology. You might find it worth your while to read a short essay of mine called 'Mind and Matter' in *Portraits from Memory*.

What you say about eugenics has my approval up to a certain point, but no further. You seem to think that governments will be enlightened and that the kind of human being they will wish to produce will be an improvement on the haphazard work of nature. If a sperm-bank, such as you envisage, had existed during the régime of Hitler, Hitler would have been the sire of all babies born in his time in Germany. Exceptional merit is, and always has been, disliked by Authority; and obviously Authority would control the sperm-bank. Consequently, in the degree to which eugenics was efficient, exceptional merit would disappear. I am entirely with you as to what eugenics *could* achieve, but I disagree as to what it would achieve.

I have somewhat similar criticisms to make on what you say about education. For example: you dismiss silly myths which make up orthodox religion, and you do not mention that throughout the Western world nobody who openly rejects them can be a schoolmaster. To take another point: education has enormously facilitated total war. Owing to the fact that people can read, while educators have been at pains to prevent them from thinking, warlike ferocity is now much more easily spread than it was in former times.

You seem to think that governments will be composed of wise and enlightened persons who will have standards of value not unlike yours and mine. This is against all the evidence. Pythagoras was an exile because Policrates disliked him; Socrates was put to death; Aristotle had to fly from Athens as soon as Alexander died. In ancient Greece it was not hard to escape from

Greece. In the modern world it is much more difficult; and that is one reason why there are fewer great men than there were in Greece.

Best wishes to both of you from both of us.

Yrs. ever
B. R.

From Sir Julian Huxley

31, Pond Street
Hampstead, N.W.3
13th March, 1963

Dear Bertie

So many thanks for your fascinating letter. I can hear you chuckling about peacocks and lipstick!

As regards the mind-body problem, I think it must be approached from the evolutionary angle. We are all of us living 'mind-body' organisations, with a long history behind us, and related to all other living organisations. To me this implies that mind and body in some way constitute a single unity.

Of course you are right as to the dangers inherent in eugenic measures or approved educational measures. On the other hand, one must do *something*! My attitude is neither purely optimistic nor purely pessimistic—it is that we and our present situation are far from perfect, but are capable of improvement, and indeed are liable to deteriorate unless something is done. This is to me the real point—that something must be done, though of course we must try to see that it is, in principle, the right thing, and also must try to safeguard it as far as possible from abuse.

Again, we must have an educational system of sorts—& I should have thought we ought to try to improve it, in spite of possible dangers—

Juliette sends her best wishes,

Yours ever
Julian H.

To and from Alice Mary Hilton

Plas Penrhyn
9 June, 1963

Dear Miss Hilton

My warm thanks for your book on *Logic, Computing Machines and Automation*. I have, so far, only had time to read parts of it, but what I have read has interested me very much. In particular, I am grateful for the nice things you say about *Principia Mathematica* and about me. The followers of Gödel had almost persuaded me that the twenty man-years spent on the *Principia* had been wasted and that the book had better been forgotten. It is a comfort to find that you do not take this view.

Yours sincerely
Bertrand Russell

174

405 East 63rd Street
New York 21, New York
July 2, 1963

Dear Lord Russell

Thank you very much for your kind letter about my book on *Logic, Computing Machines and Automation*. It was very thoughtful of you to write to me and I can hardly express my appreciation for your interest and your kindness. Although I am aware of the fact that it doesn't matter very much what I think of *Principia Mathematica*, I am convinced that future generations of mathematicians will rate it one of the two or three major contributions to science. I have the feeling that the criticism stems from a lack of understanding rather than anything else. I cannot claim that I understand this tremendous work fully but I have been trying for several years now to learn enough so that I can at least understand basic principles. I am quite certain no great mathematician (which I am certainly not) could possibly have read the *Principia* and think that 'the twenty man-years spent on the *Principia* had been wasted and that the book had better be forgotten.' I am quite certain that it won't be forgotten as long as there is any civilization that preserves the work of really great minds.

I mentioned to you in the past that I am planning to edit a series which is tentatively called *The Age of Cyberculture* and which is to include books by thinkers—scientists, philosophers, artists—who have a contribution to make to the understanding of this era we are entering. It seems to me that humanity has never been in so critical a period. Not only do we live in constant danger of annihilation, but even if we do survive the danger of nuclear extinction, we are standing on the threshold of an age which can become a paradise or hell for humanity. I am enclosing a very brief outline of the series. Because I believe so strongly that understanding and communication among the educated and thinking human beings of this world are so important I am presuming to ask you to write a contribution to this series. I am going further than that. I would like to ask you to serve on the editorial board. I know that you are a very busy man, and I am not asking this lightly. But I also know that you make your voice heard and I believe very strongly that this series will make a contribution and possibly have considerable impact to further the understanding among people whose work is in different disciplines and who must cooperate and learn to understand one another. It is through the contributors and the readers of this series that I hope that some impact will be made upon the political decision makers of this society and through them upon all of us who must realize our responsibility for choosing the right decision makers.

It would give me personally the greatest pleasure to be allowed to work with the greatest mind of this—and many other—century.

I would like you to know that your recording has just become available in this country ('Speaking Personally, Bertrand Russell') and that we have listened to it with great enjoyment and have spent several happy and most wonderful evenings in the company of friends listening to your words.

Thank you again for all of your kindness.

Sincerely
Alice Mary Hilton

To John Paulos

2nd August, 1966

Dear Mr Paulos

Thank you very much for your letter.

My reason for rejecting Hegel and monism in general is my belief that the dialectical argument against relations is wholly unsound. I think such a statement as 'A is west of B' can be exactly true. You will find that Bradley's arguments on this subject pre-suppose that every proposition must be of the subject-predicate form. I think this the fundamental error of monism.

With best wishes,

Yours sincerely
Bertrand Russell

To Marquesa Origo

19 January, 1966

Dear Marquesa

I have been reading your book on Leopardi with very great interest. Although I have long been an admirer of his poetry, I knew nothing of his life until I read your book. His life is appallingly tragic and most of the tragedy was due to bad institutions.

I cannot agree with Santayana's remark; 'The misfortunes of Leopardi were doubtless fortunate for his genius.' I believe that in happier circumstances he would have produced much more.

I do not know Italian at all well and have read most of his poetry in Italian; as a result I have probably missed much by doing so. I am grateful to your book for filling many gaps in my knowledge.

Yours sincerely
Bertrand Russell

To Mr Hayes

25.11.1963

Dear Mr Hayes

Thank you for your letter of November 18. The idea which has been put about to the effect that I am more anti-American than anti-Russian is one of ignorant hostile propaganda. It is true that I have criticised American behaviour in Vietnam, but I have, at the same time, been vehemently protesting against the treatment of Soviet Jews. When the Russians resumed Tests I first wrote to the Soviet Embassy to express a vehement protest & then organized hostile demonstrations against the Soviet Government. I have described the East German Government as a 'military tyranny imposed by alien armed force.' I have written articles in Soviet journals expressing complete impartiality. The only matter in which I have been more favourable to Russia than to America was the Cuban crisis because Khrushchev yielded rather than embark upon a nuclear war. In any crisis involving the danger of nuclear war, if one side yielded & the other did not, I should think the side that yielded more deserving of praise than the other side, because I think nuclear war the greatest misfortune that could befall the human race.

In view of your letter, I am afraid I cannot write an article that would be acceptable to you as I have always expressed in print my criticisms of Russia as often & as emphatically as my criticisms of the West.

Yours sincerely
Bertrand Russell

From Arnold Toynbee

At 273 Santa Teresa
Stanford, Calif. 94305
United States
9 May, 1967

Dear Lord Russell

Your ninety-fifth birthday gives me, like countless other friends of yours who will also be writing to you at this moment, a welcome opportunity of expressing some of the feelings that I have for you all the time: first of all, my affection for you and Edith (I cannot think of either of you without thinking of you both together), and then my admiration and my gratitude.

I met you first, more than half a century ago, just after you had responded to the almost superhuman demand that Plato makes on his fellow philosophers. You had then stepped back out of the sunshine into the cave, to help your fellow human beings who were still prisoners there. You had just come out of prison in the literal sense (and this not for the last time). You had been put in prison, that first time, for having spoken in public against conscription.

It would have been possible for you to continue to devote yourself exclusively to creative intellectual work, in which you had already made your name by achievements of the highest distinction—work which, as we know, gives you intense intellectual pleasure, and which at the same time benefits the human race by increasing our knowledge and understanding of the strange universe in which we find ourselves. You could then have led a fairly quiet life, and you would have been commended unanimously by all the pundits. Of course, ever since then, you have continued to win laurels in this field. But you care too much for your fellow human beings to be content with your intellectual career alone, a splendid one though it is. You have had the greatness of spirit to be unwilling to stay 'above the battle'. Ever since, you have been battling for the survival of civilization, and latterly, since the invention of the atomic weapon, for the survival of the human race.

I am grateful to you, most of all, for the encouragement and the hope that you have been giving for so long, and are still giving as vigorously and as fearlessly as ever, to your younger contemporaries in at least three successive generations. As long as there are people who care, as you do, for mankind, and who put their concern into action, the rest of us can find, from the example that you have set us, courage and confidence to work, in your spirit, for trying to give mankind the future that is its birthright, and for trying to help it to save itself from self-destruction.

This is why Thursday, 18 May, 1967, is an historic date for the hundreds of millions of your contemporaries who are unaware of this, as well as for the hundreds of thousands who do know what you stand for and what you strive for. You have projected yourself, beyond yourself, into the history of the extraordinary species of which you are so outstanding a representative. Every living creature is self-centred by nature; yet every human living creature's mission in life is to transfer the centre of his concern from himself to the ultimate reality, whatever this may be. That is the true fulfilment of a human being's destiny. You have achieved it. This is why I feel constant gratitude to you and affection for you, and why 18 May, 1967, is a day of happiness and hope for me, among your many friends.

Yours ever
Arnold Toynbee

From Field Marshal Sir Claude Auchinleck, G C B

Oswald House
Northgate
Beccles, Suffolk
1 May 64

My dear Lord Russell

I apologise for not having written earlier to thank you for your hospitality and, for me, a most interesting and inspiring visit. I have read the paper you gave me—'A New Approach to Peace' which I found most impressive. There is nothing in it with which I could not whole-heartedly agree and support. I understand the relationship and functions of the Atlantic Peace Foundation and the Bertrand Russell Peace Foundation and I hope to be able to make a small contribution to the expenses of the former.

If I can be of help in any other way, perhaps you or your Secretary will let me know. It is an honour to have met you.

With best wishes and hopes for your success.

Yours sincerely
C. J. Auchinleck

From U Thant on the formation of the Bertrand Russell Peace Foundation

Secretary General

It is good to know that it is proposed to start a Foundation in the name of Lord Russell, to expand and continue his efforts in the cause of peace.

Lord Russell was one of the first to perceive the folly and danger of unlimited accumulation of nuclear armaments. In the early years he conducted practically a one-man crusade against this tendency and he now has a much larger following. While there may be differences of views about the wisdom of unilateral disarmament, and other similar ideas, I share the feeling of Lord Russell that the unrestricted manufacture, testing, perfecting, and stock-piling of nuclear armaments represent one of the greatest dangers to humanity and one of the most serious threats to the survival of the human race.

178

I hope, therefore, that this effort to put on an institutional basis the crusade for peace that Lord Russell has conducted for so long and with such dedication will be crowned with success.

U Thant

SPONSORS OF THE BERTRAND RUSSELL PEACE FOUNDATION

H.I.M. Haile Selassie
Prof. Linus Pauling, Nobel
    Prize for Chemistry
    and for Peace
Pres. Kenneth Kaunda
Pres. Kwame Nkrumah
Pres. Ayub Khan
Pres. Julius K. Nyerere
Pres. Leopold Senghor
The Duke of Bedford

Dr Max Born, Nobel Prize for Physics
Lord Boyd Orr, FRS, Nobel Peace Prize
Pablo Casals, Puerto Rico, Cellist
Danilo Dolci, Sicily
Her Majesty Queen Elizabeth of the
    Belgians
Prime Minister Jawaharlal Nehru
Vanessa Redgrave, Actress
Dr Albert Schweitzer, Lambarene,
    Nobel Peace Prize

February 1964

A NEW APPROACH TO PEACE

by

BERTRAND RUSSELL

The nuclear age in which we have the misfortune to live is one which imposes new ways of thought and action and a new character in international relations. Ever since the creation of the H-bomb, it has been obvious to thoughtful people that there is now a danger of the extermination of mankind if a nuclear war between two powerful nations or blocs of nations should break out. Not only would such a war be a total disaster to human hopes, but, so long as past policies persist, a nuclear war may break out at any minute. This situation imposes upon those who desire the continuation of our species a very difficult duty. We have, first, to persuade Governments and populations of the disastrousness of nuclear war, and when that has been achieved, we have to induce Governments to adopt such policies as will make the preservation of peace a possibility.

Of these two tasks, the first has been very largely accomplished. It has been accomplished by a combination of methods of agitation: peace marches, peace demonstrations, large public meetings, sit-downs, etc. These were conducted in Britain by the CND and the Committee of 100, and in other countries by more or less similar bodies. They have testified—and I am proud that I was amongst them—that nuclear war would be a calamity for the whole human race, and have pointed out its imminence and its dangers. They have succeeded in making very widely known, even to Governments, the dangers of nuclear war. But it is time for a new approach. The dangers must not be forgotten

179

but now the next step must be taken. Ways and means of settling questions that might lead to nuclear war and other dangers to mankind must be sought and made known, and mankind must be persuaded to adopt these new and different means towards securing peace.

The culmination, so far, of the conflict between rival nuclear groups was the Cuban crisis. In this crisis, America and Russia confronted each other while the world waited for the destruction that seemed imminent. At the last moment, the contest was avoided and it appeared that neither side was willing to put an end to the human race because of disagreement as to the politics of those who would otherwise be living in Cuba. This was a moment of great importance. It showed that neither side considered it desirable to obliterate the human race.

We may, therefore, take it that the Governments of the world are prepared to avoid nuclear war. And it is not only Governments, but also vast sections, probably a majority, of the populations of most civilised countries which take this view.

The first part of the work for peace has thus been achieved. But a more difficult task remains. If there is not to be war, we have to find ways by which war will be avoided. This is no easy matter. There are many disputes which, though they may begin amicably, are likely to become more and more bitter, until at last, in a fury, they break out into open war. There is also the risk of war by accident or misinformation. Furthermore, there are difficulties caused by the one-sided character of information as it reaches one side or the other in any dispute. It is clear that peace cannot come to the world without serious concessions, sometimes by one side, sometimes by the other, but generally by both. These difficulties in the pursuit of peace require a different technique from that of marches and demonstrations. The questions concerned are complex, the only possible solutions are distasteful to one side or both, and negotiators who discuss such questions will need to keep a firm hold of their tempers if they are to succeed.

All this should be the work of Governments. But Governments will not adequately do the necessary work unless they are pushed on by a body or bodies which have an international character and are especially concerned with a search for peaceful solutions. It is work of this kind that we hope to see performed by the new Foundations, which I hereby recommend to you.

Of the two Foundations one is called The Atlantic Peace Foundation. Being a Foundation for purposes of research in matters of war and peace, it has been registered as a charity and is recognised as such by the British Inland Revenue. Income Tax at the standard rate is, therefore, recoverable on any subscription given to it under a seven-year contract, which means that such subscriptions are increased by about sixty per cent. This Foundation works in co-operation with the Bertrand Russell Peace Foundation. The latter implements the purposes of the Atlantic Peace Foundation. For this reason, I shall refer to only a single Foundation in the rest of this discussion.

It may be said: 'But such work as that is the work of the United Nations.' I agree that it should be the work of the United Nations and I hope that, in time, it will become so. But the United Nations has defects, some of them remediable, others essential in a body which represents an organisation of States. Of the former kind of defect, the most notable is the exclusion of China; of the latter kind, the equality of States in the Assembly and the veto power of certain States in the Security Council. For such reasons the United Nations, alone, is not adequate to work for peace.

It is our hope that the Foundations which we have created will, in time, prove adequate to deal with all obstacles to peace and to propose such solutions of difficult questions as may commend themselves to the common sense of mankind. Perhaps this hope is too ambitious. Perhaps it will be some other body with similar objects that will achieve the final victory. But however that may be, the work of our Foundation will have ministered to a fortunate ending.

The problems which will have to be settled are two kinds. The first kind is that which concerns mankind as a whole. Of this the most important are two: namely, disarmament and education. The second class of problems are those concerning territorial adjustments, of which Germany is likely to prove the most difficult. Both kinds must be solved if peace is to be secure.

There have been congresses concerned with the subject of disarmament ever since nuclear weapons came into existence. Immediately after the ending of the Second World War, America offered to the world the Baruch Proposal. This was intended to break the American monopoly of nuclear weapons and to place them in the hands of an international body. Its intentions were admirable, but Congress insisted upon the insertion of clauses which it was known the Russians would not accept. Everything worked out as had been expected. Stalin rejected the Baruch Proposal, and Russia proceeded to create its own A-bomb and, then, its own H-bomb. The result was the Cold War, the blockade of Berlin, and the creation by both sides of H-bombs which first suggested the danger to mankind in general. After Stalin's death, a new attempt at complete disarmament was made. Eisenhower and Khrushchev met at Camp David. But warlike elements in the Pentagon continued their work of spying, and the Russian destruction of U-2 put an end to the brief attempt at friendship. Since that time, disarmament conferences have met constantly, but always, until after the Cuban Crisis, with the determination on both sides that no agreement should be reached. Since the Cuban Crisis there has again been a more friendly atmosphere, but so far, without any tangible result except the Test-Ban Treaty. This Treaty was valuable, also, as showing that agreement is possible between East and West. The success of the negotiations involved was largely due to Pugwash, an international association of scientists concerned with problems of peace and war.

The present situation in regard to disarmament is that both America and Russia have schemes for total nuclear disarmament, but their schemes differ, and no way has, so far, been discovered of bridging the differences. It should be one of the most urgent tasks of the Foundation to devise some scheme of disarmament to which both sides could agree. It is ominous, however, that the Pentagon has again allowed one of its planes to be shot down by the Russians over Communist territory.

If peace is ever to be secure, there will have to be great changes in education.

At present, children are taught to love their country to the exclusion of other countries, and among their countrymen in history those whom they are specially taught to admire are usually those who have shown most skill in killing foreigners. An English child is taught to admire Nelson and Wellington; a French child, to admire Napoleon; and a German child, Barbarossa. These are not among those of the child's countrymen who have done most for the world. They are those who have served their country in ways that must be forever closed if man is to survive. The conception of Man as one family will have to be taught as carefully as the opposite is now taught. This will not be an easy transition. It will be said that boys under such a regimen will be soft and effeminate. It will be said that they will lose the manly virtues and will be destitute of courage. All this will be said by Christians in spite of Christ's teaching. But, dreadful as it may appear, boys brought up in the old way will grow into quarrelsome men who will find a world without war unbearably tame. Only a new kind of education, inculcating a new set of moral values, will make it possible to keep a peaceful world in existence.

There will, after all, be plenty of opportunity for adventure, even dangerous adventure. Boys can go to the Antarctic for their holidays, and young men can go to the moon. There are many ways of showing courage without having to kill other people, and it is such ways that should be encouraged.

In the teaching of history, there should be no undue emphasis upon one's own country. The history of wars should be a small part of what is taught. Much the more important part should be concerned with progress in the arts of civilisation. War should be treated as murder is treated. It should be regarded with equal horror and with equal aversion. All this, I fear, may not be pleasing to most present-day educationists. But, unless education is changed in some such way, it is to be feared that men's natural ferocity will, sooner or later, break out.

But it is not only children who need education. It is needed, also by adults, both ordinary men and women and those who are important in government. Every technical advance in armaments has involved an increase in the size of States. Gunpowder made modern states possible at the time of the Renaissance by making castles obsolete. What castles were at that time, national States are now, since weapons of mass destruction have made even the greatest States liable to complete destruction. A new kind of outlook is, therefore, necessary. Communities, hitherto, have survived, when they have survived, by a combination of internal co-operation and external competition. The H-bomb has made the latter out of date. World-wide co-operation is now a condition of survival. But world-wide co-operation, if it is to succeed, requires co-operative feelings in individuals. It is difficult to imagine a World Government succeeding if the various countries of which it is composed continue to hate and suspect each other. To bring about more friendly feelings across the boundaries of nations is, to begin with, a matter of adult education. It is necessary to teach both individuals and Governments that as one family mankind may prosper as never before, but as many competing families there is no prospect before mankind except death. To teach this lesson will be a large part of the educative work of the Foundation.

There are throughout the world a number of territorial questions, most of which divide East from West. Some of the questions are very thorny and must be settled before peace can be secure. Let us begin with Germany.

At Yalta it was decided that Germany should be divided into four parts: American, English, French and Russian. A similar division was made of Berlin within Germany. It was hoped that all would, in time, come to agree and would submit to any conditions imposed by the victorious allies. Trouble, however, soon arose. The city of Berlin was in the midst of the Russian zone and no adequate provision had been made to secure access to the Western sector of Berlin for the Western allies. Stalin took advantage of this situation in 1948 by the so-called 'Berlin Blockade' which forbade all access to West Berlin by road or rail on the part of the Western allies. The Western allies retorted by the 'Air Lift' which enabled them to supply West Berlin in spite of the Russian blockade. Throughout the period of the Berlin blockade both sides were strictly legal. Access to West Berlin by air had been guaranteed in the peace settlement, and this the Russians never challenged. The whole episode ended with a somewhat ambiguous and reluctant agreement on the part of the Russians to allow free intercourse between West Berlin and West Germany. This settlement, however, did not satisfy the West. It was obvious that the Russians could at any moment occupy West Berlin and that the only answer open to the West would be nuclear war. Somewhat similar considerations applied, rather less forcibly, to the whole of Western Germany. In this way, the problem of Germany became linked with the problem of nuclear disarmament: if nuclear disarmament was accepted by the West without adequate assurances as to disarmament in regard to conventional weapons, then Germany's defence against the East would become difficult if not impossible.

The German problem also exists in regard to Eastern Germany—and here it represents new complexities. What had been the Eastern portion of the German Reich was divided into two parts. The Eastern half was given to Russia and Poland, while the Western half was given to a Communist regime in East Germany. In the part given to Russia and Poland all Germans were evicted. Old and young, men, women and children were ruthlessly sent in over-crowded trains to Berlin, where they had to walk from the Eastern terminus to the Western terminus in queues which were apt to take as much as thirty-six hours. Many Germans died in the trains and many in the Berlin queues, but for the survivors there was no legal remedy.

And how about the part of Germany which was assigned to the East German Government? The East German Government was a Communist Government, while the population was overwhelmingly anti-Communist. The Government was established by the Russians and sustained by their armed forces against insurrection. Eastern Germany became a prison, escape from which, after the construction of the Berlin Wall, was only possible at imminent risk of death.

It cannot be expected that Germany will tamely accept this situation. The parts of the old German Reich which were given to Russia or Poland were, for the most part, inhabited by Poles and must be regarded as justly lost to Germany whatever may be thought of the hardships suffered by excluded

Germans. But the position of the Germans in what is now the Eastern portion of Germany is quite different. Eastern Germany is virtually a territory conquered by the Russians and governed by them as they see fit. This situation, combined with the natural nationalistic sympathy felt by the West Germans, is an unstable one. It depends upon military force and nothing else.

So far, we have been concerned with the German case, but the Nazis, during their period in power, inspired in all non-Germans a deep-rooted fear of German power. There is reason to dread that, if Germany were reunited, there would be a repetition of the Nazi attempt to rule the world. This apprehension is apparently not shared by the Governments of the West, who have done everything in their power to strengthen West Germany and make it again capable of another disastrous attempt at world dominion. It cannot be said that this apprehension is unreasonable.

What can be done to secure a just and peaceful solution of this problem? The West might suggest that Germany should be free and reunited and the East might, conceivably, agree, if Germany were disarmed. But the Germans would never agree to a punitive disarmament inflicted upon them alone. Only general disarmament would make German disarmament acceptable to the Germans. In this way, the question of Germany becomes entangled with the problem of disarmament. It is difficult to imagine any solution of the German problem which would be acceptable both to Germans and to the rest of the world, except reunification combined with *general* disarmament.

The next most difficult of territorial disputes is that between Israel and the Arabs. Nasser has announced that it is his purpose to exterminate Israel and that, within two years, he will be in possession of missiles for this purpose. (*Guardian*, 16.3.64.) The Western world is sure to feel that this cannot be allowed to happen, but most of Asia and, possibly, Russia would be prepared to look on passively so long as the Arabs continued to be victorious. There seems little hope of any accommodation between the two sides except as a result of outside pressure. The ideal solution in such a case is a decision by the United Nations which the countries concerned would be compelled to adopt. I am not prepared to suggest publicly the terms of such a decision, but only that it should come from the United Nations and be supported by the major powers of East and West.

In general, when there is a dispute as to whether the Government of a country should favour the East or the West, the proper course would be for the United Nations to conduct a plebiscite in the country concerned and give the Government to whichever side obtained a majority. This is a principle which, at present, is not accepted by either side. Americans do not accept it in South Vietnam, though they conceal the reason for their anti-Communist activities by pretending that they are protecting the peasantry from the inroads of the Vietcong. The attitude of the United States to Castro's Government in Cuba is very ambiguous. Large sections of American opinion hold that throughout the Western Hemisphere no Government obnoxious to the United States is to be tolerated. But whether these sections of opinion will determine American action is as yet, doubtful. Russia is, in this respect, equally to blame, having enforced Communist Governments in Hungary and Eastern Germany against the wishes of the inhabitants. In all parts of the world, self-deter-mination by hither-to subject nations will become very much easier if there is general disarmament.

The ultimate goal will be a world in which national armed forces are limited to what is necessary for internal stability and in which the only forces capable of acting outside national limits will be those of a reformed United Nations. The approach to this ultimate solution must be piecemeal and must involve a gradual increase in the authority of the United Nations or, possibly, of some new international body which should have sole possession of the major weapons of war. It is difficult to see any other way in which mankind can survive the invention of weapons of mass extinction.

Many of the reforms suggested above depend upon the authority of the United Nations or of some new international body specially created for the purpose. To avoid circumlocution I shall speak of the United Nations to cover both those possibilities. If its powers are to be extended, this will have to be done by means of education which is both neutral and international. Such education will have to be carried out by an organisation which is, itself, international and neutral. There are, at present, in various countries, national associations working towards peace, but, so far as we are aware, the Foundation with which we are concerned is the first international association aiming at the creation of a peaceful world. The other Foundations are limited in scope—being either national or aimed towards dealing with only one or two aspects or approaches to peace. We shall support them where we can, and shall hope for their support in those areas of our work which impinge upon theirs. We shall also endeavour to diminish the acerbity of international controversy and induce Governments and important organs of public opinion to preserve at least a minimum of courtesy in their criticism of opponents.

The Government of this Foundation will be in the hands of a small body of Directors. This body is, as yet, incomplete, but should as soon as possible be representative of all the interests concerned in the prevention of war. It is supported by a body of Sponsors who approve of its general purposes, but, for one reason or another, cannot take part in the day to day work. There is to be a Board of Advisers, each having special knowledge in some one or more fields. Their specialised knowledge shall be drawn upon as it may be relevant. The Headquarters of the Foundation will remain in London, which will also house the International Secretariat. In the near future, it is intended to establish offices in various parts of the world. Probably the first two, one in New York and one in Beirut, will be established in the immediate future. Others will follow as soon as suitable personnel can be recruited. This is, in many parts of the world, a difficult task. Many Governments, although they do not venture publicly to advocate nuclear war, are opposed to any work against it in their own territories, and many individuals, while genuinely desirous of peace, shrink from such national sacrifices as the Foundation's general policy may seem to make desirable. It is obvious that a general peace policy must demand moderation everywhere, and many friends of peace, while admitting the desirability of concessions by countries other than their own, are apt to shrink from advocating necessary concessions by their own country.

Willingness for such concessions is a necessary qualification for membership of the Secretariat and for the Head of any subsidiary office. Each subsidiary office will have to collect information and first-hand knowledge on all local matters from both the ordinary population and the authorities. They will have to assess this knowledge with a view to its importance in work towards peace. And they will have to disseminate accurate knowledge and to educate both authorities and the public in attitudes and actions desirable in work towards peace. Each office will also have the task of finding suitable workers to support its own part of the general work and to collect money both for its own and the general work. It should be part of the work of the subsidiary offices to pass on information and advice so that the Central Secretariat can draw up soundly based schemes for the settlement of disputes that stand a good chance of being accepted by the disputants.

To accomplish these tasks will not be possible without a considerable expenditure in secretarial help, in offices, in means of travel, in means of publicising findings and, ultimately, when and if funds permit, in establishing a radio and newspaper of our own. Until such funds permit, the exploration of possibilities and estimates of location plant and personnel for these needed means of publicity—in itself no mean task—must occupy the Foundation.

It will be seen that the Foundation as we hope it may become must be a gradual work. It cannot spring into being full-armoured like Athene. What exists at present is only a small seed of what we hope may come to be. We have a Head Office in London. We have a small Secretariat which is international, neutral and energetic, but too small for the work that has to be done. We have pamphlets and leaflets stating our views on various topical issues. These we supplement, when we can, by letters and articles in the Press. But what can be done in this way is, as yet, very limited since most newspapers are opposed to what must be done in this or that disturbed region if peace is to be secured there. Nevertheless, even now, we have found that there is much that we can accomplish. We can collect information, partly by means of already published facts, and partly by travels in the course of which we visit the Governments and learn their point of view. In the short five months of its existence, the Foundation has sent emissaries to various troubled spots and to the Governments concerned. We have already an enormous correspondence, partly with sympathisers in all parts of the world, and partly also, with Heads of States. From all these we derive both information and advice. Partly, too, our correspondence has been concerned with appeals for the liberation of political prisoners and the amelioration of the lot of minorities in various countries, East and West, South and North. In these last respects, our work has already met with great and unexpected success. In recounting the success of the Foundation during these first five months, however, we labour under the handicap of being unable to be specific. Negotiations such as we are conducting, as will readily be understood, cannot be talked of, since to talk of them would nullify their efficacy.

As everybody who has ever attempted to create a large organisation will understand, our chief effort during these early months has been concerned with obtaining funds, and this must continue for a considerable time since much of the work we wish to do involves very considerable expense. We are opening accounts in various countries to pay for local expenditure. We have done various things to raise money, such as a sale of paintings and sculpture generously donated to us by their creators. We are sponsoring a film. We have hope of money from various theatrical performances. But these alone will not suffice, unless supplemented by gifts from individuals and organisations. It is obvious that the more money we can collect the more nearly and adequately we can carry out our aims. We are firmly convinced that the Foundation can achieve the immense work it has undertaken provided sufficient funds become available. We are working for a great cause—the preservation of Man. In this work one might expect to have the support of every human being. This, alas, is not yet the case. It is our hope that, in time, it will become so.

From and to Erich Fromm

Gonzalez Cosio No. 15
Mexico 12, D.F.
May 30th, 1962

Lord Bertrand Russell
care of Mrs Clara Urquhart
London, W.1

Dear Bertrand Russell
I know how frightfully busy you must be before the Moscow Conference, but I also believe that you will understand it if I approach you for your advice and help with regard to the fate of a man, Heinz Brandt, who was arrested last June by the East German police in East Berlin, or Potsdam, and was sentenced to thirteen years of hard labour (Zuchthaus) on the 10th of May at a secret trial for espionage against the D.D.R.

Brandt was a German communist before Hitler, for eleven years was in Hitler's prisons and concentration camps and severely tortured in the latter. After the War he went to East Germany and was a journalist there for the communist party. He got more and more into opposition with that party, and eventually fled to West Germany where he took a job in Frankfort as a journalist on the newspaper of the Metal Workers' Union. He was sent last year by his union to attend a union conference in West Berlin, and apparently was kidnapped or lured into East Berlin by the East German police, since nobody who knows him believes that he would have gone voluntarily to East Germany. The remarkable thing about him is that, in spite of having turned against communism he did not do what so many others have done, to become a rabid spokesman against communism in West Germany. On the contrary, he was one of the most passionate and ardent fighters against West German rearmament, for peace and for an understanding with the Soviet Union. Although his union in Frankfort is not only the biggest but also the most peace-minded union in West Germany, his courageous stand made him enemies in many places and yet he fought for his ideals without the slightest compromise.

187

I know that Brandt was left in a nervous condition from the tortures he underwent in the Nazi camps, he has a wife and three young children, and the sentence amounts to a life-long one or even a death sentence, considering his present age of around 55 and his condition. . . .

There was a great deal of protest and indignation going on since he was arrested and again now after he was sentenced. Naturally his case has been used for fanatical anti-communist propaganda by various circles. We, on the other hand, have done all we could to prevent this kind of misuse, and we have addressed ourselves in cables to Khrushchev and Ulbricht asking for Brandt's release. (These cables were signed by a number of American pacifists and leading peace workers and also by some from France (Claude Bourdet) and Germany (Professor Abendroth).) After being sentenced, it seems that the only hope for his liberation would lie in the fact that enough people, and sufficiently influential ones from the Western Hemisphere, would approach the Soviet people with the request to exert influence on the Ulbricht government to pardon Brandt and return him to his family in West Germany. I thought myself that the coming Congress in Moscow would be a good opportunity for such an attempt. I intend to go there as an observer. I cabled Professor Bernal some time ago and asked him whether, if I went, I would be free to bring up the Brandt case, and he cabled back that this was so. Naturally, the success of this action depends on one fact: How many other non-communists and Western peace people will support this step? I hope very much that you could decide to lend your support also.

I enclose the declaration of the West German Socialistischer Deutscher Studentenbund. Similar declarations have been signed by Professor W. Abendroth, Professor H. J. Heydorn, H. Brakemeier and E. Dähne. (It may be known to you that the Socialistischer Deutscher Studentenbund has been expelled from the West German Democratic Party precisely because of its stand against West German rearmament.)

I would have liked very much to talk with you before the Moscow conference, about how one could best organize a step in favour of Brandt. (I assume you will go to Moscow). Would you be kind enough to drop me a line how long you will be in London, and when you will be in Moscow, and if you could see me for an hour to discuss this case either before you leave or in Moscow?

Yours sincerely
Erich Fromm

Encl.
cc—Mrs Clara Urquhart

1 July 1962

Dear Erich Fromm

I wish to apologise to you most sincerely for leaving your letter of May 30th unanswered until now. I shall do anything you advise with respect to Brandt. I have recently received two communications from Khruschchev and can easily incorporate the question of Brandt in my reply.

I am not going to Moscow but I am sending a personal representative and four members of the Committee of 100 are going as delegates. I should very much wish to see you in London. I shall be in London until around July 10 when I expect to be returning to Wales. I should be delighted to see you in London at my home. Please contact me as soon as you come to London. Good wishes.

Yours sincerely
Bertrand Russell

To Nikita Khrushchev

4 July, 1962

Dear Mr Khrushchev

I am venturing to send to you a copy of a letter which I have written to the Moscow Conference on Disarmament, dealing with the case of Heinz Brandt. I hope you will agree with me that clemency, in this case, would further the cause of peace.

My warmest thanks for your kind letter on the occasion of my 90th birthday, which gave me great satisfaction.

Yours sincerely
Bertrand Russell

To the President of the Moscow Conference on Disarmament

4 July, 1962

Sir

I wish to bring to the attention of this Conference the case of Heinz Brandt who has been sentenced in East Germany to thirteen years of prison with hard labour. I do not know the exact nature of the charges against him. At first, he was to have been charged with espionage, but, when he was brought to trial, this charge was dropped. Heinz Brandt has been throughout his active life a devoted and self-sacrificing worker for peace and against West German re-armament. For eleven years during Hitler's regime, he was in prisons and concentration camps, including Auschwitz and Buchenwald. To all friends of peace and disarmament in West Germany, his arrest and condemnation by the East German Authorities were a severe blow, while to the militarists of West Germany they supplied new arguments and new reasons for bitterness. I have no doubt that, in the interests of disarmament with which this Congress is concerned, his release would be profoundly beneficial. I hope that the Congress will pass a resolution asking for his release on these grounds.

Bertrand Russell

To Walter Ulbricht

12 August, 1963

Dear Herr Ulbricht

Recently I was honoured with an award for peace by your government in the name of Carl von Ossietzky. I hold Ossietzky's memory in high regard and I honour that for which he died. I am passionately opposed to the Cold

War and to all those who trade in it, so I felt it important to accept the honour accorded me.

You will understand, therefore, the motives which lead me to, once more, appeal to you on behalf of Heinz Brandt. I am most deeply disturbed that I have not received so much as an acknowledgement of my previous appeals on his behalf. Heinz Brandt was a political prisoner, placed in concentration camp along with Ossietzky. He has suffered many long years of imprisonment because he has stood by his political beliefs. I do not raise the question here of the comparative merit or demerit of those beliefs. I but ask you to consider the damage that is done to the attempts to improve relations between your country and the West and to soften the Cold War by the continued imprisonment of Heinz Brandt. I appeal to you, once more, on grounds of humanity, to release this man, and I should be grateful if you would inform me of your intentions with regard to him.

Although I value the Ossietzky Medal, I am placed in an ambiguous position by the continued imprisonment of Heinz Brandt.

Yours sincerely
Bertrand Russell

On October 30, 1963, the Secretary of the East German State Council wrote to me at great length to explain that 'the spy Brandt', 'condemned for treason' had received the 'justified sentence' of thirteen years' hard labour, the sentence to expire in June, 1974. Brandt had served only two years of this sentence, and no long sentence could be conditionally suspended until at least half of it had been served. 'Reduction of the sentence by act of grace' was not justified because of the seriousness of the crimes. Herr Gotsche's letter concluded: 'I may assume that you, too, dear Mr Russell, will appreciate after insight . . . that in this case the criminal law must be fully applied . . . in the interest of humanity.'

To Walter Ulbricht

7 January 1964

Dear Mr Ulbricht

I am writing to you to tell you of my decision to return to your Government the Carl von Ossietzsky medal for peace. I do so reluctantly and after two years of private approaches on behalf of Heinz Brandt, whose continued imprisonment is a barrier to coexistence, relaxation of tension and understanding between East and West.

My representative, Mr Kinsey, spoke recently with officials of your governing council in East Berlin and he carried a message from me.

I regret not to have heard from you on this subject. I hope that you will yet find it possible to release Brandt through an amnesty which would be a boon to the cause of peace and to your country.

Yours sincerely
Bertrand Russell

29 May 1964

Dear Premier Ulbricht

I am writing to convey my great pleasure at the news of the release of Heinz Brandt from prison. I realise that this was not an easy decision for your Government to make but I am absolutely convinced that it was a decision in the best interests of your country and of the cause of peace and good relations between East and West.

I wish to offer my appreciation and approval for this important act of clemency.

Yours sincerely
Bertrand Russell

From and to Tony and Betty Ambatielos

Filonos 22
Piraeus. Greece
7 May 1964

Dear Lord Russell

It will give my husband and I the greatest pleasure if, during a visit we hope to make to Britain soon, we are able to meet you and thank you personally for all your support over the years. Meantime, however, we send you this brief letter as a token of our deep gratitude and esteem.

We will be indebted to you always for assisting in bringing about Tony's release and we know that his colleagues who were freed at the same time would wish us to convey their feelings of gratitude towards you also. It is unfortunate that when so many hundreds were at last freed, nearly one hundred were and are still held. But we are all confident that with the continued interest and support of such an esteemed and stalwart friend as yourself, they too can be freed in the not too distant future.

With kind regards to Lady Russell and all good wishes and thanks,

Yours sincerely
Betty Ambatielos

Dear Lord Russell

I wish to send you these few lines to express my very deep gratitude and respect to you for the way you championed the cause of the political prisoners.

Your name is held in very high esteem among all of us.

Please accept my personal thanks for all you have done.

Yours sincerely
Tony Ambatielos

13 May, 1964

Dear Mr and Mrs Ambatielos

Thank you very much for your letter. I should be delighted to see you both in Wales or London. I have been corresponding with Papandreou, pressing him for the release of remaining prisoners and the dropping of recent charges in Salonika.

With kind regards,

Yours sincerely
Bertrand Russell

From and to Lord Gladwyn

30, Gresham Street
London, E.C.2
3rd November, 1964

Dear Lord Russell

I have read with great interest, on my return from America your letter of September 11th which was acknowledged by my secretary. It was indeed kind of you to send me the literature concerning the 'Bertrand Russell Peace Foundation' and the paper entitled 'Africa and the Movement for Peace' and to ask for my views, which are as follows:—

As a gener l observation, I should at once say that I question your whole major premise. I really do not think that general nuclear war is getting more and more likely: I believe, on the contrary, that it is probably getting less and less likely. I do not think that either the USA or the USSR has the slightest intention of putting the other side into a position in which it may feel it will have to use nuclear weapons on a 'first strike' for its own preservation (if that very word is not in itself paradoxical in the circumstances). Nor will the Chinese for a long time have the means of achieving a 'first strike', and when they have they likewise will not want to achieve it. We are no doubt in for a difficult, perhap. even a revolutionary decade and the West must stand together and discuss wise joint policies for facing it, otherwise we may well lapse into mediocrity, anarchy or barbarism. If we do evolve an intelligent common policy not only will there be no general nuclear war, but we shall overcome the great evils of hunger and overpopulation. Here, however, to my mind, everything depends on the possibility of organizing Western unity.

Nor do I believe that 'war by accident', though just conceivable, is a tenable hypothesis. Thus the so-called 'Balance of Terror' (by which I mean the ability of each of the two giants to inflict totally unacceptable damage on the other even on a 'second strike') is likely to result in the maintenance of existing territorial boundaries (sometimes referred to as the 'Status Quo') in all countries in which the armed forces of the East and West are in physical contact, and a continuance of the so-called 'Cold War', in other words a struggle for influence between the free societies of the West and the Communist societies of the East, in the 'emergent' countries of South America, Africa and Asia. I developed this general thesis in 1958 in an essay called 'Is Tension Necessary?' and events since then have substantially confirmed it. The Balance of Terror has not turned out to be so 'delicate' as some thought; with the passage of time I should myself say that it was getting even less fragile.

In the 'Cold War' struggle the general position of the West is likely to be strengthened by the recent ideological break between the Soviet Union and

China, which seems likely to persist in spite of the fall of Khrushchev. Next to the 'Balance of Terror' between Russia and America I should indeed place the split as a major factor militating in favour of prolonged World Peace, in the sense of an absence of nuclear war. The chief feature of the present land-scape, in fact (and it is a reassuring one), is that America and Russia are becoming less afraid of each other. The one feels that the chances of a sub-version of its free economy are substantially less: the other feels that no attack can now possibly be mounted against it by the Western 'Capitalists'.

Naturally, I do not regard this general situation as ideal, or even as one which is likely to continue for a very long period. It is absurd that everybody, and more particularly the USA and the USSR, should spend such colossal sums on armaments, though it seems probable that, the nuclear balance having been achieved, less money will be devoted to reinforcing or even to maintaining it. It is wrong, in principle, that Germany should continue to be divided. Clearly general disarmament is desirable, though here it is arguable that it will not be achieved until an agreed settlement of outstanding political prob-lems, and notably the reunification of Germany is peacefully negotiated. The truth may well be that in the absence of such settlements both sides are in practice reluctant to disarm beyond a certain point, and without almost impossible guarantees, and are apt to place the blame for lack of progress squarely on the other. What is demonstrably untrue is that the West are to blame whereas the Soviet Union is guiltless. In particular, I question your statement (in the African paper) that the Soviet Union has already agreed to disarm and to accept adequate inspection in all the proper stages, and that failure to agree on disarmament is solely the responsibility of the West. The facts are that although the Soviet Government has accepted full verification of the destruction of all armaments due for destruction in the various stages of both the Russian and the American Draft Disarmament Treaties, they have *not* agreed that there should be any verification of the balance of armaments remaining in existence. There would thus, under the Russian proposal, be no guarantee at all that retained armed forces and armaments did not exceed agreed quotas at any stage. Here the Americans have made a significant concession, namely to be content in the early stages with a system of verifying in a few sample areas only: but the Soviet Government has so far turned a deaf ear to such suggestions. Then there is the whole problem of the run-down and its relation to the Agreed Principles, as regards which the Soviet intentions have not, as yet, been fully revealed. Finally the West want to have the International Peace-Keeping Force, which would clearly be required in the event of complete disarmament, under an integrated and responsible Command, but the Soviet Government is insisting, for practical purposes, on the intro-duction into the Command of a power of veto.

It follows that I cannot possibly agree with your subsequent statement either that 'if we are to alter the drift to destruction it will be necessary to change *Western* policy (my italics)'—and apparently Western policy only. At the time of the Cuba crisis you circulated a leaflet entitled 'No Nuclear War over Cuba', which started off 'You are to die'. We were to die, it appeared, unless public opinion could under your leadership be mobilized so as to alter

American policy, thus allowing the Soviet Government to establish hardened nuclear missile bases in Cuba for use against the United States. Happily, no notice was taken of your manifesto: the Russians discontinued their suicidal policy; and President Kennedy by his resolution and farsightedness saved the world. We did not die. Someday, all of us will die, but not, I think in the great holocaust of the Western imagination. The human animal, admittedly, has many of the characteristics of a beast of prey: mercifully he does not possess the suicidal tendencies of the lemmings. What we want in the world is less fear and more love. With great respect, I do not think that your campaign is contributing to either objective.

These are matters of great moment to our people and indeed to humanity. I should hope that you would one day be prepared to advance your proposals in the House of Lords where they could be subjected to intelligent scrutiny. In the meantime I suggest that we agree to publish this letter together with your reply, if indeed you should feel that one is called for.

Yours sincerely
Gladwyn

Plas Penrhyn
14 November, 1964

Dear Lord Gladwyn

Thank you for your long, reasoned letter of November 3rd. I shall take up your points one by one.

I. You point out that the danger of a nuclear war between Russia and the West is less than it was a few years ago. As regards a direct clash between NATO and the Warsaw Powers, I agree with you that the danger is somewhat diminished. On the other hand, new dangers have arisen. All the Powers of East and West, ever since Hiroshima, have agreed that the danger of nuclear war is increased when new Powers become nuclear. But nothing has been done to prevent the spread of nuclear weapons. France and Belgium, India and China and Brazil have or are about to have nuclear weapons. West Germany is on the verge of acquiring a share in Nato weapons. As for China, you say that it will be a long time before China will be effective, but I see no reason to believe this. The West thought that it would be a long time before Russia had the A-bomb. When Russia had the A-bomb, the West thought it would be a long time before they had the H-bomb. Both these expectations turned out to be illusions.

You consider war by accident so improbable that it can be ignored. There is, however, the possibility of war by mistake. This has already almost occurred several times through mistaking the moon for Soviet planes or some such mis-reading of radar signals. It cannot be deemed unlikely that, sooner or later, such a mistake will not be discovered in time.

Moreover, it is a simple matter of mathematical statistics that the more nuclear missiles there are the greater is the danger of nuclear accident. Vast numbers of rockets and other missiles, primed for release and dependent upon mechanical systems and slight margins in time, are highly subject to accident.

Any insurance company would establish this where the factors involved relate to civilian activity such as automobile transport or civilian aviation. In this sense, the danger of accidental war increases with each day that the weapons systems are permitted to remain. Nor is the danger wholly mechanical: human beings, even well 'screened' and highly trained are subject to hysteria and madness of various sorts when submitted to the extreme tensions and concentration that many men having to do with nuclear weapons now are submitted to.

Another danger is the existence of large, adventurous and very powerful groups in the United States. The us Government has run grave risks in attacks on North Vietnam forces. In the recent election some 40%, or thereabouts, of the population voted for Goldwater, who openly advocated war. Warlike groups can, at any moment, create an incident such as the U2 which put an end to the conciliatory mood of Camp David.

In estimating the wisdom of a policy, it is necessary to consider not only the possibility of a bad result, but also the degree of badness of the result. The extermination of the human race is the worst possible result, and even if the probability of its occurring is small, its disastrousness should be a deterrent to any policy which allows of it.

II. You admit that the present state of the world is not desirable and suggest that the only way of improving it is by way of Western unity. Your letter seems to imply that this unity is to be achieved by all countries of the West blindly following one policy. Such unity does not seem to me desirable. Certainly the policy to which you appear to think the West should adhere— a policy which upholds the present United States war in South Vietnam and the economic imperialism of the us in the Congo and Latin America—cannot possibly avoid a lapse into mediocrity, anarchy or barbarism, which you say you wish above all to avoid.

The United States is conducting a war in Vietnam in which it has tolerated and supervised every form of bestiality against a primitively armed peasant population. Disembowelments, mutilations, mass bombing raids with jellygasoline, the obliteration of over 75% of the villages of the country and the despatch of eight million people to internment camps have characterised this war. Such conduct cannot be described as an ordered bulwark against mediocrity, anarchy or barbarism. There is a large body of opinion in the United States itself that opposes this war, but the Government persists in carrying it on. The unity that you advocate would do little to encourage the us Government to alter its policy. The us policy in the Congo promises to be similar to that in Vietnam in cruelty. The Western nations show no signs of encouraging any other policy there. (I enclose two pamphlets dealing with Vietnam and the Congo in case you have not seen them.)

Universal unity, however, such as might be achieved by a World Government I am entirely persuaded is necessary to the peace of the world.

III. You find fault with me on the ground that I seem to hold the West always to blame and the Soviet Union always guiltless. This is by no means the case. While Stalin lived, I considered his policies abominable. More recently, I protested vigorously against the Russian tests that preceded the

Test Ban Treaty. At present, I am engaged in pointing out the ill-treatment of Jews in the Soviet Union. It is only in certain respects, of which Cuba was the most important, that I think the greatest share of blame falls upon the United States.

IV. Your comments on the Cuban crisis are, to me, utterly amazing. You say that the way the solution was arrived at was that 'the Russians discontinued their suicidal policy; and President Kennedy by his resolution and far-sightedness saved the world.' This seems to me a complete reversal of the truth. Russia and America had policies leading directly to nuclear war. Khrushchev, when he saw the danger, abandoned his policy. Kennedy did not. It was Khrushchev who allowed the human race to continue, not Kennedy.

Apart from the solution of the crisis, Russian policy towards Cuba would have been justifiable but for the danger of war, whereas American policy was purely imperialistic. Cuba established a kind of Government which the us disliked, and the us considered that its dislike justified attempts to alter the character of the Government by force. I do not attempt to justify the establishment of missiles on Cuban soil, but I do not see how the West can justify its objection to these missiles. The us has established missiles in Quemoy, in Matsu, in Taiwan, Turkey, Iran and all the countries on the periphery of China and the Soviet Union which host nuclear bases. I am interested in your statement that the Soviet Government was establishing hardened nuclear missile bases in Cuba, especially as neither Mr Macmillan nor Lord Home stated that the missiles in Cuba were nuclear, fitted with nuclear warheads or accompanied by nuclear warheads on Cuban soil.

In view of the conflict at the Bay of Pigs, it cannot be maintained that Cuba had no excuse for attempts to defend itself. In view of Kennedy's words to the returned Cuban exiles after the crisis, it cannot be said that Cuba still has no excuse.

You speak of 'the free world'. Cuba seems a case in point. The West seems little freer than the East.

You allude to my leaflet 'Act or Perish'. This was written at the height of the crisis when most informed people were expecting universal death within a few hours. After the crisis passed, I no longer considered such emphatic language appropriate, but, as an expression of the right view at the moment, I still consider it correct.

V. You say, and I emphatically agree with you, that what the world needs is less fear and more love. You think that it is to be achieved by the balance of terror. Is it not evident that, so long as the doctrine of the balance of terror prevails, there will be continually new inventions which will increase the expense of armaments until both sides are reduced to penury? The balance of terror consists of two expensively armed blocs, each saying to the other, 'I should like to destroy you, but I fear that, if I did, you would destroy me.' Do you really consider that this is a way to promote love? If you do not, I wish that you had given some indication of a way that you think feasible. All that you say about this is that you see no way except disarmament, but that disarmament is not feasible unless various political questions have first been settled.

My own view is that disarmament could now come about. Perhaps you know Philip Noel-Baker's pamphlet 'The Way to World Disarmament—Now!' In it he notes accurately and dispassionately the actual record of disarmament negotiations. I enclose it with this letter in case you do not know it. He has said, among other things that Soviet proposals entail the presence of large numbers of inspectors on Soviet territory during all stages of disarmament. In 1955 the Soviet Union accepted in full the Western disarmament proposals. The Western proposals were withdrawn at once upon their acceptance by the Soviet Union. It is far from being only the West that cries out for disarmament: China has pled for it again and again, the last time a few days ago.

As to the expense of present arms production programmes, I, naturally, agree with you. Arms production on the part of the great powers is in excess of the gross national product of three continents—Africa, Latin America and Asia.

I also agree that disarmament would be easier to achieve if various political questions were first settled. It is for this reason that the Peace Foundation of which I wrote you is engaged at present in an examination of these questions and discussions with those directly involved in them in the hope of working out with them acceptable and feasible solutions. And it is with a view to enhancing the love and mitigating the hate in the world that the Foundation is engaged in Questions relating to political prisoners and members of families separated by political ruling and red tape and to unhappy minorities. It has had surprising and considerable success in all these fields during the first year of its existence.

As to publication, I am quite willing that both your letter and mine should be published in full.

> *Yours sincerely*
> *Russell*

enc:
'Vietnam and Laos' by Bertrand Russell and William Warbey, M P
'The Way to World Disarmament—Now!' by Philip Noel-Baker
Unarmed Victory by Bertrand Russell
'The Cold War and World Poverty' by Bertrand Russell
'Freedom in Iran' by K. Zaki
'Oppression on South Arabia' by Bertrand Russell
'Congo—a Tragedy' by R. Schoenman

No reply was ever received by me to this letter to Lord Gladwyn who, so far as I know, never published either of the above letters.

16 QUESTIONS ON THE ASSASSINATION

The official version of the assassination of President Kennedy has been so riddled with contradictions that it has been abandoned and rewritten no less than three times. Blatant fabrications have received very widespread coverage by the mass media, but denials of these same lies have gone unpublished.

Photographs, evidence and affidavits have been doctored out of recognition. Some of the most important aspects of the case against Lee Harvey Oswald have been completely blacked out. Meanwhile the FBI, the police and the Secret Service have tried to silence key witnesses or instruct them what evidence to give. Others involved have disappeared or died in extraordinary circumstances.

It is facts such as these that demand attention, and which the Warren Commission should have regarded as vital. Although I am writing before the publication of the Warren Commission's report, leaks to the press have made much of its contents predictable. Because of the high office of its members and the fact of its establishment by President Johnson, the Commission has been widely regarded as a body of holy men appointed to pronounce the Truth. An impartial examination of the composition and conduct of the Commission suggests quite otherwise.

The Warren Commission has been utterly unrepresentative of the American people. It consisted of two Democrats, Senator Russell of Georgia and Congressman Boggs of Louisiana, both of whose racist views have brought shame on the United States; two Republicans, Senator Cooper of Kentucky and Congressman Gerald R. Ford of Michigan, the latter of whom is leader of his local Goldwater movement, a former member of the FBI and is known in Washington as the spokesman for that institution; Allen Dulles, former director of the CIA; and Mr McCloy, who has been referred to as the spokesman for the business community. Leadership of the filibuster in the Senate against the Civil Rights Bill prevented Senator Russell attending a single hearing during this period. The Chief Justice of the United States Supreme Court, Earl Warren, who rightly commands respect, was finally persuaded, much against his will, to preside over the Commission, and it was his involvement above all else that helped lend the Commission an aura of legality and authority. Yet many of its members were also members of those very groups which have done so much to distort and suppress the facts about the assassination. Because of their connection with the Government, not one member would have been permitted under American law to serve on a jury had Oswald faced trial. It is small wonder that the Chief Justice himself remarked: 'You may never know all of the facts in your life time.' Here, then, is my first question: *Why were all the members of the Warren Commission closely connected with the U.S. Government?*

If the composition of the Commission was suspect, its conduct confirmed one's worst fears. No counsel was permitted to act for Oswald, so that cross-examination was barred. Later, under pressure, the Commission appointed the President of the American Bar Association, Walter Craig, one of the leaders of the Goldwater movement in Arizona, to represent Oswald. To my knowledge he did not attend a single hearing, but satisfied himself with representation by observers. In the name of national security, the Commission's hearings were held in secret, thereby continuing the policy which has marked the entire course of the case. This prompts my second question: *If, as we are told, Oswald was the lone assassin, where is the issue of national security?* Indeed, precisely the same question must be put here as was posed in France during the Dreyfus case: *If the Government is so certain of its case, why has it conducted all its enquiries in the strictest secrecy?*

At the outset the Commission appointed six panels through which it would conduct its enquiry. They considered: (1) What did Oswald do on November 22, 1963? (2) What was Oswald's background? (3) What did Oswald do in the US Marine Corps, and in the Soviet Union? (4) How did Ruby kill Oswald? (5) What is Ruby's background? (6) What efforts were taken to protect the President on November 22? This raises my fourth question: *Why did the Warren Commission not establish a panel to deal with the question of who killed President Kennedy?*

All the evidence given to the Commission has been classified 'Top Secret', including even a request that hearings be held in public. Despite this the Commission itself leaked much of the evidence to the press, though only if the evidence tended to prove Oswald was the lone assassin. Thus Chief Justice Warren held a press conference after Oswald's wife Marina, had testified, he said, that she believed her husband was the assassin. Before Oswald's brother Robert, testified, he gained the Commission's agreement never to comment on what he said. After he had testified for two days, Allen Dulles remained in the hearing room and several members of the press entered. The next day the newspapers were full of stories that 'a member of the Commission' had told the press that Robert Oswald had just testified that be believed that his brother was an agent of the Soviet Union. Robert Oswald was outraged by this, and said that he could not remain silent while lies were told about his testimony. He had never said this and he had never believed it. All that he had told the Commission was that he believed his brother was in no way involved in the assassination.

The methods adopted by the Commission have indeed been deplorable, but it is important to challenge the entire role of the Warren Commission. It stated that it would not conduct its own investigation, but rely instead on the existing governmental agencies—the FBI, the Secret Service and the Dallas police. Confidence in the Warren Commission thus presupposes confidence in these three institutions. *Why have so many liberals abandoned their own responsibility to a Commission whose circumstances they refuse to examine?*

It is known that the strictest and most elaborate security precautions ever taken for a President of the United States were ordered for November 22 in Dallas. The city had a reputation for violence and was the home of some of the most extreme right-wing fanatics in America. Mr and Mrs Lyndon Johnson had been assailed there in 1960 when he was a candidate for the Vice-Presidency. Adlai Stevenson had been physically attacked when he spoke in the city only a month before Kennedy's visit. On the morning of November 22, the Dallas *Morning News* carried a full-page advertisement associating the President with communism. The city was covered with posters showing the President's picture and headed 'Wanted for Treason'. The Dallas list of subversives comprised 23 names, of which Oswald's was the first. All of them were followed that day, except Oswald. *Why did the authorities follow as potential assassins every single person who had ever spoken out publicly in favour of desegregation of the public school system in Dallas, and fail to observe Oswald's*

199

entry into the book depository building while allegedly carrying a rifle over four feet long?

The President's route for his drive through Dallas was widely known and was printed in the Dallas *Morning News* on November 22. At the last minute the Secret Service changed a small part of their plans so that the President left Main Street and turned into Houston and Elm Streets. This alteration took the President past the book depository building from which it is alleged that Oswald shot him. How Oswald is supposed to have known of this change has never been explained. *Why was the President's route changed at the last minute to take him past Oswald's place of work?*

After the assassination and Oswald's arrest, judgement was pronounced swiftly: Oswald was the assassin, and he had acted alone. No attempt was made to arrest others, no road blocks were set up round the area, and every piece of evidence which tended to incriminate Oswald was announced to the press by the Dallas District Attorney, Mr Wade. In such a way millions of people were prejudiced against Oswald before there was any opportunity for him to be brought to trial. The first theory announced by the authorities was that the President's car was in Houston Street, approaching the book depository building, when Oswald opened fire. When available photographs and eye-witnesses had shown this to be quite untrue, the theory was abandoned and a new one formulated which placed the vehicle in its correct position.

Meanwhile, however, DA Wade had announced that three days after Oswald's room in Dallas had been searched, a map had been found there on which the book depository building had been circled and dotted lines drawn from the building to a vehicle on Houston Street. After the first theory was proved false, the Associated Press put out the following story on November 27: 'Dallas authorities announced today that there never was a map. Any reference to the map was a mistake.'

The second theory correctly placed the President's car on Elm Street, 50 to 75 yards past the book depository, but had to contend with the difficulty that the President was shot from the front, in the throat. How did Oswald manage to shoot the President in the front from behind? The FBI held a series of background briefing sessions for *Life* magazine, which in its issue of December 6 explained that the President had turned completely round just at the time he was shot. This, too, was soon shown to be entirely false. It was denied by several witnesses and films, and the previous issue of *Life* itself had shown the President looking forward as he was hit. Theory number two was abandoned.

In order to retain the basis of all official thinking, that Oswald was the lone assassin, it now became necessary to construct a third theory with the medical evidence altered to fit it. For the first month no Secret Service agent had ever spoken to the three doctors who had tried to save Kennedy's life in the Parkland Memorial Hospital. Now two agents spent three hours with the doctors and persuaded them that they were all misinformed: the entrance wound in the President's throat had been an exit wound, and the bullet had not ranged down towards the lungs. Asked by the press how they could have been so mistaken, Dr McClelland advanced two reasons: they had not seen the autopsy report—and they had not known that Oswald was behind the President! The autopsy report, they had been told by the Secret Service, showed that Kennedy had been shot from behind. The agents, however, had refused to show the report to the doctors, who were entirely dependent upon the word of the Secret Service for this suggestion. The doctors made it clear that they were not permitted to discuss the case. The third theory, with the medical evidence rewritten, remains the basis of the case against Oswald. *Why has the medical evidence concerning the President's death been altered out of recognition?*

Although Oswald is alleged to have shot the President from behind, there are many witnesses who are confident that the shots came from the front. Among them are two reporters from the Fort Worth *Star Telegram*, four from the Dallas *Morning News*, and two people who were standing in front of the book depository building itself, the director of the book depository and the vice-president of the firm. It appears that only two people immediately entered the building, the director, Mr Roy S. Truly, and a Dallas police officer, Seymour Weitzman. Both thought that the shots had come from in front of the President's vehicle. On first running in that direction, Weitzman was informed by 'someone' that he thought the shots had come from the building, so he rushed back there. Truly entered with him in order to assist with his knowledge of the building. Mr Jesse Curry, however, the Chief of Police in Dallas, has stated that he was immediately convinced that the shots came from the building. If anyone else believes this, he has been reluctant to say so to date. It is also known that the first bulletin to go out on Dallas police radios stated that 'the shots came from a triple overpass in front of the presidential automobile'. In addition, there is the consideration that after the first shot the vehicle was brought almost to a halt by the trained Secret Service driver, an unlikely response if the shots had indeed come from behind. Certainly Mr Roy Kellerman, who was in charge of the Secret Service operation in Dallas that day, and travelled in the presidential car, looked to the front as the shots were fired. The Secret Service have removed all the evidence from the car, so it is no longer possible to examine the broken windscreen. *What is the evidence to substantiate the allegation that the President was shot from behind?*

Photographs taken at the scene of the crime could be most helpful. One young lady standing just to the left of the presidential car as the shots were fired took photographs of the vehicle just before and during the shooting, and was thus able to get into her picture the entire front of the book depository building. Two FBI agents immediately took the film from her and have refused to this day to permit her to see the photographs which she took. *Why has the FBI refused to publish what could be the most reliable piece of evidence in the whole case?*

In this connection it is noteworthy also that it is impossible to obtain the originals of photographs of the various alleged murder weapons. When *Time* magazine published a photograph of Oswald's arrest—the only one ever seen—the entire background was blacked out for reasons which have never been explained. It is difficult to recall an occasion for so much falsification of photographs as has happened in the Oswald case.

The affidavit by police officer Weitzman, who entered the book depository building, stated that he found the alleged murder rifle on the sixth floor. (It was at first announced that the rifle had been found on the fifth floor, but this was soon altered.) It was a German 7.65mm. Mauser. Later the following day, the FBI issued its first proclamation. Oswald had purchased in March 1963 an Italian 6.5mm. carbine. DA Wade immediately altered the nationality and size of his weapon to conform to the FBI statement.

Several photographs have been published of the alleged murder weapon. On February 21, *Life* magazine carried on its cover a picture of 'Lee Oswald with the weapon he used to kill President Kennedy and Officer Tippett.' On page 80, *Life* explained that the photograph was taken during March or April of 1963. According to the FBI, Oswald purchased his pistol in September 1963. The *New York Times* carried a picture of the alleged murder weapon being taken by police into the Dallas police station. The rifle is quite different. Experts have stated that it would be impossible to pull the trigger on the rifle in *Life*'s picture. The *New York Times* also carried the same photograph as *Life*, but left out the telescopic sights. On March 2, *Newsweek* used the same photograph but painted in an entirely new rifle. Then on April 13, the Latin American edition of *Life* carried the same picture on its cover as the US edition had on February 21, but in the same issue on page 18 it had the same picture with the rifle altered. *How is it that millions of people have been misled by complete forgeries in the press?*

Another falsehood concerning the shooting was a story circulated by the Associated Press on November 23 from Los Angeles. This reported Oswald's former superior officer in the Marine Corps as saying that Oswald was a crack shot and a hot-head. The story was published everywhere. Three hours later AP sent out a correction deleting the entire story from Los Angeles. The officer had checked his records and it had turned out that he was talking about another man. He had never known Oswald. To my knowledge this correction has yet to be published by a single major publication.

The Dallas police took a paraffin test of Oswald's face and hands to try to establish that he had fired a weapon on November 22. The Chief of the Dallas Police, Jesse Curry, announced on November 23 that the results of the test 'proves Oswald is the assassin'. The Director of the FBI in the Dallas–Fort Worth area in charge of the investigation stated: 'I have seen the paraffin test. The paraffin test proves that Oswald had nitrates and gun-powder on his hands and face. It proves he fired a rifle on November 22.' Not only does this unreliable test not prove any such thing, it was later discovered that the test on Oswald's face was in fact negative, suggesting that it was unlikely he fired a rifle that day. *Why was the result of the paraffin test altered before being announced by the authorities?*

Oswald, it will be recalled was originally arrested and charged with the murder of Patrolman Tippett. Tippett was killed at 1.06 p.m. on November 22 by a man who first engaged him in conversation, then caused him to get out of the stationary police car in which he was sitting and shot him with a pistol. Miss Helen L. Markham, who states that she is the sole eye-witness to this crime, gave the Dallas police a description of the assailant. After signing her affidavit, she was instructed by the FBI, the Secret Service and many police officers that she was not permitted to discuss the case with anyone. The affidavit's only description of the killer was that he was a 'young white man'. Miss Markham later revealed that the killer had run right up to her and past her, brandishing the pistol, and she repeated the description of the murderer which she had given to the police. He was, she said, 'short, heavy and had bushy hair.' (The police description of Oswald was that he was of average height, or a little taller, was slim and had receding fair hair.) Miss Markham's affidavit is the entire case against Oswald for the murder of Patrolman Tippett, yet District Attorney Wade asserted: 'We have more evidence to prove Oswald killed Tippett than we have to show he killed the President.' The case against Oswald for the murder of Tippett, he continued, was an absolutely strong case. *Why was the only description of Tippett's killer deliberately omitted by the police from the affidavit of the sole eye-witness?*

Oswald's description was broadcast by the Dallas police only 12 minutes after the President was shot. This raises one of the most extraordinary questions ever posed in a murder case: *Why was Oswald's description in connection with the murder of Patrolman Tippett broadcast over Dallas police radio at 12.43 p.m. on November 22, when Tippett was not shot until 1.06 p.m.?*

According to Mr Bob Considine, writing in the New York *Journal American*, there had been another person who had heard the shots that were fired at Tippett. Warren Reynolds had heard shooting in the street from a nearby room and had rushed to the window to see the murderer run off. Reynolds himself was later shot through the head by a rifleman. A man was arrested for this crime but produced an alibi. His girl-friend, Betty Mooney McDonald, told the police she had been with him at the time Reynolds was shot. The Dallas police immediately dropped the charges against him, even before Reynolds had time to recover consciousness and attempt to identify his assailant. The man at once disappeared, and two days later the Dallas police arrested Betty Mooney McDonald on a minor charge and it was announced that she had hanged herself in the police cell. She had been a striptease artist in Jack Ruby's nightclub, according to Mr Considine.

Another witness to receive extraordinary treatment in the Oswald case was his wife, Marina. She was taken to the jail while her husband was still alive and shown a rifle by Chief of Police Jesse Curry. Asked if it was Oswald's, she replied that she believed Oswald had a rifle but that it didn't look like that. She and her mother-in-law were in great danger following the assassination because of the threat of public revenge on them. At this time they were unable to obtain a single police officer to protect them. Immediately Oswald was killed, however, the Secret Service illegally held both women against their will. After three days they were separated and Marina has never again been accessible to the public. Held in custody for nine weeks and questioned almost daily by the FBI and Secret Service, she finally testified to the Warren Commission and, according to Earl Warren, said that she believed her husband was the assassin. The Chief Justice added that the next day they intended to show Mrs Oswald the murder weapon and the Commission was fairly confident that she would identify it as her husband's. The following day Earl Warren announced that this had indeed happened. Mrs Oswald is still in the custody of the Secret

Service. To isolate a witness for nine weeks and to subject her to repeated questioning by the Secret Service in this manner is reminiscent of police behaviour in other countries, where it is called brain-washing. *How was it possible for Earl Warren to forecast that Marina Oswald's evidence would be exactly the reverse of what she had previously believed?*

After Ruby had killed Oswald, DA Wade made a statement about Oswald's movements following the assassination. He explained that Oswald had taken a bus, but he described the point at which Oswald had entered the vehicle as seven blocks away from the point located by the bus driver in his affidavit. Oswald, Wade continued, then took a taxi driven by a Darryll Click, who had signed an affidavit. An enquiry at the City Transportation Company revealed that no such taxi driver had ever existed in Dallas. Presented with this evidence, Wade altered the driver's name to William Wahley. Wade has been DA in Dallas for 14 years and before that was an FBI agent. *How does a District Attorney of Wade's great experience account for all the extraordinary changes in evidence and testimony which he has announced during the Oswald case?*

These are only a few of the questions raised by the official versions of the assassination and by the way in which the entire case against Oswald has been conducted. Sixteen questions are no substitute for a full examination of all the factors in this case, but I hope that they indicate the importance of such an investigation. I am indebted to Mr Mark Lane, the New York criminal Lawyer who was appointed Counsel for Oswald by his mother, for much of the information in this article. Mr Lane's enquiries, which are continuing, deserve widespread support. A Citizens' Committee of Inquiry has been established in New York[1] for such a purpose, and comparable committees are being set up in Europe.

In Britain I invited people eminent in the intellectual life of the country to join a 'Who killed Kennedy Committee', which at the moment of writing consists of the following people: Mr John Arden, playwright; Mrs Carolyn Wedgwood Benn, from Cincinnati, wife of Anthony Wedgwood Benn, MP; Lord Boyd-Orr, former director-general of the UN Food and Agricultural Organisation and a Nobel Peace Prize winner; Mr John Calder, publisher; Professor William Empsom, Professor of English Literature at Sheffield University; Mr Michael Foot, Member of Parliament; Mr Kingsley Martin, former editor of the *New Statesman*; Sir Compton Mackenzie, writer; Mr J. B. Priestley, playwright and author; Sir Herbert Read, art critic; Mr Tony Richardson, film director; Dr Mervyn Stockwood, Bishop of Southwark; Professor Hugh Trevor-Roper, Regius Professor of Modern History at Oxford University; Mr Kenneth Tynan, Literary Manager of the National Theatre; and myself.

We view the problem with the utmost seriousness. US Embassies have long ago reported to Washington world-wide disbelief in the official charges against Oswald, but this has never been reflected by the American press. No US television programme or mass circulation newspaper has challenged the permanent basis of all the allegations—that Oswald was the assassin, and that he acted alone. It is a task which is left to the American people.

[1] Room 422, 156 Fifth Avenue, New York, N.Y. (telephone: YU 9-6850).

THE LABOUR PARTY'S FOREIGN POLICY

A speech delivered at the London School of Economics on 15th February, 1965
by Bertrand Russell

Before his speech, which begins overleaf, Lord Russell made this emergency statement on the situation in Vietnam:

'The world is on the brink of war as it was at the time of the Cuban Crisis. American attacks on North Vietnam are desperate acts of piratical madness. The people of South Vietnam want neutrality and independence for their country. America, in the course of a war of pure domination in the South, attacked a sovereign state in the North because the us has been defeated by the resistance of the entire population in South Vietnam.

We must demand the recall of the Geneva Conference for immediate negotiations. I urge world protest at every us Embassy. And in Britain the craven and odious support for American madness by the Labour Government must be attacked by meetings, marches, demonstrations and all other forms of protest.

If this aggressive war is not ended now, the world will face total war. The issue must be resolved without a nuclear war. This is only possible by world outcry now against the United States. The American proposition that an independent Vietnam free of us control is worse than a nuclear war is madness. If America is allowed to have its cruel way, the world will be the slave of the United States.

Once more America summons mankind to the brink of world war.

Once more America is willing to run the risk of destroying the human race rather than bow to the general will.

Either America is stopped now or there will be crisis after crisis until, in utter weariness, the world decides for suicide.'

My purpose in what I am about to say is to examine the relations between the foreign policy of the Labour Party before the General Election and the policy of the Labour Government in regard to international politics. I should like to recall to you, first, the preamble to that section—almost the last—in the Labour Manifesto of last September, entitled 'New Prospects for Peace'. I take it from *The Times* of September 12th.

It begins with a very brief history of East–West relations since 1945 and says that even in 'the grimmest periods. . . . Labour always regarded the Cold War strategies as second best . . . and remained faithful to its long-term belief in the establishment of East–West co-operation as the basis for a strengthened United Nations developing towards World Government.'

It castigates the Tory Government for their old-fashioned policies, especially the Tory failure to relax tensions and to halt the spread of nuclear weapons. 'The Labour Government will do all that is possible to rectify these policies.'

The Manifesto then considers the means to be taken to 'relax tensions'. 'First and foremost', it says, 'will come our initiative in the field of disarmament. We are convinced that the time is opportune for a new breakthrough in the disarmament negotiations, releasing scarce resources and manpower desperately needed to raise living standards throughout the world.'

'We shall appoint a Minister in the Foreign Office with special responsibility for disarmament to take a new initiative in the Disarmament Committee in association with our friends and allies.'

'We have', it says, 'put forward constructive proposals:
   (1) To stop the spread of nuclear weapons.
   (2) To establish nuclear free zones in Africa, Latin America and Central Europe.
   (3) To achieve controlled reductions in manpower and arms.
   (4) To stop the private sale of arms.
   (5) To establish an International Disarmament Agency to supervise a disarmament treaty.'

The Labour Government has, to be sure, appointed a Minister in the Foreign Office with special responsibility for disarmament and even an arms control and disarmament research unit headed by a reader in international relations at the LSE. It has, indeed, appointed so many new Ministers and departments for various phases of disarmament and defence and offence that one is hard put to it to know to whom to apply for what.

As to the five proposals. Nothing, so far as the Press has told us, has been done about implementing any of them. Far from taking measures to stop the spread of nuclear weapons, the Labour Government has done quite the opposite. Nor has it taken measures to achieve controlled reductions in manpower and arms—it has turned down any suggestion of reducing the British Army in Germany. Little seems to have come out of the propositions of Mr Rapacki concerning a nuclear free zone in Central Europe. Chinese proposals—pleas, even—for a nuclear free zone in Asia and/or the Pacific have been passed over in apparent scorn. I know of no measures taken to stop the private sale of arms or to establish an International Disarmament Agency.

A few lines further on in the Manifesto, the following sentence occurs; 'Labour will stand by its pledge to end the supply of arms to South Africa.' 'Britain,' it says, 'of all nations, cannot stand by as an inactive observer of this tragic situation.' Admirable statements, and backed by previous admirable statements: the *Sunday Times* of January 26, 1964, reports Mrs Barbara Castle as saying, in regard to a possible order from South Africa for Bloodhound bombers, 'If an order is placed before the election we shall do all we can to stop it.' Mr Wilson has, in the past, referred to the arms traffic with South Africa as 'this bloody traffic in these weapons of oppression', and called on the people of Britain to 'Act now to stop' it. . . . But, on November 25, 1964, Mr Wilson announced that the Labour Government had determined to honour the contract entered into during the rule of the Tory Government for 16 Buccaneers for South Africa.

Following the five proposals that I have cited, the Manifesto says: 'In a further effort to relax tension, a Labour Government will work actively to bring Communist China into its proper place in the United Nations; as well as making an all-out effort to develop East–West trade as the soundest economic basis for peaceful co-existence.' Britain has achieved nothing since the advent of the Labour Government towards the admission of China into the UN nor has it appreciably increased East–West trade. Traders are usually ahead of politicians, Tory traders no less than Labour traders.

The Manifesto continues with an item which, in the light of the Government's actions, does not read well: it says, 'Peaceful co-existence, however, can only be achieved if a sincere readiness to negotiate is combined with a firm determination to resist both threats and pressures'. It is difficult to equate this statement with the refusal, curt and out-of-hand, given by the Labour Government to the proposals of the Chinese Government for summit discussions of disarmament and other international matters which our Press told us took place soon after the Labour Government's advent.

That the Labour Government 'will continue to insist on guarantees for the freedom of West Berlin' we do not yet know—the matter has not come to the fore during Labour's rule. Nor do we yet know how far the Labour Government will be able to implement its admirable suggestions concerning the UN nor how far it will be able to take us towards world government, which the Manifesto says is the final objective—as I believe it should be. So far, Britain under the Labour Government has done nothing to strengthen the UN, though it has been, according to *The Guardian* (27 January, 1965) 'giving close study to the question of designating specific military units for potential use in United Nations peace-keeping operations'. In the light of events during the past two or three months, I cannot, however, feel very hopeful as I read what the Manifesto has to say on these matters, much as I agree with it regarding them.

I propose to take up further on in my discussion of the Labour Government's policy the question of how far the measures which it has so far indulged in tend to relax the tensions of the Cold War, as the Manifesto says the Party wishes to do. But I will continue for a moment with the next items mentioned in the Manifesto; the Party's 'Defence Policy Outline' and its 'New Approach' to defence.

It excoriates the 'run down defences' of the Tory Government whose wastefulness and insistence upon sticking to such affairs as Blue Streak, Skybolt and Polaris, and whose inefficient policy in regard to the aircraft industry has resulted in our defences being obsolescent and meagre. It proposes to institute a revision of the Nassau agreement to buy Polaris know-how and missiles from the United States. But, in face of the storm about TSR 2 bombers and of the fact that it is continuing plans for Polaris submarines and is discussing a nuclear umbrella for South East Asia, one wonders how far the Government intends to go with such plans. It seems extraordinary that, having set itself such a programme as the Manifesto suggests, it had not examined the problems of conversion very carefully and come to some sort of plan to avoid or minimise the hardships that would be entailed in the way of unemployment and waste of machinery and money. But no evidence has been given the ordinary newspaper reader that any such basic studies were made.

It is possible that the Government will strengthen conventional regular forces in order to contribute its share to NATO and keep its peace-keeping commitments to the Commonwealth and the UN as the Manifesto says it stresses doing. This seems, however, unless it runs concurrently with cutting down in other quarters, to be contrary to the controlled reduction in arms which it also says it will strive for.

The next item is both bewildering and interesting. The Manifesto says: 'We are against the development of national nuclear deterrents and oppose the current American proposal for a new mixed-manned nuclear surface fleet (MLF). We believe in the inter-dependence of the Western alliance and will put constructive proposals for integrating all NATO's nuclear weapons under effective political control so that all the partners in the Alliance have a proper share in their deployment and control.' A little further on, when discussing the folly of the Conservatives in entering into the Nassau agreement and in talking about an 'independent British deterrent', it says: This nuclear pretence runs the risk of encouraging the 'spread of nuclear weapons to countries not possessing them, including Germany'. And yet, when the Prime Minister announced what one must suppose are the 'new constructive proposals' which the Manifesto told us to expect, they turned out to be the Atlantic Nuclear Force (ANF). The ANF is to be not merely, as was the MLF, a mixed-manned force of surface ships, but is to include other nuclear delivery systems, including aircraft and submarines. It therefore encourages the spread of nuclear weapons more enthusiastically than does the MLF—which I agree was a deplorable suggestion—and certainly encourages the spread of nuclear weapons to Germany. The remedy is, therefore, far worse than the disaster it professes to correct.

If you would like a glimpse of the chicanery indulged in, I advise you to read the reports of the Parliamentary debate on defence in the week beginning 14th December, and the report in *The Times* of 18 December entitled 'Britain to waive control of Polaris weapons', 'Our bombers over Asia' in the *Daily Worker* of the same date, and 'Britain to retain part of V-bomber force' in *The Guardian* of the previous day. Amongst other information to be gained from these various sources are the facts that Britain proposes to give a certain number of its ships and V-bombers by devious routes to NATO, but will keep others to be used by Britain outside the NATO area. The Government thereby persuades the populace that it is keeping its promise to do away with its independent deterrent and at the same time can, independently, form 'a nuclear umbrella' over South East Asia. By means of the ANF we soothe German feelings, since the Germans will participate equally with us in the control and benefits of this nuclear force and will, therefore, be distracted from pushing for an independent nuclear deterrent of their own. This scheme of the ANF has been put to the public through the Press in such a way that the layman is entirely baffled and cannot understand either what the ANF consists in or how very contrary it is to professed beliefs of the Labour Party as given in the Manifesto or as understood by the lay members of the Party. It is a bare-faced turn-about carried off, in so far as the Government has succeeded in carrying it off, by being wrapped up in a welter of words and the happy slogans that the Prime Minister did not knuckle under to the US in the matter of the MLF and Britain is once more taking the initiative in constructive pacific proposals.

The Manifesto concludes with eight paragraphs in which it first gives itself a reason for not carrying out its promises at once by saying that it does not yet know what damage inflicted upon the country by the Tories it will have to repair. It seems a little odd, perhaps, that the members of the Labour Party who aspired to office were so taken by surprise by the financial state of the country—a situation that was fairly apparent to many laymen—and had not prepared any adequate plans to cope with it. But I do not intend to go into economics and finances here. The Manifesto goes on to say that a Labour Government will first of all have to make itself more efficient than the Government which it supersedes. Presumably the rash of new offices and holders of office in the present Government is its answer to the need of efficiency. Secondly, it says that the Government will seek to establish a true partnership between the people and their Parliament; and thirdly it must foster, throughout the nation, a new and more critical spirit. 'The Government can give a lead,' it says, 'by subjecting to continuing and probing review of its own Departments of State, the administration of justice and the social services.' And here I should like to recount an experience of mine that appears to run counter to the promise contained in the statement from the Manifesto I have just cited. Three eminent Russians were appointed by the Russian Government to discuss various topics of international interest with me. In November these three Russians applied for visas to enter Britain. The Home Office at first refused visas for all three, but after protest, allowed visas for two of them. In regard to the most eminent of the three, the Chief Archivist of the Supreme Soviet, the Home Office remained adamant. I wrote to the Home Office—and I am, of course, speaking of the Labour Home Office—begging them to rescind their ban upon a visa for the Chief Archivist. After many weeks during which I was unable to learn anything of the fate of my letter, I received a reply from the Home Secretary saying that he did not feel able to grant my request. I wrote again and wrote also to the Prime Minister. After some time, I received from the Home Secretary the same reply as before, and from the Prime Minister a notification that he agreed with the Home Secretary and would not ask him to reconsider. On no occasion from beginning to end, has any reason been given me or to the Russians for the ban. If this experience is typical, it hardly bears out the claim of the Manifesto that the Government would, or does welcome criticism or open discussion with its electors and members of its Party.

The Manifesto ends with a stirring pronouncement that the Labour Government 'must put an end to the dreary commercialism and personal selfishness which have dominated the years of Conservative government' and says that 'the Labour Party is offering Britain a new way of life that will stir our hearts'.

There is a lot of ironic fun to be got out of that Manifesto now that we have seen its fruits.

So much for the Manifesto upon which the present Government was elected and for how far it has carried out its promises in certain respects. I propose now to return to one of its most important promised intentions: its determination to relax the tensions of the Cold War. And I beg of you to ask yourselves, as I recount what has been happening in certain areas of international activity, whether you consider that this activity to which the present

Government has contributed and proposes to continue to contribute is calculated to relax any tensions whatever.

You doubtless know a good deal about the war in South Vietnam, but I will give a very brief outline of its progress and character. South Vietnam was part of French Cochin-China, but after a long process of civil war, the French were excluded from the whole region. A conference was summoned to meet at Geneva in 1954. The conclusions reached were sensible, and, if they had been carried out, no trouble would have arisen. Vietnam was to be independent and neutral, and was to have a parliamentary government established by a General Election. The Americans did not like this. They professed to suspect that Vietnam would become part of the Communist bloc if left to itself and that North Vietnam was already, and has continued to be, part of the Communist bloc, in spite of reiterated statements by the Government of North Vietnam that they wish to be neutral.

The Americans sent observers who decided that South Vietnam was too disturbed for a general election. There were in South Vietnam three parties; the peasants, who constituted the large majority; the Buddhists; and a tiny minority of Christians, who had been supporters of the French. The Americans decided to support this small faction. They did so at first by sending technical aid and material and 'Advisers'. It was soon seen, however, that the 'Advisers' were taking far more than a passive part in the war that ensued between the American-supported minority and the Buddhists and peasants. The war has continued now for many years and the American-supported Government—or, more outspokenly, the Americans—have steadily lost ground. It has been warfare of an incredibly brutal kind, brutal to a degree seldom equalled by any civilised Power.

Eight million people have been put in barbed wire concentration camps involving forced labour. The country—civilians, animals and crops, as well as warriors and jungle—has been sprayed with jelly gasoline and poison chemicals. Fifty thousand villages were burnt in 1962 alone. The following account was published in the Dallas *Morning News* on January 1, 1963: 'Supposedly the purpose of the fortified villages is to keep the Vietcong out. But barbed wire denies entrance and exit. Vietnamese farmers are forced at gunpoint into these virtual concentration camps. Their homes, possessions and crops are burned. In the province of Kien-Tuong, seven villagers were led into the town square. Their stomachs were slashed, their livers extracted and put on display. These victims were women and children. In another village, expectant mothers were invited to the square by Government forces to be honoured. Their stomachs were ripped open and their unborn babies removed.' And the anti-Communist Democratic Party of Vietnam told the International Control Commission that: 'Decapitation, eviscerations and the public display of murdered women and children are common.' It is, as the *Nation* of January 19, 1963, called it, 'a dirty, cruel war', and one can only agree with the leader of the Vietnamese Democratic Party when he said in an interview on CBS (reported in the Vietnamese Democratic Bulletin for September, 1963): 'It is certainly an ironic way to protect the peasant masses from Communism.'

It is generally admitted that there is no hope that the Americans can win this war. Obviously failing in South Vietnam, they are now considering extending the war to North Vietnam in spite of the fact that China has declared its support of Vietnam if that should happen, and Russia may follow suit. The Labour Party had, hitherto, been opposed to this policy which involves risk of world war. As late as June 4, 1964, the *Daily Worker* said that Mr Wilson, at the end of talks in Moscow, was opposed to carrying the war into North Vietnam as well as to North Vietnamese infiltration into the South. But, since the formation of his Government, the Labour Party has agreed with America to support that country in its war of conquest. *The Guardian* reports on December 10, 1964, that Mr Wilson told President Johnson that Britain wholly supported the legitimate role the United States is playing in South Vietnam. The Labour Government is doing this in spite of the fact that the vast majority of the inhabitants of South Vietnam are opposed to this American war and want to achieve peace and neutrality—as the North Vietnamese have repeatedly asserted that they also wish—and in spite of the extreme unparalleled brutality of the war, and in spite of the fact—and this is to be noted—that the Americans have no shred of right in South Vietnam and are conducting a war of a type to which the Labour Party has always been passionately opposed. Moreover, if the Americans extend the war to North Vietnam, as they threaten to do, we and they will be involved in a war with China of which the consequences are bound to be horrible—possibly all-out nuclear war. For all these consequences, the Labour Government will share the responsibility.

A similar situation is developing in the Congo. Katanga is incredibly rich in valuable minerals, especially cobalt. Cobalt would be necessary for the Doomsday Bomb. When the Congo became independent, the Western Powers, especially America and Belgium, made a determined effort to preserve for the West the products of Katanga. Lumumba, who was the Congo's choice as Prime Minister, was murdered, and Tshombe, under Western pressure, was made Prime Minister of the whole country. The country rose against this decision, and the Americans and Belgians sent a military expedition to enforce their will. This expedition, the British, under the leadership of the Labour Government, supported, and they allowed it to use Ascension Island as a convenient spot from which to conduct the invasion. There is, in consequence, a war of devastation in progress throughout the Congo. The likelihood is that this will degenerate into guerilla warfare which will continue without securing victory for the West. Perhaps an excerpt from the writing of one of those who was a mercenary fighting for the West in the Congo would bring home the sort of war we are supporting there. I quote this from *News of the World* for 22 November, 1964:

'On the way to Stanleyville one of our vehicles broke down. We took our gear off it and retreated into the bush. Late in the afternoon we went back to the vehicle, but found it completely wrecked. . . .

'The young English lieutenant was furious. "We will give the bastards a real lesson." He ordered us to move at once on the nearest village and take it apart.

'It was a familiar enough command. It seemed to me we had been taking villages apart, innocent villages of peaceful farming folk who did not want any part of this war, all the way along the track from far down in the south.

'We would turn up unexpectedly, open fire without warning, race through the place, burning every pathetic shanty and shack to the ground regardless of who might be inside. The idea was to spread the image of our determination and ruthlessness; to terrorize the whole area; to give the rebels an example of what they were in for. . . .

'It seemed almost certain that the villagers knew nothing about the activities of the rebels. I doubted they even knew the lorry had been destroyed.

'It was just before dusk when we came. Unsuspecting women were hustling around, carrying water and going about the last of their day's chores. Children were playing in the dust, laughing and shouting to one another.

'We paused for a few minutes, and then came the order to fire. There was a great crackle of shots from machine guns and our deadly new Belgian rifles. Women screamed and fell. Little children just stood there, dazed, or cartwheeled hideously as bullets slammed into them.

'Then, as usual, we raced into the place, still firing as we went. Some of us pitched cans of petrol on to the homes before putting a match to them. Others threw phosphorous hand grenades, which turned human beings into blazing inextinguishable torches of fire.

'For a while, as we raced along, there was bedlam. Shrieks, moans, shrill cries for mercy. And, above all, the throaty, half-crazed bellowing of those commandoes among us who quite obviously utterly loved this sort of thing.

'Then, as we moved away beyond the village, the comparative silence, the distant, hardly distinguishable cries of the wounded, the acrid smell of burning flesh.'

The account continues, but I do not think that I need pursue it to illustrate my point. The cardinal point in the training of these mercenaries—and again I quote—is 'that never, in any circumstances, should prisoners be taken. "Even if men, women and children come running to you" I was told, "even if they fall on their knees before you, begging for mercy, don't hesitate. Just shoot to kill." '

I need hardly say that this young man was sickened of being a hired assassin and ceased to be one. But, in England, under the aegis of the Labour Government, we are continuing to support this slaughter. On November 20, 1964, *The Times* announced that Mr George Thomson, our Minister of State at the Foreign Office, was informed during the previous week by the Belgian Government that they were engaged in contingency planning with the us Government. Britain then gave her permission to use Ascension Island. *The Times* also announced that Belgian troops were flown to Ascension Island with British permission. The *Daily Express* of 30 November, 1964, reports: 'At one stage the Cabinet considered sending British troops. Britain was the first to suggest armed intervention to Belgium. But officials in Whitehall now say that the terrain in rebel-held areas prevents large-scale troop landings.' And on December 15, 1964, Mr George Thomson stated: 'We give outright support to Tshombe.' Yet, two days later our Minister of Defence (one of them, anyway) 'referred to "primitive barbarism" in the Congo and said that we had to see that other parts of Africa and Asia were not plunged into "a similar state of chaos." ' Does this mean that we are to uphold similar bloody and unjustified slaughter otherwhere in Africa, carried on with the permission and help of the Labour Government? The record is one of which I as an Englishman cannot be proud. As a member of the Party responsible, I am sickened.

But to move on: Similar troubles are being stirred up by British initiative in the war between Malaysia and Indonesia, a war likely to be as bloody and atrocious as the two of which I have been speaking and to last as long, with no victory possible. On page 65 of the report of the 62nd Annual Conference of the Labour Party, July 1963, you will find that Labour supported the Malaysia Bill for the relinquishment of British sovereignty over North Borneo, Sarawak and Singapore. Labour felt—and I quote—'that the federation of Malaysia would play an important stabilising role in S.E. Asia.' On December 10 of this last year, *The Guardian* reports that Mr Wilson told President Johnson that Britain has 8,000 troops in Borneo, 20,000 in Malaysia as a whole: and the *New Statesman* of January 15, 1965, says that 'the bulk of Britain's fleet, some 700 ships including a Commando "bushfire" ship and aircraft carriers' are now in the waters near Malaysia and Indonesia. 'The Commonwealth Brigade is in Malaya facing Sumatra.'

But these are not the only places where the Labour Government is supporting Western imperialism. In both British Guiana and Aden and the South Arabian Protectorates it is following the policies of the Tory Government although it has sent its Colonial Secretary travelling to the trouble spots to study the situations once again.

All these are shameful attempts to support the tottering supremacy of Britain and America against the wishes of the populations concerned, and against the vast movement for independence which is agitating formerly subject peoples. It is a terrible fact that the Labour Government is supporting these hopeless and cruel attempts at subjugation. It is an almost worse fact that it is running the risk for us of these wars escalating to large nuclear wars. Its reception of China's overtures towards peace and disarmament is a dreary pointer to its attitude. Soon after the Labour Government took office, Premier Chou En-lai wrote to our Prime Minister proposing that the governments of the world should undertake not to use nuclear weapons, and suggesting a summit conference. Mr Wilson replied: 'I do not believe the procedure you have suggested is the best way to make progress in present circumstances.' He criticised China on two grounds: for carrying out a nuclear test in the atmosphere and for her approach being 'not realistic'. This attitude on the part of the Prime Minister hardly seems a means of relaxing tensions or of resolving differences between East and West or of halting the spread of nuclear weapons—all of which the electoral Manifesto said the Labour Government would try to do. Again it is following the dangerous policies of the past. In the past few years the West has rebuffed several overtures made by China towards nuclear disarmament and denuclearised zones. If China is not included in disarmament discussions there is little hope for peace in the world. The Labour Government might have taken—might still take—a new and more realistic attitude, taking the promises of the East, as well as the West, at face value, at least as a basis for discussion, until they have been proved to be hollow. But our new Minister for Disarmament seems to be interested chiefly in how to keep up our armed forces more cheaply than hitherto. (See his speech at Salisbury 2 February, 1965, and the extracts from it which the Labour Party appears to think important.)

In none of the actions of the Labour Government has there been evidence of the promised effort to relax the tensions of the Cold War.

What the Labour Government has accomplished in the way of carrying out the promises made in its electoral Manifesto is to appoint a Minister for Disarmament in the Foreign Office. Possibly, also, it has made the Government more efficient by the vast proliferation of new offices, ministries and committees which it has instituted.

It has done nothing apparent to implement Labour's promises in the very important fields of disarmament negotiations, the establishment of nuclear-free zones, the reduction of man-power and arms, the private sale of arms, a drastic re-examination and modification of our defence policy, a re-negotiation of the Nassau agreement, the admission of China into the UN, or the revivification of the morale and the increase of the powers of the UN. Nor does it show any signs of the self-criticism or of the welcome to criticism by their fellow Labour Party members which it advocated.

Moreover, it has directly contravened its definite statements in regard to arms for South Africa and to opposition to the spread of nuclear arms. And, perhaps worst of all, it has increased by many times and in many ways the Cold War tensions between East and West.

What are we to think of this betrayal? Is it the result of a kind of black-mail owing to the parlous state of the economy and finances of the country? But, surely, those who were about to take office must have examined the economic and financial condition of the country and the extent of its dependence upon the United States, and made plans to carry out their promises with the results of their examination in mind. Had they not the courage to attack their problems boldly—or, indeed, with the probable end-results of their actions in mind, realistically?

What hope is there for Parliamentary democracy when the leaders of a Party, upon achieving office, act in direct contradiction to their electoral promises? Those Labour Party members who do not like treachery have hitherto kept quiet in the interests of unity. But what is the use of unity in evil? The cardinal virtues in gangs of criminals are unity and loyalty. Before we are committed irrevocably—and we are rapidly being so committed—to policies leading to disaster for ourselves and for all the inhabitants of the world, we should make known in unmistakable terms our abhorrence of present policies. To wait much longer will be to wait too long. If the Labour Party is to regain any part of its former championship of vitally necessary reforms, those who voted for it on the basis of its electoral Manifesto will have to insist that the leading members of this present Government must lose hope of ever holding office again. Whatever they may have done or not done in regard to their pre-election promises, they have got us into, and propose to keep us in, at least two of the most cruel and useless wars that there have ever been—wars of extermination. Against this policy we must protest in every possible way.

SPEECH TO FIRST MEETING OF MEMBERS OF THE WAR CRIMES TRIBUNAL, NOVEMBER 13, 1966

Allow me to express my appreciation to you for your willingness to participate in this Tribunal. It has been convened so that we may investigate and assess the character of the United States' war in Vietnam.

The Tribunal has no clear historical precedent. The Nuremberg Tribunal, although concerned with designated war crimes, was possible because the victorious allied Powers compelled the vanquished to present their leaders for trial. Inevitably, the Nuremberg trials, supported as they were by State power, contained a strong element of *realpolitik*. Despite these inhibiting factors, which call in question certain of the Nuremberg procedures, the Nuremberg Tribunal expressed the sense of outrage, which was virtually universal, at the crimes committed by the Nazis in Europe. Somehow, it was widely felt, there had to be criteria against which such actions could be judged, and according to which Nazi crimes could be condemned. Many felt it was morally necessary to record the full horror. It was hoped that a legal method could be devised, capable of coming to terms with the magnitude of Nazi crimes. These ill-defined but deeply-felt, sentiments surrounded the Nuremberg Tribunal.

Our own task is more difficult, but the same responsibility obtains. We do not represent any State power, nor can we compel the policy-makers responsible for crimes against the people of Vietnam to stand accused before us. We lack *force majeure*. The procedures of a trial are impossible to implement.

I believe that these apparent limitations are, in fact, virtues. We are free to conduct a solemn and historic investigation, uncompelled by reasons of State or other such obligations. Why is this war being fought in Vietnam? In whose interest is it being waged? We have, I am certain, an obligation to study these questions and to pronounce on them, after thorough investigation, for in doing so we can assist mankind in understanding why a small agrarian people have endured for more than twelve years the assault of the largest industrial power on earth, possessing the most developed and cruel military capacity.

I have prepared a paper, which I hope you will wish to read during your deliberations. It sets out a considerable number of reports from Western newspapers and such sources, giving an indication of the record of the United States in Vietnam. These reports should make it clear that we enter our enquiry with considerable *prima facie* evidence of crimes reported not by the victims but by media favourable to the policies responsible. I believe that we are justified in concluding that it is necessary to convene a solemn Tribunal, composed of men eminent not through their power, but through their intellectual and moral contribution to what we optimistically call 'human civilisation'.

I feel certain that this Tribunal will perform an historic role if its investigation is exhaustive. We must record the truth in Vietnam. We must pass judgment on what we find to be the truth. We must warn of the consequences of this truth. We must, moreover, reject the view that only indifferent men are impartial men. We must repudiate the degenerate conception of individual intelligence, which confuses open minds with empty ones.

I hope that this Tribunal will select men who respect the truth and whose life's work bears witness to that respect. Such men will have feelings about the *prima facie* evidence of which I speak. No man unacquainted with this evidence through indifference has any claim to judge it.

I enjoin this Tribunal to select commissions for the purpose of dividing the areas of investigation and taking responsibility for their conduct, under the Tribunal's jurisdiction. I hope that teams of qualified investigators will be chosen to study in Vietnam the evidence of which we have witnessed only a small part. I should like to see the United States Government requested to present evidence in defence of its actions. The resistance of the National Liberation Front and of the Democratic Republic of Vietnam must also be assessed and placed in its true relation to the civilisation we choose to uphold. We have about five months of work before us, before the full hearings, which have been planned for Paris.

As I reflect on this work, I cannot help thinking of the events of my life, because of the crimes I have seen and the hopes I have nurtured. I have lived through the Dreyfus Case and been party to the investigation of the crimes committed by King Leopold in the Congo. I can recall many wars. Much injustice has been recorded quietly during these decades. In my own experience I cannot discover a situation quite comparable. I cannot recall a people so tormented, yet so devoid of the failings of their tormentors. I do not know any other conflict in which the disparity in physical power was so vast. I have no memory of any people so enduring, or of any nation with a spirit of resistance so unquenchable.

I will not conceal from you the profundity of my admiration and passion for the people of Vietnam. I cannot relinquish the duty to judge what has been done to them because I have such feelings. Our mandate is to uncover and tell all. My conviction is that no greater tribute can be provided than an offer of the truth, born of intense and unyielding enquiry.

May this Tribunal prevent the crime of silence.

THE AIMS AND OBJECTIVES OF THE TRIBUNAL
NOVEMBER 1966

The conscience of mankind is profoundly disturbed by the war being waged in Vietnam. It is a war in which the world's wealthiest and most powerful State is opposed to a nation of poor peasants, who have been fighting for their independence for a quarter of a century. It appears that this war is being waged in violation of international law and custom.

Every day, the world Press and, particularly, that of the United States, publishes reports which, if proved, would represent an ever growing violation of the principles established by the Nuremberg Tribunal and rules fixed by international agreements.

Moved and shocked by the suffering endured by the Vietnamese people and convinced that humanity must know the truth in order to deliver a serious and impartial judgement on the events taking place in Vietnam and where the responsibility for them lies, we have accepted the invitation of Bertrand Russell to meet, in order to examine these facts scrupulously and confront them with the rules of law which govern them.

It has been alleged that in the first nine months of 1966, the air force of the United States has dropped, in Vietnam, four million pounds of bombs daily. If it continues at this rate to the end of the year, the total will constitute a greater mass of explosives than it unloded on the entire Pacific theatre during the whole of the Second World War. The area bombarded in this way is no bigger than the states of New York and Pennsylvania. In the South, the us forces and their docile Saigon allies have herded eight million people, peasants and their families, into barbed wire encampments under the surveillance of the political police. Chemical poisons have been, and are being, used to defoliate and render barren tens of thousands of acres of farmland. Crops are being systematically destroyed—and this in a country where, even in normal times, the average man or woman eats less than half the food consumed by the average American (and lives to less than one third of his age).

Irrigation systems are deliberately disrupted. Napalm, phosphorus bombs and a variety of other, sadistically designed and hitherto unknown weapons are being used against the population of both North and South Vietnam. More than five hundred thousand Vietnamese men, women and children have perished under this onslaught, more than the number of soldiers the United States lost in both world wars, although the population of Vietnam had already been decimated during the Japanese and French occupations and the famine which followed the Second World War.

Even though we have not been entrusted with this task by any organised authority, we have taken the responsibility in the interest of humanity and the preservation of civilisation. We act on our own accord, in complete independence from any government and any official or semi-official organisation, in the firm belief that we express a deep anxiety and remorse felt by many of our fellow humans in many countries. We trust that our action will help to arouse the conscience of the world.

We, therefore, consider ourselves a Tribunal which, even if it has not the power to impose sanctions, will have to answer, amongst others, the following questions:

1. Has the United States Government (and the Governments of Australia, New Zealand and South Korea) committed acts of aggression according to international law?

2. Has the American Army made use of or experimented with new weapons or weapons forbidden by the laws of war (gas, special chemical products, napalm, etc.)?

3. Has there been bombardment of targets of a purely civilian character, for example hospitals, schools, sanatoria, dams, etc., and on what scale has this occurred?

4. Have Vietnamese prisoners been subjected to inhuman treatment forbidden by the laws of war and, in particular, to torture or to mutilation? Have there been unjustified reprisals against the civilian population, in particular, the execution of hostages?

5. Have forced labour camps been created, has there been deportation of the population or other acts tending to the extermination of the population and which can be characterised juridically as acts of genocide?

If the Tribunal decides that one, or all, of these crimes have been committed, it will be up to the Tribunal to decide who bears the responsibility for them.

This Tribunal will examine all the evidence that may be placed before it by any source or party. The evidence may be oral, or in the form of documents. No evidence relevant to our purposes will be refused attention. No witness competent to testify about the events with which our enquiry is concerned will be denied a hearing.

The National Liberation Front of Vietnam and the Government of the Democratic Republic of Vietnam have assured us of their willingness to co-operate, to provide the necessary information, and to help us in checking the accuracy and reliability of the information. The Cambodian Head of State, Prince Sihanouk, has similarly offered to help by the production of evidence. We trust that they will honour this pledge and we shall gratefully accept their help, without prejudice to our own views or attitude. We renew, as a Tribunal, the appeal which Bertrand Russell has addressed in his name to the Government of the United States. We invite the Government of the United States to present evidence or cause it to be presented, and to instruct their officials or representatives to appear and state their case. Our purpose is to establish, without fear or favour, the full truth about this war. We sincerely hope that our efforts will contribute to the world's justice, to the re-establishment of peace and the liberation of the oppressed peoples.

*   *   *

RESOLUTION OF THE TRIBUNAL

We are grateful to the Bertrand Russell Peace Foundation for the work which it has already done. We are sure that the preliminary steps already taken by it will help us to complete our task within a reasonable time and with considerable more efficiency than it would have been possible if its preliminary work had not helped our deliberations.

APPEAL FOR SUPPORT FOR THE INTERNATIONAL WAR
CRIMES TRIBUNAL

For several years Western news media have unwittingly documented the record of crime committed by the United States in Vietnam, which comprises an overwhelming *prima facie* indictment of the American war. The terrible series of photographs, and accounts of torture, mutilation and experimental war has impelled Bertrand Russell to call us together to conduct an exhaustive inquiry into the war in all its aspects. Scientists, lawyers, doctors and world renowned scholars will serve on commissions investigating the evidence. Witnesses will be brought from Vietnam to give their first-hand testimony. Investigating teams will travel throughout Vietnam and Indochina, gathering data on the spot. The documentation published in the West and elsewhere will be relentlessly examined. This five months' intensive work, requiring travelling scientific inquiry, and the detailed research, will cost a vast amount of money. Twelve weeks of public hearings will be even more expensive.

The International War Crimes Tribunal is determined to be financially independent. This can only be accomplished through the contributions of every individual who supports the work of the Tribunal and recognizes the profound importance of the full realisation of its task.

We command no state power; we do not represent the strong; we control no armies or treasuries. We act out of the deepest moral concern and depend upon the conscience of ordinary people throughout the world for the real support—the material help, which will determine whether people of Vietnam are to be abandoned in silence or allowed the elementary right of having their plight presented to the conscience of Mankind.

POSTSCRIPT[1]

THE SERIOUS part of my life ever since boyhood has been devoted to two different objects which for a long time remained separate and have only in recent years united into a single whole. I wanted, on the one hand, to find out whether anything could be known; and, on the other hand, to do whatever might be possible toward creating a happier world. Up to the age of thirty-eight I gave most of my energies to the first of these tasks. I was troubled by scepticism and unwillingly forced to the conclusion that most of what passes for knowledge is open to reasonable doubt. I wanted certainty in the kind of way in which people want religious faith. I thought that certainty is more likely to be found in mathematics than elsewhere. But I discovered that many mathematical demonstrations, which my teachers expected me to accept, were full of fallacies, and that, if certainty were indeed discoverable in mathematics, it would be in a new kind of mathematics, with more solid foundations than those that had hitherto been thought secure. But as the work proceeded, I was continually reminded of the fable about the elephant and the tortoise. Having constructed an elephant upon which the mathematical world could rest, I found the elephant tottering, and proceeded to construct a tortoise to keep the elephant from falling. But the tortoise was no more secure than the elephant, and after some twenty years of very arduous toil, I came to the conclusion that there was nothing more that *I* could do in the way of making mathematical knowledge indubitable. Then came the First World War, and my thoughts became concentrated on human misery and folly. Neither misery nor folly seems to me any part of the inevitable lot of man. And I am convinced that intelligence, patience, and eloquence can, sooner or later, lead the human race out of its self-imposed tortures provided it does not exterminate itself meanwhile.

On the basis of this belief, I have had always a certain degree of optimism, although, as I have grown older, the optimism has grown more sober and the happy issue more distant. But I remain completely incapable of agreeing with those who accept fatalistically the view that man is born to trouble. The causes of unhappiness in the past and in the present are not difficult to ascertain. There have been poverty, pestilence,

[1] Published separately as 'Reflections on my Eightieth Birthday' in *Portraits from Memory*.

220

and famine, which were due to man's inadequate mastery of nature. There have been wars, oppressions and tortures which have been due to men's hostility to their fellow men. And there have been morbid miseries fostered by gloomy creeds, which have led men into profound inner discords that made all outward prosperity of no avail. All these are unnecessary. In regard to all of them, means are known by which they can be overcome. In the modern world, if communities are unhappy, it is often because they have ignorances, habits, beliefs, and passions, which are dearer to them than happiness or even life. I find many men in our dangerous age who seem to be in love with misery and death, and who grow angry when hopes are suggested to them. They think hope is irrational and that, in sitting down to lazy despair, they are merely facing facts. I cannot agree with these men. To preserve hope in our world makes calls upon our intelligence and our energy. In those who despair it is frequently the energy that is lacking.

The last half of my life has been lived in one of those painful epochs of human history during which the world is getting worse, and past victories which had seemed to be definitive have turned out to be only temporary. When I was young, Victorian optimism was taken for granted. It was thought that freedom and prosperity would spread gradually throughout the world by an orderly process, and it was hoped that cruelty, tyranny, and injustice would continually diminish. Hardly anyone was haunted by the fear of great wars. Hardly anyone thought of the nineteenth century as a brief interlude between past and future barbarism. For those who grew up in that atmosphere, adjustment to the world of the present has been difficult. It has been difficult not only emotionally but intellectually. Ideas that had been thought adequate have proved inadequate. In some directions valuable freedoms have proved very hard to preserve. In other directions, especially as regards relations between nations, freedoms formerly valued have proved potent sources of disaster. New thoughts, new hopes, new freedoms, and new restrictions upon freedom are needed if the world is to emerge from its present perilous state.

I cannot pretend that what I have done in regard to social and political problems has had any great importance. It is comparatively easy to have an immense effect by means of a dogmatic and precise gospel, such as that of Communism. But for my part I cannot believe that what mankind needs is anything either precise or dogmatic. Nor can I believe with any wholeheartedness in any partial doctrine which deals only with some part or aspect of human life. There are those who hold that everything depends upon institutions, and that good institutions will inevitably bring the millennium. And, on the other hand, there are those who believe that what is needed is a change of heart, and that, in comparison, institutions are of little account. I cannot accept either view. Institutions mould character, and character transforms institutions. Reforms in both must march hand in hand. And if individuals are to retain that measure of initiative and flexibility which they ought to have, they must not be all forced into one rigid mould; or, to change the metaphor, all drilled into one army. Diversity is essential in spite of the fact that it precludes univeral acceptance of a single gospel. But to preach such a doctrine is difficult especially in arduous times. And perhaps it cannot be effective until some bitter lessons have been learned by tragic experience.

My work is near its end, and the time has come when I can survey it as a whole. How far have I succeeded, and how far have I failed? From an early age I thought of myself as dedicated to great and arduous tasks. Nearly three-quarters of a century ago, walking alone in the Tiergarten through melting snow under the coldly glittering March sun, I determined to write two series of books: one abstract, growing gradually more concrete; the other concrete, growing gradually more abstract. They were to be crowned by a synthesis, combining pure theory with a practical social philosophy. Except for the final synthesis, which still eludes me, I have written these books. They have been acclaimed and praised, and the thoughts of many men and women have been affected by them. To this extent I have succeeded.

But as against this must be set two kinds of failure, one outward, one inward.

To begin with the outward failure: the Tiergarten has become a desert; the Brandenburger Tor, through which I entered it on that March morning, has become the boundary of two hostile empires, glaring at each other across a barrier, and grimly preparing the ruin of mankind. Communists, Fascists, and Nazis have successively challenged all that I thought good, and in defeating them much of what their opponents have sought to preserve is being lost. Freedom has come to be thought weakness, and tolerance has been compelled to wear the garb of treachery. Old ideals are judged irrelevant, and no doctrine free from harshness commands respect.

The inner failure, though of little moment to the world, has made my mental life a perpetual battle. I set out with a more or less religious belief in a Platonic eternal world, in which mathematics shone with a beauty like that of the last Cantos of the *Paradiso*. I came to the conclusion that the eternal world is trivial, and that mathematics is only the art of saying the same thing in different words. I set out with a belief that love, free and courageous, could conquer the world without fighting. I came to support a bitter and terrible war. In these respects there was failure.

But beneath all this load of failure I am still conscious of something that I feel to be victory. I may have conceived theoretical truth wrongly, but I was not wrong in thinking that there is such a thing, and that it deserves our allegiance. I may have thought the road to a world of free and happy human beings shorter than it is proving to be, but I was not wrong in thinking that such a world is possible, and that it is worth while to live with a view to bringing it nearer. I have lived in the pursuit of a vision, both personal and social. Personal: to care for what is noble, for what is beautiful, for what is gentle; to allow moments of insight to give wisdom at more mundane times. Social: to see in imagination the society that is to be created, where individuals grow freely, and where hate and greed and envy die because there is nothing to nourish them. These things I believe, and the world, for all its horrors, has left me unshaken.

INDEX

Abbotsbury, 105
ABC of Relativity, The, 15
A-bomb, 181, 194
Aborigines, 27
Acheson, Dean, 90
Acropolis, 67
'Act or Perish', 112, 137–9, 196
Adenauer, Konrad, 146
Adrian, Lord Edgar, 75
'Africa and the Movement for Peace' (BRPF), 192
Alderley, 106
Aldermaston March, 103–4, 114, 125
'A Liberal Decalogue', 60–1
Alice Springs, 27
Allen and Unwin Ltd., George, 125, 167
Ambatielos, Betty, 156; *L. from and to*, 191–2
Ambatielos, Tony, *L. from and to*, 191–2
America, 22, 27–8, 41, 56, 102, 163, 213; *and Baruch proposal*, 17–18, 181; McCarthyism in, 20; *and Rosenberg executions*, 59; *and Sobell case*, 81–2; *and Cuban crisis*, 125, 150, 180; *anti-nuclear protests in*, 133; *and civil defence* 137; *nuclear policy of* 141–4, 192–4, 196, 207–8; *and armament lobby*, 147–9; *and China*, 151; *and Kennedy assassination* 165, 198–9, 204; *and Vietnam war* 168–72, 195, 205, 210–11, 215–19; *whether B.R. is anti-* 176; *Britain's dependence on*, 214
American Committee for Cultural Freedom, 82
American Emergency Civil Liberties Committee, 157
American Mercury, 39
Anglo-Boer War, 94, 97
Anrep, Boris, 66
Arabs, 157, 184; *and Palestine refugees*, 157
Arbuthnot, Helen, 49
Arcadia, 67
Archbishop of Melbourne, 27
Arden, John, 204
A Religious Rebel (Ls. of Mrs Pearsall Smith), 47
Aristotle, 30, 173
Ascension Island, 211–12
Athens, 67–8
Atlantic Peace Foundation (*see also* Bertrand Russell Peace Foundation), 160, 171, 178, 180–1
Atomic Scientists' Association, 77
Atomic War (*see also* H-Bomb), 61–3

Attlee, Clement *L. from*, 45
Auchinleck, Field Marshall Sir Claude, *L. from*, 178
Austen, Jane, 106
Australia, 217; *visit to*, 26–8
Australian Institute of International Affairs, 26
Austria, 84, 86
'Authority and the Individual', 22
Ayer, A. J., 123; *Ls. to and from*, 130–1

Bahba, Dr, (*see* Dr H. J. Bhabha)
Bahrein, Sheikh of, 158
Barnes, Albert C., 16, 39–40, 42
Barnes Institute, 39
Baruch Proposal, 17, 181
Bay of Pigs, 196
Beaconsfield, Lord, 57
Bean, T. E., 123
Beaverbrook, Lord, 55
Bedford, 12th Duke of, *L. from*, 44
Bedford, 13th Duke of, 123, 162, 179
Behaviour and Social Life of Honeybees, The (Ribband), 92
Belgium, 211–12
Benn, Caroline Wedgwood, 204
Berenson, Bernard, 47–8, 51, 73–4; *Ls. from*, 87–9
Berenson, Mary, 74, 87
Berlin, 20, 47, 145, 148, 150, 207; *air lift*, 19, 183; *blockade*, 181, 183; *Wall*, 183; *East and West*, 183, 187
Bernal, J. D., 121, 188
Bertrand Russell Peace Foundation, 159–62, 165, 167, 171, 178–87, 192, 197
Bertrand Russell Speaks His Mind, 107
'Best Answer to Fanaticism-Liberalism, The', (*see* 'A Liberal Decalogue'),
Bhabha, Dr H. J., 80, 107
Bikini Test, 20, 99–100
Biquard, Paul, 77
Black Maria, 116,118
Blake, William, 89
Blunt, Wilfred Scawen, 50–1
Boggs, Congressman, 198
Bohr, Niels, 75, 106, 136
Bolt, Robert, 163
Bonaparte, Napoleon, 65
Boothby, Lord, 107
Born, Max, 78, 99, 179; *Ls. from and to*, 135–7
Bow Street Magistrates Court, 115–17; *statement at*, 145